Managing
ADHD
in the
K–8
Classroom

A Teacher's Guide

Managing ADHD
in the
K–8
Classroom

Grad L. Flick

CORWIN
A SAGE Company

For information:

Corwin
A SAGE Company
2455 Teller Road
Thousand Oaks, California 91320
(800) 233-9936
Fax: (800) 417-2466
www.corwin.com

SAGE Ltd.
1 Oliver's Yard
55 City Road
London EC1Y 1SP
United Kingdom

SAGE India Pvt. Ltd.
B 1/I 1 Mohan Cooperative
    Industrial Area
Mathura Road, New Delhi 110 044
India

SAGE Asia-Pacific Pte. Ltd.
33 Pekin Street #02-01
Far East Square
Singapore 048763

Printed in the United States of America

Library of Congress Cataloging-in-Publication Data

Managing ADHD in the K–8 classroom : a teacher's guide/by Grad L. Flick.
    p. cm.
Includes bibliographical references and index.
ISBN 978-1-4129-6910-9 (pbk.)

    1. Attention-deficit-disordered children—Education. 2. Attention-deficit-disordered children—Behavior modification. 3. Attention-deficit hyperactivity disorder. 4. Teachers of children with disabilities. I. Flick, Grad L. II. Title.

LC4713.2.M37 2010
371.94—dc22   2009033587

This book is printed on acid-free paper.

11 12 13 14 15 10 9 8 7 6 5 4 3

Acquisitions Editor:	David Chao
Editorial Assistant:	Sarah Bartlett
Production Editor:	Jane Haenel
Copy Editor:	Paula L. Fleming
Typesetter:	C&M Digitals (P) Ltd.
Proofreader:	Gretchen Treadwell
Indexer:	Maria Sosnowski
Cover and Graphic Designer:	Karine Hovsepian

Contents

Acknowledgments

I wish to thank my typist, Katie Hopkins, for general typing and preparation of the manuscript. Many thanks also go to my wife, Alma Flick, PhD, for not only being there but also for keeping our five dogs quiet. I wish to acknowledge my editorial assistant, Brynn Saito, for sending and receiving the manuscript and also for responding to my many requests. Lastly, I wish to thank my editor, David Chao, for his support and encouragement in seeing this manuscript through its various stages. Kudos also go to my current Cardiac Rehab Team.

PUBLISHER'S ACKNOWLEDGMENTS

Corwin gratefully acknowledges the contributions of the following individuals:

Margaret H. Blackwell, Executive Director
Student Services and Exceptional Children Programs
Chapel Hill-Carrboro City Schools
Chapel Hill, NC

Gloria Avolio DePaul, School Counselor
School District of Hillsborough County
Tampa, FL

Debi Gartland, Professor of Special Education
Towson University
Towson, MD

Mari Gates, Fifth-Grade Teacher
Henry B. Burkland Intermediate School
Middleboro, MA

Richard Hanf, HI Resource Teacher and Exceptional Needs Specialist
Westview Elementary/Middle Schools
Goose Creek, SC

James Javorsky, Associate Professor
Department of Human Development and Child Studies
Oakland University
Rochester, MI

Kathy J. Johnson, Fourth-Grade Teacher
North Callaway R-I School District
Williamsburg, MO

Ken Klopack, Art and Gifted Educational Consultant
Chicago Public Schools
Chicago, IL

Dana B. Leonard, Life Skills Teacher
Ledford High School
Thomasville, NC

Sarah Miller, Special Education Teacher
Orange Beach Elementary School
Orange Beach, AL

Stephen A. Wright, Doctoral Candidate and Research Assistant
Virginia Commonwealth University
Richmond, VA

About the Author

 **Grad L. Flick,** PhD, is a Licensed Clinical Psychologist in the states of Mississippi and Arkansas. He has a doctorate from the University of Miami (1969) with an APA-approved internship in clinical psychology at the University of Florida Medical Center. He has specialization in neuropsychology and certification in biofeedback and stress management. He is also an employee assistance program (EAP) provider and has training in critical incident stress debriefing. Dr. Flick has been in private practice for over 38 years and has seen thousands of children, adolescents, and adults. Currently, he is director of Seacoast Psychological Associates Inc. and the ADD Clinic. The ADD Clinic offers assessment and treatment for children, adolescents, and adults who have ADHD. Dr. Flick has numerous scientific presentation and publication credits, has conducted many workshops for both parents and teachers on ADHD, and has given lectures to various parent and teacher organizations on ADHD and child management.

Dr. Flick is the author of seven books on ADHD, including *Power Parenting for Children with ADD/ADHD* (1996) and the *ADD/ADHD Behavior Change Resource Kit* (1998). He has research and clinical experience with children who present attention, learning, and/or behavioral disorders; along with his wife, Alma Flick, PhD, they have parented a child who has both ADHD and a learning disability.

This book is dedicated to Shelly, Geri, Celeste, Summer, and Doug.
Without my Cardiac Rehab Team, I would probably not be here. Thank you again.

Overview of ADHD

Key Points

❖ About this book

❖ Options for teachers

❖ Age range

❖ Sequence of steps

Jordan was a nine-year-old fourth grader who was diagnosed with mild attention deficit hyperactivity disorder (ADHD) (primarily inattentive) and a learning disability (LD). He was not taking any medication. Jordan failed to complete his work, was disruptive (teasing and taunting his peers), and sometimes stole things off the desks of his classmates. He also acted like the "class clown." He often got others to laugh at him and to giggle.

How would you address these problems?

ABOUT THIS BOOK

This book primarily targets general education teachers and special education teachers. It provides a behavioral approach to the treatment of children in school who present behavioral problems associated with ADHD. Treatment typically begins with an appropriate diagnosis using the most accurate instruments and rating scales. After a diagnosis is made, a decision is usually rendered about whether medication should be used. This decision is typically based on the degree of functional impairment of the problem behavior along with the number of symptoms, and it is generally made by the physician involved (e.g., pediatrician, neurologist, general practitioner).

The practice advocated in this book will be to employ behavioral interventions with targeted symptoms, without concern for diagnosis. If these interventions are not sufficient, a consult may be considered for medication. If this is still not effective, a referral may then be made for a Functional Behavioral Assessment (FBA) and a formal Behavioral Intervention Plan (BIP).

A symptomatic approach (Flick, 1998) is used in this book. This means that treatment is based on the problem behaviors that are most troublesome, not on diagnoses. Consequently, the approach to be discussed in this book will be about those symptoms or problem behaviors that are most difficult to deal with in the classroom and how teachers may be involved in a child's behavioral interventions. This behavioral approach has been demonstrated to be effective in dealing with these most troublesome behaviors in critical school situations. One of the major problems in managing children with ADHD and associated problems has always been the lack of appropriate transfer of skills learned in the clinician's office to situations in school, where their application is more critical. In this case, skills and appropriate behaviors are learned within the same context where they will be used (i.e., the classroom or school in general).

Should the initial accommodations, specific suggestions, or behavioral interventions fail, then the child may be referred for an FBA and a formal BIP. The procedures outlined in this book are therefore to be used *prior* to any formal intervention. However, background is provided should a teacher wish to explore the use of other behavioral interventions.

AGE RANGE

This behavioral approach targets children with ADHD, as symptoms are manifested in children 6–14 years of age; basically, children in kindergarten through eighth grade (K–8). This approach does not address two age ranges that have appeared in the literature, specifically (a) preschool children with ADHD and (b) adults with ADHD. The former group will be the focus of a separate publication covering diagnosis, assessment, and treatment; the latter age range, covering both older adolescents as well as adults, will also be addressed in a future publication.

OPTIONS FOR TEACHERS

Teachers of children with ADHD may have varied experiences with behavioral techniques. Therefore, this book will not only review these basic behavioral techniques but also cover specific applications of behavioral principles that are used with some of the most troublesome behaviors associated with ADHD.

This book will not present comprehensive coverage of diagnostic and assessment procedures. However, some of the major instruments, rating scales, and checklists will be listed. These procedures may often be used in the diagnostic/assessment phase and the monitoring phase concurrently with behavioral interventions and/or medications as each procedure is implemented.

Those teachers who are most familiar with the diagnostic/assessment instruments as well as the behavioral principles used in interventions may wish to use this material as a review. Each chapter will include a list of key points along with a case history presentation on ADHD. These presentations are designed to stimulate the teacher's thinking regarding the behavioral treatment of ADHD. Case vignettes are also presented to illustrate some of the behaviors characteristic of ADHD. Possible solutions for each case history may be found in Appendix A. It is important for the teacher to remember that these solutions are just *possible* solutions; a teacher may elect to use an alternate intervention that would work just as well.

CLINICAL MANUAL

This book is a clinical manual for all teachers. It is not a scientifically based treatise on ADHD; neither are all of the behavioral interventions developed with regard to evidence-based treatments. Basically, two treatments for ADHD symptoms have a rock-solid base of effectiveness: (1) behavioral interventions and (2) medication. Behavioral interventions include (a) parent training, (b) school interventions, and (c) child-focused treatments. While parent training and child-focused treatments are clearly important, the topic of this book is behavioral interventions in the school (or classroom) (Barkley, 2005; DuPaul, Stoner, & O'Reilly, 2002; DuPaul & White, 2004).

SEQUENCE OF STEPS

When behavioral problems occur, and especially those associated with ADHD, teachers need some guidelines regarding how to deal with them.

Step 1: Implement the procedures that are easiest to use—the accommodations (with an Individual Education Plan, or IEP, in place) or a 504 Plan.

Step 2: Employ the general and specific suggestions provided.

Step 3: Use a procedure or a combination of procedures that address the problem behavior (i.e., the behavioral interventions).

Step 4: Refer the child for a Functional Behavioral Assessment (FBA) and a formal Behavioral Intervention Plan (BIP).

These four steps are outlined in the flowchart in Figure 1.1.

Remember, the goal for teachers is to deal with the problem behavior(s) *before* reaching the step where the student must be referred for an FBA and BIP. This clinical manual provides a list of accommodations, general and specific suggestions, and the behavioral techniques needed to implement behavioral interventions for children with ADHD.

Figure 1.1 Procedural Flowchart: Dealing With Behavior Problems

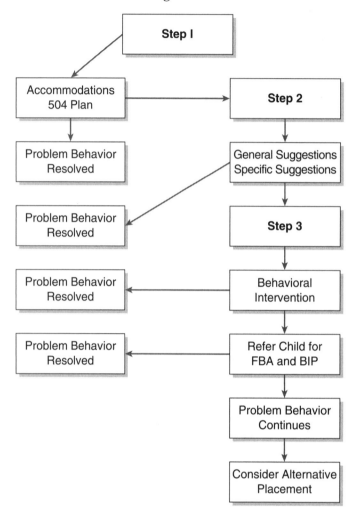

2

Attention Deficit Hyperactivity Disorder (ADHD)

Key Points

- Core characteristics of ADHD
- Biological bases of ADHD
- Current *DSM-IV-TR* diagnostic criteria
- Comorbidity
- Developmental trends

- The ADHD controversy
- ADHD: A real disorder
- Overdiagnosis of ADHD
- Myths about ADHD
- Long-term outcomes for ADHD

José was a six-year-old child in the first grade. He was classified as Other Health Impaired with ADHD. This child was average in intelligence but had trouble with both expressive and receptive language. He was taking Adderall-XR. José was noncompliant; grabbed things; and hit, bit, and pinched others. José resisted going to the resource room, and teachers struggled to get him there.

How would you address these problems?

ADHD stands for attention deficit hyperactivity disorder; ADD is an older term that is an abbreviation for attention deficit disorder. While many professionals use these terms interchangeably, the term ADHD will be used throughout this book. ADHD, considered a chronic condition, is the most researched and commonly diagnosed psychiatric disorder of childhood (Barkley, 2005).

—————————— ✀ ——————————

Up to 40 percent of all referrals to mental health centers involve ADHD (Barkley, 2000).

ADHD is characterized by a triad of symptoms (hyperactivity, inattention, and/or impulsivity) that cause functional impairment in a child's social, educational, and relational roles, as well as impairment of self-concept and self-esteem (Barkley, 1990). Not every child shows all of the associated or even core characteristics; the pattern may have many variations (Flick, 1998).

CORE CHARACTERISTICS OF ADHD

This section views each of the core behaviors and associated characteristics of ADHD behavior in more detail and includes some typical observations made by parents and teachers of children with ADHD.

Attentional processes are more complex than we sometimes think. Teachers tell parents, "Jimmy just needs to pay attention in class; he doesn't keep his mind on his work." This all-too-common statement complains simplistically about a complex process. One may ask, "What does 'paying attention' mean?" The teacher may believe that he or she has communicated a specific problem to the parent, but a host of questions arise from this general statement about not paying attention. Specifically, a parent may wish to know: When does the problem occur? In a specific class or in all classes? With one teacher or with all teachers? Only in one subject area (e.g., reading)? How long can the child attend? Does it matter where the child is seated? Does it matter how well the teacher is organized? How well the teacher communicates? Are attentional problems only evident when changing from one type of task in a subject area to another? Did this problem just develop, or has it been evident for some time?

One might ask many of these same questions for other problem areas that need to be addressed. At times, difficulties with attention may be evident both at school and at home; for some children, however, they may appear only at school. The degree of functional impairment also needs to be assessed to determine whether the child has ADHD or whether some other condition is being manifested.

Inattention

The most basic trait of students with ADHD is lack of focused attention. The term *focused attention* has been used by researchers in ADHD for some time (Flick, 1998; Goldstein & Incognoli, 1997; Goldstein & Teeter-Ellison, 2002; Lovecky, 2004; Novak, Solanto, & Abikoff, 1995). The description "a lack of focused attention" is used to reflect a *deficit in selective attention*, defined as difficulty focusing on the relevant stimuli and ignoring the irrelevant characteristics of a task. A *deficit in sustained attention* is defined as a gradual decline over time in the degree of attention given to as task. Definitions of increasingly more complex forms of attention are given in the enclosed box.

Five Levels of Attention

Level	Definition
Focused Attention	The ability to respond discretely to specific visual, auditory, or tactile stimuli
Sustained Attention	The ability to maintain a consistent behavioral response during continuous or repetitive activity

Level	Definition
Selective Attention	The ability to maintain a cognitive set that requires activation and inhibition of responses dependent upon discrimination of stimuli
Alternating Attention	The capacity for mental flexibility that allows for moving between tasks having different cognitive requirements
Divided Attention	The ability to respond simultaneously to multiple tasks

Adapted from Sohlberg & Mateer, 1989.

It's not that children with ADHD don't attend; in fact, they attend to everything (Flick, 1998). All stimuli impinge on their senses with equal potency. Such students appear to satiate quickly on tasks, but in actuality, they may get distracted by another stimuli and go off on a tangent, failing to finish the task at hand. Their attentional processes are quite variable: some days the child may be "in tune" and finish all his work; other days he may seem to "be in a fog."

Situational factors play an important part; in school, the child with ADHD may struggle to focus attention on classroom assignments, but at home, the same child may be the champion of video games. Exciting computer graphics, flashing lights, loud sounds, and bright colors may serve to attract and maintain the attention of most children with ADHD. Likewise, novel and interesting tasks, including those spiced with humor, may help maintain the child's attention. Such children also have little difficulty focusing in a one-on-one setting, but when they're in the complex environment of a noisy classroom, they may have numerous problems with compliance and task performance.

Also, one subgroup of inattentive children may become distracted by their own internal thoughts and sensations, rather than by external stimuli. These are the "quiet underachievers," kids who rarely create a behavioral disturbance in class. Instead, they simply go into a "trancelike" state and may focus on some internal yet creative thought process—in short, they daydream.

According to Tsal, Shalev, and Mevorach (2005), deficits in sustained attention were the most pronounced symptoms of children with ADHD, but different study participants showed different clusters of attention deficits.

However, not all instances of inattention are attributable to ADHD. Some children may develop attentional problems secondary to a learning disability in language, reading, spelling, writing, or math. These children may become quite frustrated and overly stressed when asked to complete tasks that are difficult for them. Those asked to read and answer questions about a subject in which they have little knowledge and minimal interest may feel inadequate and experience stress sufficient to result in avoidance behavior (i.e., doing something to remove themselves from the situation, including "tuning out"). Similar conditions may exist for a child who may be overwhelmed with work beyond his or her capacity or developmental level (e.g., a child with a developmental delay or mental retardation) or for a child who has some preoccupation with depressive or anxious thoughts.

Impulsivity

This core symptom reflects a general lack of self-control. It is doubtful that children with ADHD plan their trouble-making behavior. Although they may be aware of right and wrong and may be able to cite a rule at home or in the classroom, they often "act before they think." By this time it's too late—they've already "done it" and are "in trouble" again. At times, their behavior is perplexing to parents, who wonder how someone of average or better intelligence can act so "unintelligent" and careless at times. While the child may feel quite guilty over the wrongdoing, this guilt is unlikely, by itself, to prevent future acting-out behavior. The average child who gets punched in line at school may first look to see if the teacher is watching before punching back. However, the child with ADHD in the same situation responds impulsively and reflexively; he or she often gets caught and is, thus, labeled "the aggressor."

Also, because of their impulsive style, children with ADHD have a higher incidence of "accident proneness." In conversations, such children can't wait to talk; they often interrupt and talk over others. Described as frustrated and impatient, they blurt out answers in class before raising their hands, and they frequently have a short fuse and may vent their anger explosively. These children start working on projects before learning all of the directions, rush through their work, and make many careless errors in the process. Socially and in play activities, these kids experience difficulty taking turns and have problems with rules that involve control; they are generally unaware of the effects of their action on others. Such children also learn slowly from their mistakes, since their behavior is primarily reflexive and they are genuinely unaware of "how they get in trouble."

Hyperactivity

Perhaps the most salient behavioral characteristic in this ADHD symptom pattern is hyperactivity. Some mothers of children with ADHD have noted that hyperactivity was often present "even before birth." Problematic hyperactivity may not be recognized as a real symptom until the first time a child is placed in a situation that requires some self-control of movement. Sometimes this doesn't occur until the child is in preschool or, most likely, kindergarten.

While all youngsters are generally more active during the early years, those children with ADHD are apt to be described as "restless," and they find it especially hard to settle down for quiet activity such as reading or nap time. These children appear to be "driven" and go from one thing to another, seemingly becoming easily bored and needing more stimulation. Enhanced self-stimulation, such as humming, making noise, and talking, could come from excess overt motor activity.

By the time the child is in a structured setting, like a classroom, hyperactive behavior has become an obvious problem that often cannot be ignored. According to Smallwood (1997), ADHD with hyperactivity may be distinctly different neurologically from the ADHD subtype without hyperactivity (i.e., ADHD, primarily inattentive type).

Inconsistency

This is perhaps one of the most visible characteristics of ADHD. Basically, a child is described by parents and teachers alike as having good days and bad days. On some days, the student may complete all assigned work; on other days, none. Often, this pattern itself sets the child up for failure. Dr. Russell Barkley (2000) has eloquently reported, "Children [with ADHD] do well in school twice and we hold it against them the rest of their life" (child psychiatrist as cited by Barkley, p. 47). Parents may often wonder if their child has a "split personality," since performance is so inconsistent. Such fluctuations may parallel the variability of underlying physiological processes, which in turn are affected by many factors, both internal and external. Inconsistency is a clearly a significant feature of ADHD.

Related to inconsistency is the notion that these children also seem to have a great deal of difficulty with change and transitions. It is not uncommon for teachers to observe an increase in behavioral problems in a child who is generally well controlled on medications but is experiencing change in his or her life:

- Significant change in the family, such as marital separation or divorce.
- A seemingly minor change, such as resetting the clock forward one hour for spring or one hour backward for fall.
- A change that might normally be perceived as "good." (For example, one child became very upset and cried when his parents traded their old car for a new one.)

Typically, ADHD is categorized as "other health impaired" when a child is evaluated by special education.

IDEA's Definition of "Other Health Impairment"

To be eligible for special education, a student must meet the definition criteria for at least 1 of 13 disability categories listed in the federal regulations. Some students may meet more than one definition. Many students with ADHD now may qualify for special education services under the "Other Health Impairment" category within the Individuals with Disabilities Education Act (IDEA). IDEA defines *other health impairment* as follows:

... having limited strength, vitality or alertness, including a heightened alertness to environmental stimuli, that results in limited alertness with respect to the educational environment, that is due to chronic or acute health problems such as asthma, attention deficit disorder or attention deficit hyperactivity disorder, diabetes, epilepsy, a heart condition, hemophilia, lead poisoning, leukemia, nephritis, rheumatic fever, and sickle cell anemia; and adversely affects a child's educational performance.

Source: 34 Code of Federal Regulations §300.7 (c) (9)

BIOLOGICAL BASES OF ADHD

Over the past 35 years, much has been learned about the neurobiological bases of ADHD, beginning with the early work of Satterfield and Dawson (1971) on psychophysiological parameters up to the current work on brain imaging. Integration of research from several disciplines, including genetic studies, neuroanatomical evidence, and neuropsychological findings, all points to strong biological bases for ADHD (e.g., Krain & Castellanos, 2006; Rubia, 2007; Smalley, 2008; Todd et al., 2005; Tsai, Wang, & Hong, 2001).

There is a 25 to 35 percent chance that if one member in a family has ADHD, other family members have it as well.

CURRENT *DSM-IV-TR* CRITERIA

Parents and teachers often label a child as hyperactive based on personal observations. According to Cruz and Bahna (2006), a diagnosis should be based on criteria in the American Psychiatric Association's (APA) *Diagnostic and Statistical Manual of Mental Disorders* (2000). ADHD is a complex, multifactorial disorder. Underlying factors include any combination of genetic factors, perinatal events, environmental causes, neurobiological mediations, and psychosocial influences—in short, it has multiple etiologies.

The formulation of the criteria established to diagnose ADHD in *DSM-IV-TR* represents improvement over that in prior edition *DSM-III-R* with regard to the selection of specific items used. However, there still are problems, since these diagnostic entities are formulated by a committee. As committees change, so too do diagnostic criteria, items, and nosology. Many revisions of definitions have occurred, and more are expected in future editions. There is also a problem in that Categories I and III, while different diagnostically, have been given the same diagnostic descriptions. These descriptions about ADHD, as well as most comorbid conditions, have been adapted with permission from the *DSM-IV-TR* (APA). Perhaps the *DSM-V* (due in 2010) will clarify some of these issues.

DSM-IV-TR Diagnostic Features

There are three main behavioral dimensions of ADHD: inattention, impulsivity, and hyperactivity. Diagnostic classification thus results from the presence of either inattention or impulsivity-hyperactivity or all three (Criterion A). Criterion B stipulates that these symptoms must be present prior to seven years of age. To meet Criterion C, these symptoms must impair one's functioning in more than one setting; that is, school, home, or work (adult). For Criterion D, there must be evidence that one is impaired socially, academically, or occupationally. In Criterion E, the clinician must be able to rule out the presence of other disorders that might account for these symptoms, including—without limitation—pervasive developmental disorder and schizophrenia or other psychiatric disorder, including mood disorder, anxiety disorder, dissociative disorder, and personality disorder.

Diagnostic Criteria for ADHD

"When problems with attention, hyperactivity, and impulsiveness develop in childhood and persist, in some cases into adulthood, this mental disorder may be diagnosed" (APA, 2000).

Following is the list of the symptoms of ADHD.

Diagnostic Criteria for Attention-Deficit/Hyperactivity Disorder

A. Either (1) or (2):

  1. *Inattention:* six (or more) of the following symptoms of inattention have persisted for at least 6 months to a degree that is maladaptive and inconsistent with developmental level:

    a. Often fails to give close attention to details or makes careless mistakes in schoolwork, work, or other activities

    b. Often has difficulty sustaining attention in tasks or play activities

    c. Often does not seem to listen when spoken to directly

    d. Often does not follow through on instructions and fails to finish school work, chores, or duties in the workplace (not due to oppositional behavior or failure to understand instructions)

    e. Often has difficulty organizing tasks and activities

    f. Often avoids, dislikes, or is reluctant to engage in tasks that require sustained mental effort (such as schoolwork or homework)

g. Often loses things necessary for tasks or activities (e.g., toys, school assignments, pencils, books, or tools)

h. Is often easily distracted by extraneous stimuli

i. Is often forgetful in daily activities

2. *Hyperactivity-impulsivity:* six (or more) of the following symptoms of hyperactivity-impulsivity have persisted for at least 6 months to a degree that is maladaptive and inconsistent with developmental level:

Hyperactivity

a. Often fidgets with hands or feet or squirms in seat

b. Often leaves seat in classroom or in other situations in which remaining seated is expected

c. Often runs about or climbs excessively in situations in which it is inappropriate (in adolescents or adults, may be limited to subjective feelings of restlessness)

d. Often has difficulty playing or engaging in leisure activities quietly

e. Is often "on the go" or often acts as if "driven by a motor"

f. Often talks excessively

Impulsivity

g. Often blurts out answers before questions have been completed

h. Often has difficulty awaiting turn

i. Often interrupts or intrudes on others (e.g., butts into conversations or games)

B. Some hyperactive-impulsive or inattentive symptoms that caused impairment were present before age 7 years.

C. Some impairment from the symptoms is present in two or more settings (e.g., at school [or work] and at home).

D. There must be clear evidence of clinically significant impairment in social, academic, or occupational functioning.

E. The symptoms do not occur exclusively during the course of a Pervasive Developmental Disorder, Schizophrenia, or other Psychotic Disorder and are not better accounted for by another mental disorder (e.g., Mood Disorder, Anxiety Disorder, Dissociative Disorders, or a Personality Disorder).

Code Based on Type

314.01 Attention-Deficit/Hyperactivity Disorder, Combined Type: if both Criteria A1 and A2 are met for the past 6 months

314.00 Attention-Deficit/Hyperactivity Disorder, Predominantly Inattentive Type: if Criterion A1 is met but Criterion A2 is not met for the past 6 months

314.01 Attention-Deficit/Hyperactivity Disorder, Predominantly Hyperactive-Impulsive Type: if Criterion A2 is met but Criterion A1 is not met for the past 6 months

Coding note: For individuals (especially adolescents and adults) who currently have symptoms that no longer meet full criteria, "In Partial Remission" should be specified.

To be diagnosed as having ADHD, the child must show maladaptive and/or developmentally inappropriate symptoms of inattention, hyperactivity, or impulsivity (or some combination) for a period of at least six months. Also, these symptoms should be present before age seven and should occur in at least two settings (e.g., home and school). Children with ADHD report having a number of significant problems (Barkley, 2002; Barkley, Fisher, Smallish, & Fletcher, 2002).

There are three basic subtypes of ADHD: (1) predominantly inattentive type, (2) predominantly hyperactive-impulsive type, and (3) combined type (see Figure 2.1). A fourth category is called ADHD not otherwise specified, or ADHD (NOS), where the child shows significant symptoms of ADHD but does not meet the criteria for the diagnostic category.

Figure 2.1 Subtypes of ADHD

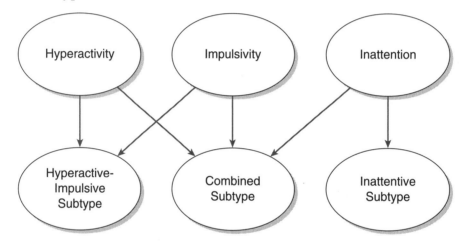

Instability of the *DSM-IV-TR* Subtypes

There are a number of reports on the instability of the *DSM-IV-TR* subtypes (Graetz, Sawyer, Hazell, Arney & Baghurst, 2001; Lahey, Pelham, Loney, Lee, & Willcutt, 2005; Lahey & Willcutt, 2002; Rowland et al., 2008; Willcutt, Chhabildas, & Pennington, 2001). The overall conclusion is that the combined subtype and the primarily inattentive subtype are stable over time for research purposes but may not be sufficiently stable for clinical purposes. Also, children researched remain in the hyperactive-impulsive subtype but sometimes shift to the combined subtype as they age.

The following are descriptions of each type.

Predominantly Inattentive Type

It is estimated that about 20 to 30 percent of all those with ADHD fall into this category. Here, there is difficulty focusing and maintaining attention and concentration. Children with ADHD may easily become distracted and are either receiving positive reinforcement for their inattention or may be allowed to avoid something unpleasant (e.g., math). Such children experience difficulty completing their work and persisting on tasks that may not be interesting. These symptoms of inattention and information-processing problems remain problematic from childhood to adolescence and sometimes beyond (Biederman, Mick, & Faraone, 2000; Wilens, Beiderman, & Spencer, 2002). Children with this type of ADHD exhibit a slow cognitive tempo, and such problems do not respond to medication

(Barkley, 2005; Carlson & Mann, 2002; Hartman, Willcutt, Rhee, & Pennington, 2004). Characteristically, these students receive poor grades because their assignments are either late, incomplete, or forgotten altogether. Children with this type of ADHD often show symptoms of anxiety or depression as comorbid disorders (Nigg, 2006; Tannock, 2000).

The finding of slower processing speed in this subtype is consistent with other research suggesting a slower reaction time and a "sluggish cognitive tempo." These features may indicate that the optimal pace of presentation of classroom instruction is slower for children with predominantly inattentive subtype than for other children (Solanto, 2004).

Predominantly Hyperactive-Impulsive Type

In this type, developmentally inappropriate levels of vocal or motor activity are present. Impulsivity may best be described as "acting before thinking." This is the least common sub-type, affecting less than 15 percent of all children with ADHD (Wilens et al., 2002). Acting before thinking causes problems in any situation where there are rules (e.g., blurting out an answer in school or having trouble waiting one's turn in play activities). When this type is associated with conduct disorder, there is an elevated risk of substance abuse and emotional and/or behavioral problems (Fischer, Barkley, Smallish, Fletcher, 2002; Wilens et al., 2002).

Combined Type

This is the most frequently diagnosed subtype, affecting about 50 to 75 percent of all children with ADHD (Nigg, 2006; Wilens et al., 2002). Such individuals experience both cognitive and behavioral problems. Children with this subtype appear to be the most impaired of children with ADHD and have problems with attention as well as problems in behavior (Wilens et al., 2002).

ADHD Subtypes

Overall, children who are diagnosed with ADHD show poor motivation for classroom tasks and generally display avoidance of activities that require sustained effort (Milich, 1994). Such results appear characteristic of both combined and inattentive subtypes of ADHD. All children with ADHD are less reliant upon external feedback and are seen as more dependent, as more easily discouraged, and as having lower expectations for themselves.

> All three ADHD subtypes were rated as having more emotional and behavioral problems and lower psychosocial quality of life, with combined types consistently rated the most impaired. Combined types received higher ratings that hyperactive-impulsive and inattentive types on externalizing behavior problems, descriptions of family activities, and symptom specific impairments with school lunch and peer-related activities. Inattentive types were rated as having lower self-esteem, more social and school-related problems, but fewer externalizing problems than hyperactive-impulsive types. (Graetz, Sawyer, Hazell, Arney, & Baghurst, 2001)

These authors conclude that their findings support the belief that *DSM-IV-TR* subtypes are distinct clinical entities with multiple impairments.

Functional Impairment

Symptoms don't automatically imply impairment. So one could carry a diagnosis of ADHD and not be impaired. Barkley, Fischer, Smallish, and Fletcher (2006) defined symptoms of ADHD as "the behavioral expressions associated with this disorder—they are the actions demonstrated by those having the disorder that are believed to reflect that disorder." Impairments result from the interaction of symptoms and their severity, and this interaction may affect the child's school and/or play situations, as well as the child's overall adaptive behavior. The *DSM-IV-TR* does not provide criteria for defining impairment (Johnson & Conners, 2002). In many cases, a child may not be bothered by a symptom (e.g., losing important things), yet other significant people in the child's life may. The evaluator must determine whether a symptom results in impairment.

Risks and Protective Factors

A number of risks and protective factors are important in the development and diagnosis of ADHD. These are briefly outlined in the following table.

Risk and Protective Factors for ADHD

	Risk Factors	*Protective Factors*
Biological	Genetic predisposition	No family genetic evidence
	Maternal smoking	No maternal smoking
	Maternal alcohol/drug use	No maternal alcohol/drug use

	Delivery complications:
	
	    Preeclampsia
	    Low birth weight
	    Premature labor
	    Complicated C-section
		No delivery complications

Family	Poor attachment/low maternal social support	Good attachment/high maternal social support
	Low socioeconomic status	High socioeconomic status
	Poor nutrition	Good nutrition
	Lack of educational resources	Educational resources
	Poor family environment	Positive family environment
	Low level of ability	High level of ability
Psychological	Comorbid ODD, conduct disorder, or anxiety disorder	No evidence of comorbid disorders or an anxiety disorder
Environmental	Parent with ADHD	No parent with ADHD
	Single-parent home	Two-parent home
	Presence of lead/heavy metals	No evidence of lead/heavy metals

One can easily see that many of the risk and protective factors would be covered in the clinical diagnostic interview. Dr. Thomas Brown (2005) stated that "the most sensitive instrument for making a diagnosis of ADHD is a well-conducted interview."

Gender Issues in ADHD

In general, ADHD appears different in male and females, especially in terms of their behavior (Nigg, 2002). Overall, the ratio of males to females is from about 4:1 up to 9:1. This difference could either be due to a referral bias or, perhaps, to behavior exhibited; males are more likely to engage in aggressive behavior, while females are more likely to show a slow cognitive tempo of the inattentive subtype (Biederman, Faraone, Monuteaux, Buber & Cadogen, 2004; Ellison, 2002). In general, ADHD in females appears to be the same disorder as in males; however, females with ADHD may have a higher risk of psychopathology (Gross-Tsur et al., 2006). Gender issues have been comprehensively addressed by Quinn and Nadeau in *Gender Issues and AD/HD: Research, Diagnosis and Treatment* (2002); those interested in exploring these issues may wish to refer to this source.

Sibling Relationships

A study by Kendall (1999) revealed that in families where one child has ADHD, there were three major categories of sibling experience: (1) disruption, (2) the effects of disruption, and (3) strategies to manage disruption.

Living with a sibling who has ADHD family life was described as chaotic, conflictual, and exhausting because of not knowing what to expect. Aggression, hyperactivity, emotional immaturity, academic problems, family conflicts, poor peer relations, and problems with relatives were noted as evidence of disruption. Other effects of disruption were being victimized by the sibling with ADHD, being expected to take care of that sibling, and a loss of parental attention (since so much time was devoted to the sibling with ADHD). With regard to the strategies to manage disruption, some siblings fought back, while others just "went with the flow." One doesn't normally think about the other sibling (without ADHD), but perhaps it is important to consider that child's perspective.

Many children with ADHD have serious problems:

- About 20 percent have set fires.
- About 30 percent have engaged in theft.
- About 40 percent tried tobacco and alcohol at an early age.
- About 25 percent have been expelled from high school for misconduct.

—Adapted from Barkley, 2000

According to a study by Biederman and colleagues (1996), the ADHD group had comorbid conduct disorder (22 percent), oppositional defiant disorder (65 percent), major depressive disorder (29 percent), bipolar disorder (11 percent), various anxiety disorders (27 percent), tic disorders (17 percent), and enuresis (30 percent).

BEHAVIORAL FEATURES

Behavioral features exhibited with ADHD include low frustration tolerance, temper problems, stubbornness, persistence, emotional liability, depression, procrastination, peer rejection, poor self-concept, and poor self-esteem. Which behavioral features are manifested and to what degree vary according to developmental status, age, and gender. Nonetheless, a common component seen in many children with ADHD is devaluation and dislike of academics (probably because of the behavior constraints, not necessarily the learning process itself).

Parents and teachers often perceive the child with ADHD as lazy and lacking in responsibility. For such children, much conflict may occur with parents and other authority figures, since much of their oppositional behavior is viewed inaccurately as outright disobedience. It is rare, however, for a child, especially an older child, to exhibit only ADHD characteristics. Because of the numerous problems encountered, the child with ADHD may also develop many *learned* inappropriate behaviors, which then are associated with the biologically based ADHD behaviors. In essence, the child with ADHD presents a complex clinical picture and often has one or more comorbid conditions associated with ADHD.

COMORBIDITY CONDITIONS

Numerous psychological, medical, and neurological conditions are often associated with ADHD and must be considered in making a differential diagnosis. Often these conditions may share symptoms with ADHD or may involve ADHD-like (mimic) behaviors. Behavioral symptoms that mimic ADHD are discussed by Kutscher and Puder (2008) and Swingle (2008).

Some of the potential overlaps with other diagnostic conditions are shown in Figure 2.2. This list of overlapping symptoms demonstrates that quite often, the clinician is presented with a very complex symptom picture. A clinician must be able to determine the primary condition and sort out what may be secondary or tertiary (i.e., comorbid) conditions. A clinician must also be able to distinguish between ADHD symptoms and other conditions that mimic ADHD behavioral symptoms.

Figure 2.2   Overlaps Between ADHD and Other Conditions

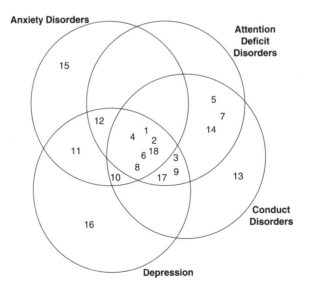

Following are two lists: one of medical conditions and the other of psychological conditions that may be comorbid with ADHD or that may be considered in differential diagnosis. These lists are followed by a list of some of the disorders that commonly co-occur with ADHD (i.e., comorbid conditions).

	Symptomatic Behavioral Characteristic	Attention Deficit	Anxiety Disorder	Depression	Conduct Disorder
1	Poor Concentration	X	X	X	X
2	Restless	X	X	?	X
3	Fails to Complete Tasks	X		X	X
4	Day Dreams	X	X	X	X
5	Impulsive	X			X
6	Poor Sleep	X	X	X	X
7	Aggressive	?		?	X
8	Mood Disturbance	X	X	X	X
9	Poor Self-Concept	X		X	X
10	Quiet and Withdrawn	?		X	
11	Guilt Over Transgressions		X	X	
12	Memory Problems	X	X	X	
13	Stealing/Lying				X
14	Poor Social Skills	X			X
15	Fearful/Avoidance	?	X	?	
16	Crying	?	?	X	
17	Sensation Seeking (High-Risk)	X		?	X
18	Difficulty Focusing on Task	X	?	?	?

Key: X = Symptom Usually Present; ? = Symptom Possible; Blank = Not Usually Present

Mimic Syndrome and Medical Conditions Comorbid With ADHD

Reaction to anticonvulsants (phenobarbital, Dilantin)
Head trauma
Otitis media
Reaction to theophylline (for asthma)
Anemia
Tourette's syndrome
Fragile X syndrome
Movement disorder (Sydenham's chorea)

Sinusitis
Epilepsy
Pinworms
Narcolepsy
Thyroid disorder
Structural brain lesion
Isoniazid
Sleep apnea
Lead

Mimic Syndrome and Psychological Conditions Comorbid With ADHD

Adjustment disorder   Oppositional defiant disorder
Learning disability   Bipolar disorder
Anxiety disorder   Obsessive compulsive disorder
Conduct disorder   Mental retardation
Depression/dysthymia

Disorders That Commonly Co-Occur With ADHD

Oppositional Defiant Disorder (ODD): A pattern of negative, hostile, and defiant behavior. Symptoms include frequent loss of temper, arguing (especially with adults), refusal to obey rules, intentionally annoying others, and blaming others. The person is angry, resentful, possibly spiteful, and touchy. (Many of these symptoms disappear with ADHD treatments.)

Conduct Disorder (CD): A pattern of behavior that persistently violates the basic rights of others or society's rules. Behaviors may include aggression toward people and animals, destruction of property, deceitfulness or theft, or serious rule violations.

Anxiety: Excessive worry that occurs frequently and is difficult to control. Symptoms include feeling restless or on edge, feeling fatigued easily, difficulty concentrating, irritability, muscle tension, and sleep disturbances.

Depression: A condition marked by having trouble concentrating, having problems sleeping, and feelings of dejection and guilt. There are many types of depression. With ADHD, one might commonly see dysthmia, which consists of having a depressed mood for many days, over- or undereating, sleeping too much or too little, low energy, low self-esteem, poor concentration, and feeling hopeless. Other forms of depression may also be present.

Learning Disabilities: Problems with reading, writing, or mathematics. When given standardized tests, the student's ability or intelligence is substantially higher than his or her achievement. Underachievement is generally considered age-inappropriate.

Note: Children with ADHD frequently have problems with reading fluency and mathematical calculations. ADHD learning problems have to do with attention, memory, and executive function difficulties rather than dyslexia, dysgraphia, or dyscalculia, which are learning disabilities. The point here is not to overlook either. Depending on how learning disabilities are defined, between 10–90% of youth with AD/HD also have a learning disability (Robin, 1998).

DEVELOPMENTAL TRENDS: CHILD TO ADULT

According to Barkley (2000),

> up to 80% of school-age children given a clinical diagnosis for ADHD will continue to have the disorder in adolescence, and between 30% and 65% will have it into adulthood, depending on how the disorder is defined in any particular study. (pp. 90–91)

Thus, ADHD must be considered a chronic disorder.

The Preschool Child

Many mothers of children with ADHD report that they noticed their children were more active even before birth. During infancy, the early ADHD pattern may be characterized by unpredictable behavior, shrill crying, irritability, and overactivity. Sleep problems have also been noted, as these infants show only brief periods of quiet sleep. Later, in the preschool years, these children begin to exhibit greater motoric restless behavior, rapid changes in mood, temper tantrums, poor sleep patterns, a low tolerance for frustration, and short attention spans. Many of these youngsters also show speech and language problems and are described as more clumsy. They generally experience much difficulty in group settings, especially with aggressive behaviors; as a result, many of these children are sometimes "asked to leave preschool!" (Flick, 1998).

- About 30 to 50 percent of students with ADHD are retained a grade.
- About 35 percent of students with ADHD fail to graduate from high school.
- About 25 to 30 percent of older adolescents and adults develop problems with substance abuse and drugs.

—Adapted from Barkley, 2000

The School-Age Child

By school age, the behavior pattern appears to become worse. These youngsters enter the classroom and are expected to sit quietly, focus on their assigned tasks, and get along with others in the class. Problems are now likely to occur at home *and* at school. Homework, routinely assigned to children at an early age, becomes another potential battlefield. Additionally, children with ADHD, who generally have much difficulty with rule-governed behavior, find handling chores at home and completing assignments at school difficult. They experience either mere tolerance or outright rejection from others as social problems tend to increase. By late childhood, social conflicts are well established. Barkley (2000) pointed out that

> between 7 and 10 years of age, at least 30–50% [of children with ADHD] are likely to develop symptoms of conduct disorder and antisocial behavior, such as lying, petty thievery, and resistance to authority. Twenty-five percent or more may have problems with fighting with other children. (p. 93)

Longitudinal studies of children with ADHD from school age to adolescence report high rates of continuing ADHD; however, studies into adulthood are inconsistent. Mannuzza, Klein, Klein, Bessler, & Shrout (2002) reported on four factors that seem to influence adult ADHD rates: (1) the assessment process, (2) the attrition rate, (3) the reporting source, and (4) the criteria used for the disorder.

Teens with ADHD are four times more likely to have serious auto accidents and three times more likely to be cited for speeding (Barkley, 2000).

Adolescence

During this period of development, it is not unusual for the symptom pattern to change, manifesting a marked decrease in hyperactivity but with the problems of attention and impulsivity remaining.

By adolescence, the child may also have a history of failures in academic performance (Flick, 1998; Mash & Barkley, 2005), as well as marked difficulties in social relations.

General outcomes (Flick, 1998) suggest that about 20 percent of children with ADHD manifest no problems as adults, about 60 percent show mild to moderate problems as adults, and about 20 percent manifest serious emotional or conduct problems as adults.

Many of these teenagers in search of acceptance may tend to associate with peers who have similar problems; this often results in an escalation of risk-taking behavior. Teens with ADHD are certainly more subject to peer pressure regarding the use of alcohol or other addictive substances (as many as 30 percent experiment with or abuse alcohol and marijuana) (Flick, 2000). Sadly, about 35 percent of ADHD children quit school before completion. Depression appears to be more common for adolescents with ADHD, along with poor self-concept, low self-esteem, and poor self-confidence, making future success seem unlikely. Thus, ADHD contributes to diminished motivation to finish school, as well as much concern about social acceptance.

Adulthood

Symptoms persist into adulthood for over half of children with ADHD. Barkley (2000) noted that "only 10–20% of children with ADHD reach adulthood free of any psychiatric diagnosis" (p. 94). They show a higher incidence of problems relating to achievement and vocation/work issues than the general population. Psychological problems and marital difficulties are more frequent, about 50 percent become alcoholics, and about 25 percent even show antisocial characteristics. We now know there is a higher incidence of more overall psychopathology and lower ability to function than in normal individuals without evidence of ADHD. It is certainly clear that ADHD is not simply outgrown, as was once thought.

Researchers have also found that the use of stimulant drugs for ADHD does not eliminate all difficulties in educational and daily living situations. Usage of these stimulant medications does, however, result in less social ostracism, along with a general improvement in the feelings associated with one's life and other people. The best outcomes were obtained with the use of both medication and behavioral interventions.

THE ADHD CONTROVERSY

Mention the term *attention deficit hyperactivity disorder*, and disagreement is sure to ensue. Is ADHD simply an excuse for poor schoolwork or bad behavior? Are teachers unable to discipline their students adequately unless those students are on medication? Are an excessive number of children labeled with ADHD and "drugged" to control their behavior? What is really going on here?

According to Flick (2002), ADHD and its close companion, ADHD primarily inattentive type, are some of the most widely known, extensively researched, and controversial of all behavioral disorders. Despite its definition in *DSM-IV-TR*, ADHD frequently appears to be associated with many comorbid conditions (e.g., learning disability, depression, oppositional defiant disorder), giving ADHD an almost infinite variation in appearance. Because of this variation, the question has been posed: Is ADHD a real disorder?

Misdiagnosis and overdiagnosis are issues that comprise a second controversy: Is ADHD overdiagnosed?

Assuming that the disorder is real and that an accurate diagnosis is made, there is further controversy about the optimal mode of treatment: Is methylphenidate (Ritalin) the most appropriate treatment for ADHD?

According to many clinicians, the criteria for ADHD are valid, and the key to appropriate diagnosis is analysis of the duration, intensity, and frequency of these behaviors. Most important is determining how much the symptoms affect the patient by assessing the degree of functional impairment. Someone could meet the criteria for one of the subtypes ADHD but not show impairment of academic or social behavior. One must consider whether the person is functionally impaired. An additional modifier of the ADHD condition has been described in the American Academy of Pediatrics's diagnostic criteria (American Academy of Pediatrics, 2000).

ADHD: A Real Disorder

If you asked parents and teachers of children with ADHD behaviors whether ADHD is real, the overwhelming response would be a resounding, "Yes! I have to deal with these behaviors every day." ADHD may be considered similar to common medical conditions such as hypertension or diabetes, in which the criteria for diagnosis depends

Roughly 75 to 80 percent of all those with ADHD respond to stimulant medication (Barkley, 1990).

on an arbitrary cutoff along a continuum of blood pressure or serum glucose levels. No one seems to question the authenticity of these medical conditions. When medications are withdrawn for hypertension or for diabetes, does the patient still have these medical conditions? Of course. These conditions are *managed* by medications, not cured (Flick, 2002).

The same might be said about ADHD: Medications can help with management; a "cure" is not expected. Research that establishes ADHD as a brain disorder is not unique; most psychiatric disorders (schizophrenia, depression, etc.) are now viewed in this way.

Assessment Versus Diagnosis

The behaviors that comprise ADHD are real and have been reported in the literature for many years. The term *attention deficit disorder* was originally coined by Dr. Virginia Douglas in the 1970s, based on her theory that such children do not stop to think before they act. Diagnostic criteria may change, and even the nosology of the behavioral syndrome may change (with many name changes for ADHD over the past years), but ultimately the actual behaviors are of major concern. Whether medication, behavioral strategies, or both are used, the basic question remains: Have the patient's behaviors changed?

Conclusion

Whether ADHD is a real disorder or not, the behaviors are real and must be addressed. These behaviors can significantly interfere with a child's ability to adapt to school or a home environment, resulting in functional impairment. Although developmental aspects may change over time (for example, hyperactivity may diminish with age), many of the same symptoms will still be readily apparent in adulthood.

These ADHD disorders affect roughly 3 to 5 percent of all school-age children, with a potential range of 1–10 percent. Roughly 3.5 million youngsters have ADHD (Flick, 2002).

Overdiagnosis of ADHD

Some children and adults may be misdiagnosed with ADHD when another mimic syndrome is actually present. Figure 2.2 depicts the possible overlap with other disorders that may look like ADHD but are actually other diagnostic entities (Flick, 1998). As many as 66 percent of children with ADHD have one or more comorbid disorders. The most frequently occurring comorbid disorder is learning disability (80 percent), followed by depression (70 percent), oppositional defiant disorder (65 percent), Tourette's syndrome

(50 percent), general anxiety (30 percent), conduct disorder (25 percent), and bipolar disorder (25 percent).

False Positives Versus False Negatives

False-positive and false-negative conclusions are possible in ADHD, making it difficult to estimate incidence accurately. In a false-positive situation, a comorbid syndrome may lead to an inaccurate diagnosis, indicating that one of the ADHD subtypes is present when it is not. In the case of a false negative, one of the ADHD subtypes is not diagnosed when, in fact, it is present. In either case, the actual prevalence of ADHD in certain settings may be over- or underestimated.

Factors Affecting Diagnostic Prevalence

In addition to misdiagnosis, other factors may affect diagnostic prevalence. These include the following:

Gender: Girls manifest the inattentive type more frequently and are often glossed over; boys more often exhibit the hyperactive-impulsive or combined type and are more difficult to miss. Therefore, many girls may be excluded in estimates of diagnostic prevalence (Barkley, 2005; Castellanos et al., 1996). Reports by LeFever, Kawson, and Morrow (1999) and Barkley (2000) indicated that boys are four to ten times more likely to be diagnosed with ADHD than are girls. Children as young as two years old are being diagnosed, and they are prescribed stimulants in increasing numbers (Zito et al., 2000). By 1996, more than 6 percent of school-age boys were on stimulants (Olfson, Marcus, Weissman, & Jensen, 2002). More recently, up to 19 percent of boys who reportedly had ADHD were on medication (Flick, 2002). Timimi (2002) noted that the United Kingdom is catching up to the United States in the number of cases of ADHD reported.

— ❧ —

Most reports indicate a ratio of three or four boys to each girl affected, with a range of sex ratios from 3:1 to 9:1.

Age of the child: Symptoms of ADHD must be evaluated within the context of age-based norms. The current criteria for ADHD (*DSM-IV-TR*) are not age referenced. Etiological studies have revealed that the disorder is highly heritable and may be associated with neurobiological deficits in the prefrontal cortex, parietal cortex, and related subcortical systems. ADHD patterns change over time. By discovering the developmental course of the disorder, one will know how to differentiate normal inattentive, hyperactive-impulsive behavior from ADHD in the early years. Such discriminations may depend a great deal on one's clinical experience; more specific guidelines (standardized age and gender diagnostic criteria) are needed (American Academy of Pediatrics, 2000).

— ❧ —

Rates of ADHD in other cultures have been estimated as follows: New Zealand (2–6.7 percent), Germany (8.7 percent), Japan (7.7 percent), and China (8.9 percent) (Flick, 2002).

Origin of ADHD: ADHD symptoms may result from a genetic predisposition, or symptoms may be acquired through some type of trauma (head injury, ear infections with high fever, or exposure to lead). Due to varying environmental conditions, the incidence of ADHD behaviors may vary with geographic location. Likewise, in areas where there is a higher incidence of head injury, there should be a higher incidence of ADHD-like behavior. It would therefore appear essential to have base rates for risk factors, as well as base rates for protective factors (e.g., a diet rich in calcium and iron may block the absorption of lead into the brain), when documenting the incidence of ADHD (Flick, 1998).

Cultural factors: Cultural bias is often cited as a possible factor in ADHD incidence determinations. If treatment with methylphenidate (Ritalin) reflects the actual incidence rate, the United States would rank highest because of its use of this medication. In the past, the incidence in the United States was reported as 3 to 5 percent of school children (Scahill & Schwab-Stone, 2000). Today, the best estimate of prevalence is 5 to 10 percent of school-age children. Thus, in any given U.S. classroom, two to four children may have ADHD.

Research has revealed that ADHD exists in multiple cultures. ADHD has been documented in Japan, China, South America, Europe, and India. It appears to be universal rather than specific to one culture (Hinshaw & Park, 1999). Several resources have reviewed cross-cultural issues (see Meyer, Eilertsen, Sundet, Tshifularo, & Sagvolden, 2004; Lloyd, Stead, & Cohen, 2006).

If ADHD were overdiagnosed in the United States, the incidence rates would be much higher than in other countries. Furthermore, while estimates of prevalence have ranged from 3 to 5 percent in the past, the percentage of children actually receiving treatment with stimulant medications has been closer to 3 percent. It would therefore appear that the condition of ADHD may actually be underdiagnosed, as well as undertreated.

Seven Myths About ADHD

1. *ADHD is not a real medical disorder.* ADHD has been noted to be a legitimate diagnosis as defined by *DSM-IV-TR* (APA, 2000). It has also been listed by the National Institutes of Health and the U.S. Department of Education as a specific disorder.

2. *Children who are given special accommodations because of their ADHD are getting an unfair advantage.* The special accommodations provided those with ADHD simply "level the playing field" so that kids with ADHD can learn just like their non-ADHD classmates.

3. *Children with ADHD eventually outgrow their condition.* Over 70 percent of those children with ADHD continue to manifest symptoms into adolescence. Nearly 50 percent continue to have symptoms into adulthood, when they may have vocational, legal, financial, and marital (relationship) difficulties.

4. *ADHD affects only boys.* Boys are more likely to be diagnosed primarily because of their acting out (aggressive/disruptive) behavior. However, it is now known that girls (who primarily show the inattentive type) are not immune to ADHD.

5. *ADHD is the result of bad parenting.* Effective parenting can help manage ADHD (Flick, 1996), and ineffective parenting can make ADHD symptoms worse, but parenting is not the cause of ADHD. Problems are rooted in structural and neurochemical differences in the brain, not discipline.

6. *Children who take ADHD medication are more likely to abuse drugs when they become teenagers.* Actually, untreated ADHD increases a person's risk of abusing alcohol or drugs. Appropriate treatment reduces this risk.

7. *People who have ADHD are stupid or lazy and never amount to anything.* Most children with ADHD have above-average intelligence and certainly aren't lazy. In fact, many famous people who were thought to have ADHD have overcome significant odds to achieve their goals (e.g., Amadeus Mozart, Benjamin Franklin, Abraham Lincoln).

—Adapted from *Additude*, www.additudemag.com.

LONG-TERM OUTCOMES FOR ADHD

As noted above, symptoms persist into adulthood for many children with ADHD. In an early long-term follow-up study by Borland and Heckman (1976) on hyperactive children and their brothers, it was noted that despite similar ability and educational levels, the hyperactive group had a lower socioeconomic status and increased antisocial behavior, along with social and marital problems. Goodwin, Schulsinger, Hermansen, Guze, and Winokur (1975) reported a relationship between early ADHD patterns and later alcoholism. Weiss and Hechtman (1993) noted in their long-term follow-up study that 10 percent of children with ADHD later attempted suicide as adults and 5 percent died from either suicide or "accidental injury," an incidence higher than would be expected in the normal population of their control group.

From one of the most comprehensive follow-up studies on *Hyperactive Children Grown Up* by Gabrielle Weiss and Lily Trockenberg Hechtman (1993), it was concluded that "a higher percentage of hyperactive subjects than normal controls had a history of antisocial behavior" (p. 408) and that "families of hyperactive children were found to have more psychopathology, particularly antisocial behavior, alcoholism, and hysteria, than normal control families" (p. 409). In studies of arrest rates of adolescents and young adults with ADHD, the ADHD subjects had significantly more arrests than did the controls. Also, it's been reported that young adults with ADHD are more likely than their matched controls to have been incarcerated.

Considering the link between criminal conduct (i.e., conduct disorder) and ADHD, this diagnostic condition has been used with limited success as a criminal defense. The approach taken has either been one of a "biological deficiency defense" (similar to temporal lobe epilepsy—a brain disorder) and described as "mental nonresponsibility" (insanity) or as a "diminished capacity defense." While this stance, to date, has reportedly helped more during the sentencing phase than in determining the verdict, most courts do allow such evidence, and the frequency of its use appears to have increased. A forensic neuropsychological evaluation of adolescents or adults with ADHD may, therefore, contribute to the legal process. Experienced clinicians who provide assessment and treatment of children, adolescents, and adults with ADHD would be essential for such an evaluation because of the complex array of factors (i.e., comorbid conditions) typically involved in such cases.

The long-term educational and behavioral outcome for students with ADHD is generally unfavorable. Some of the following have been correlated with negative outcomes for ADHD (Ellison, 2002): more severe symptoms/comorbid problems, aggressiveness, social interpersonal problems, trauma, low socioeconomic status, family disorder and parent psychopathology, and/or alcoholism. However, the following items have been correlated with a more positive outcome: treatment (Ellison), absence of impulsivity (Goldstein, 2002), higher intelligence (Ellison), special talents (Ellison), structure and predictability in the environment (Nadeau, 2002), an environment that accommodates ADHD (Nadeau), and a system of social support (Nadeau).

Some more recent longitudinal studies report that children with ADHD have significant academic underachievement, poor academic performance, and other educational problems (DeShazo, Lyman, & Klinger, 2002; Rapport, Scanlan, & Denney, 1999). Such children also show increases in repeated grades and the use of remedial academic services, and they are often placed in special education classes (Biederman et al., 1996). Children with ADHD are also more likely to be suspended or expelled (LeFever, Villers,

Morrow, & Vaughn, 2002). Longitudinal studies show that academic underachievement and poor educational outcomes associated with ADHD are persistent (Loe & Feldman, 2007). These authors conclude that "we remain ill informed about how to improve academic and educational outcomes of children with ADHD, despite decades of research on diagnosis, prevalence and short-term treatment effects."

A longitudinal study (Merrell & Tymms, 2005) investigated academic achievement of over 4,000 people with symptoms of ADHD. Achievement was followed up to age 11 years and compared with that of children who had no behavioral problems. Results indicated that children with ADHD started school with lower reading and math scores and continued to fall behind over time. Another study (Tymms & Merrell, 2004) found that providing teachers with suggestions on how to teach and manage students with severe ADHD symptoms had a positive impact on behavior; however, this approach did not affect academic achievement.

Longitudinal studies have also investigated the effects of stimulant medications on long-term outcomes (Pelham, 2004). The overall recommendations are that medications do little good beyond 24 months and their long-term use can stunt a child's growth. In August 2007, researchers from the Multimodel Treatment Study of Children with ADHD (MTA) reported on their first follow-up data. There were no differences between the behavior of children who were medicated and the behavior of those who were not. Data, however, did reveal that those children who took stimulant medications were about an inch shorter and six pounds lighter than those who did not (Vedantam, 2009). Brook Molina, a coauthor of the MTA study, reported that "children who stay on medications longer than two years [do not] have better outcomes than children who don't." In an e-mail to MTA coauthor William Pelham, she noted that "reviewers thought we were bending over backward (inappropriately) to dismiss the failure to find medication effects at 8 years" (as cited in Vedantam).

A study by Fabiano et al. (2007) did support the notion that using a behavioral intervention first allowed clinicians to give less medication. This idea was supported by Flick (1996) many years ago.

Pelham (2008) recommended that behavioral interventions be tried first, as these best meet the goals of treatment and minimize any adverse effects (on stature and weight) by minimizing stimulant medication use and dose. Pelham concluded by stating that "this approach has the best chance of maximizing the long-term adaptive outcomes of children with ADHD and their families." In a yet-to-be published study, Pelham found that

> 95 percent of parents who were told by clinicians to first try behavioral interventions for ADHD did so. When parents were given a prescription for a drug and then told to enroll their children in behavioral intervention programs, 75 percent did not seek out the behavioral approaches. (Cited in Vedantam, 2009)

SUMMARY

The core characteristics of ADHD are explained, and subtype descriptions, according to *DSM-IV-TR*, are provided. ADHD is a real disorder with a neurobiological basis. The outward appearance is often characterized not only by variation across subtypes but also confounded by several possible comorbid disorders. ADHD does change over the years, showing developmental differences between childhood and adulthood. Often, developmental changes occur at adolescence, when there is generally less hyperactivity. Long-term studies indicate that while stimulant medication is often helpful in the short term, long-term benefits are lacking. In many cases, ADHD may be treated without medication or with less medication when behavioral interventions are employed. Some of the latest research indicates that behavioral interventions should be used first; in all cases where stimulant medication is used, the best results occur when behavioral interventions are employed as well.

Diagnosis and Assessment of ADHD

Key Points

❖ Assessment of ADHD

❖ Rating scales

❖ Medication monitoring

❖ Behavioral alternative

❖ Primary functions of behavior

❖ Rewards

❖ Alternate placement

Maureen was a ten-year-old female with ADHD. She was taking Adderall-XR. Maureen was adopted when she was seven years old as the only child in the family. She showed poor relations with all peers, was not cooperative, and was often disruptive (e.g., yelling out) in groups. Maureen resorted to stealing small items, such as candy, pencils, and paper (taken from classmates or from her teacher).

How would you address these problems?

Diagnosis of ADHD is complex. The many overlapping symptoms make diagnosis and assessment difficult. As noted in Chapter 1, ADHD is often associated with other conditions (comorbid conditions), which may either mask the disorder or mimic it. It is unusual to find ADHD by itself. For example, a learning disability is often comorbid with ADHD or, at times, mistaken for it. When a child refuses to do work, gets off-task, or does not complete the work, the primary problem is often identified as ADHD. However, it is possible that the child may have difficulty doing the work and, as a result, gets off-task and does not complete it. Comprehensive diagnostics and assessments have been reviewed in other resources (e.g., Flick, 1998); it is not the purpose here to elaborate on diagnostic and assessment procedures.

Fortunately, teachers should not diagnose ADHD, nor should they recommend medication for a child. Diagnosis may be made by a psychologist or physician (e.g., pediatrician, psychiatrist, neurologist). Assessment is the purview of the psychologist, who identifies the strengths and weaknesses of each child.

Teachers are, however, involved in this process, first in the observations and ratings that they supply. Second, they are essential in monitoring either the effects of medication, a behavioral intervention, or both. Lastly, teachers may utilize suggestions, accommodations, or behavioral interventions to deal with behavior problems. This last function will require procedures that range from observation to intervention, regardless of what diagnostic labels are employed. Again, it should be emphasized that these interventions are to be implemented prior to a referral for more comprehensive Functional Behavioral Assessment (FBA) and Behavioral Intervention Plans (BIP).

ASSESSMENT OF ADHD

There have been several reviews of ADHD assessment (e.g., Anastopoulos & Shelton, 2001). These reviews have covered both narrowband and broadband assessment instruments.

Narrowband (Specific) Rating Scales

In general, there are few differences among these scales. These standardized ADHD rating scales are recommended by the American Medical Association (AMA) (Goldman, Genel, Bezman, & Slanetz, 1998), American Academy of Pediatrics (2000), the American Academy of Child & Adolescent Psychiatry (AACAP) (King et al., 1997), and they enjoy the consensus opinion of experts (Lahey & Willcutt, 2002). Parent and teacher versions of these scales are used; all are reliable.

Popular Rating Scales

There are many narrowband rating scales for ADHD. Some of the more frequently used rating scales that appear most helpful in comprehensive assessments are briefly reviewed here.

Vanderbilt Rating Scales

The Vanderbilt ADHD Rating Scales (VARS) are newer *DSM-IV-TR*-based scales with teacher-report (VADTRS) and parent-report (VADPRS) forms (Wolraich et al., 2003). (See Appendix B for a sample VADTRS form.) Similar to the Conners Rating Scales-Revised (CRS-R) and SNAP-IV, parent- and teacher-report forms include items measuring oppositional defiant disorder and conduct disorder, common comorbidities. A subscale for anxiety and depression, adapted from the Pediatric Behavior Scale (Lindgren & Koeppl, 1987), is also included, although this scale is not *DSM-IV-TR*-based. In addition, the VADTRS includes items that assess school functioning, and the VADPRS includes a comparable subscale to assess parents' perceptions of the youth's school and social functioning. Because studies have focused on school-aged children and the VADTRS has received more attention than the VADPRS, the focus here is on the VADTRS. Spanish and German translations of the VADTRS are available.

Conners Rating Scales

The Conners Teacher Rating Scale-Revised (CTRS-R) contains 59 items that parallel those on the VADTRS parent rating scale, except for the latter's psychosomatic scale, and was normed from ratings of over 2,000 teachers of persons age 3 to 17 years. The shorter, 28-item CTRS-RS covers the first three scales of the parallel parent form along with a global index.

The 10-item Conners Abbreviated Teacher Questionnaire is reportedly "diagnostically" sensitive not only to hyperactivity but also to conduct disorder. Since most teens have several teachers, the short form of this scale may be more useful. Specifically, it may be best to integrate rating-scale data from several teachers to assess how the teen manifests ADHD behavior in different contexts.

Spadafore Rating Scale

The Spadafore ADHD Rating Scale (Spadafore & Spadaford, 1997), standardized on 760 students, is designed for use by teachers to evaluate children ages 5 to 19. It was reportedly intended not only to detect ADHD but also to indicate the severity of problem behaviors. It consists of a 50-item behavior questionnaire (rating impulsivity, hyperactivity/attention, and social adjustment) and a 9-item ADHD index. The ADHD index includes criteria used to quantify on-task/off-task behaviors. The behavior scale is described as an effective screener that may be used to satisfy the assessment requirements of a 504 referral. However, this scale is also described as a "comprehensive evaluation" by the author of the scale (Spadafore & Spadaford), allegedly since the items cover a wide range of symptoms. No companion instrument for parents is available. An ADHD Observation Form is included to report results in five categories and requires about 10 minutes to complete. The Medication Monitor is comprehensive and may be useful by itself as a stand-alone measure that can be repeated over many weeks of treatment monitoring.

ADD-H Comprehensive Teacher Rating Scale

The ADD-H Comprehensive Teacher Rating Scale (ACTeRS) employs 24 items and 4 scales: attention, hyperactivity, social skills, and oppositional behavior. This rating scale provides separate norms for girls and boys (for ages 5 through 13). This scale is medication-sensitive, and it appears helpful in distinguishing between ADHD with and without hyperactivity. A parent form is available with similar scales, as well as an additional scale focusing on early childhood behavior. Since teacher ratings may be prone to halo and/or practice effects, some have recommended that two questionnaires be completed for a baseline measure, as ratings often improve between the first and second administration without any intervention. These rating scales are also sensitive to behavioral and pharmacological interventions.

All scales are listed in Table 3.1.

Table 3.1 Narrowband and Broadband Rating Scales for ADHD and Comorbid Conditions With Measures of Functional Impairment

Narrowband Scales (ADHD-Specific)	Age Range	# Items	Completion Time (Minutes)	Parent	Teacher
SNAP-IV	6–18	90	10	X	X
ADHD Rating Scale-IV	5–17	18	10–20	X	X
Vanderbilt Scales*	6–12	55 (P), 43 (T)	1	X	X
ADDES-e	4–18	46 (P), 60 (T)	15	X	X
ADHD Symptom Checklist-SC4	3–18	50	10–20	X	X
SWAN	4–18	30	10–15	X	X
Child Attention Profile	6–16	12	5	X	X
Home Situations Questionnaire (Revised)*	6–12	16	5	X	X
School Situations Questionnaire (Revised)*	6–12	12	5	X	X
Broadband Scales (ADHD General)	Age Range	# Items	Completion Time	Parent	Teacher
ADD-H	5–12	24	5–10	X	X
CBCL/TRF Child Attention Problems*	6–18	118	10–20	X	X
Conners Parent/Teacher Rating Scale*	3–17	80 (P), 59 (T)	5–10	X	X
BASC-2*	2–22	134–160 (P), 100–139 (T)	15–25 10–20	X	X
Academic Performance Rating Scale*	Grades 1–6	19	5		X

Functional Impairment Scales	Age Range	# Items	Completion Time	Parent	Teacher
Child & Adolescent Functional Assessment Scale	7–17	315	10	X	X
Behavioral Emotional Rating Scale	5–18	52	10	X	X
Brief Impairment Scale	4–17	23	5	X	X
Monitoring Scales	Age Range	# Items	Completion Time	Parent	Teacher
Child Attention Profile	6–16	12	5		X
The ADHD Monitoring System*		21	5		X
ADD-H*	5–12	24	5–10	X	X

*Recommended for evaluation/treatment. Please note that some scales have a different number of items for parents (P) and teachers (T).

Broadband (General) Rating Scales

These scales are not generally recommended for the diagnosis of ADHD (American Academy of Pediatrics, 2000) since the broad factors don't accurately identify children with ADHD (Brown et al., 2001). The Child Behavior Checklist (CBCL), along with the Teacher Report Form (TRF) (Achenbach & Rescorla, 2001) together with the Behavior Assessment System for Children (Reynolds & Kamphaus, 2002) are two frequently used instruments. A non-*DSM-IV*-based ADHD rating tool is the Conners Parent & Teacher Rating Scales. In general, these scales have good reliability and validity and are frequently used to assess comorbid problems and treatment outcomes (Barkley, 2000; Kolko, Bukstein, & Barron, 1999); they are sensitive to behavioral and pharmacological treatment effects. These broadband rating scales may complement individual evaluations, depending on the suspected condition(s). These scales will be especially helpful in defining the comorbid conditions.

Behavior Assessment System for Children, Second Edition (BASC-2)

The BASC-2 was developed by Cecil Reynolds and Randy Kamphaus (2004). A comprehensive set of rating scales and forms include the Teacher Rating Scales (TRS), Parent Rating Scales (PRS), Self-Report of Personality (SRP), Student Observation System (SOS), and Structured Developmental History (SDH). These scales, suitable for children age 2 through 21 years, provide a triangulation method of measuring behavior by analyzing the child's behavior from three perspectives: self, teacher, and parent. These scales are appropriate for use in identifying problem behaviors, as required by IDEA, and for developing the Functional Behavioral Assessment (FBA), Behavioral Intervention Plan (BIP), and Individualized Educational Plan (IEP). These assessments measure areas of behavior that are important for both IDEA and *DSM-IV-TR* classifications. Furthermore, these scales help to differentiate between hyperactivity and attention problems.

Child Behavior Checklist for Ages 6–18 (CBCL/6–18)

The CBCL/6–18 was authored by Thomas Achenbach and Leslie Rescorla; its development was reported in 2001. This scale uses reports from parents regarding their child's competencies (20 items) and behavioral/emotional problems (118 items). There are two open-ended items for reporting additional problems. The results provide for three competence scales (Activities, Social, and School): a Total Competence scale; eight cross-informant syndromes; and Internalizing, Externalizing, and Total Problems. The cross-informant scales are Aggressive Behavior, Anxious/Depressed, Attention Problems, Rule-Breaking Behavior, Social Problems, Somatic Complaints, Thought Problems, and Withdrawn/Depressed. The six *DSM*-oriented scales are Affective Problems, Anxiety Problems, Somatic Problems, Attention Deficit/Hyperactivity Problems, Oppositional Defiant Disorder, and Conduct Problems.

ADD-H Comprehensive Teacher's Rating Scale (ACTeRS), Second Edition

The ACTeRS is composed of 24 items that cover four factors: attention, hyperactivity, social skills, and oppositional behavior. The teacher rates the child on each item, using a five-point scale ranging from "Almost Never" to "Almost Always." Item scores can be totaled quickly and profiled to obtain percentiles for the four scales. Standardization is based on approximately 2,400 children in kindergarten through eighth grade, and separate norms are provided for boys and girls.

The scale is highly useful in evaluating and monitoring children who can't seem to pay attention in class. Because it is so quick and cost-effective, ACTeRS can be used to screen students or to confirm a suspected diagnosis of ADD or ADHD. It has proven particularly useful in differentiating children with learning disorders from those with ADHD.

For even greater diagnostic accuracy, the teacher rating scale may be supplemented with the ACTeRS Parent Form and the ACTeRS Self-Report. These give additional perspectives on the child's behavior. The Parent Form provides scores for the same four subscales as in the original ACTeRS, plus an additional scale focusing on early childhood behavior. Since this behavior is known to the parent but not the teacher, the Parent Form brings a new dimension to the assessment. The 35-item Self-Report provides scores for three scales: Attention, Hyperactivity/Impulsivity, and Social Adjustment.

DEFINING FUNCTIONAL IMPAIRMENT

Diagnosing ADHD based on symptoms ensures that the number and frequency of symptoms is tied closely to the impairment of an individual's functioning. The clinician typically defines the child's functional impairment by using information collected during the intake interview. This information is obtained either from the clinical interview, parent and teacher ratings, and/or the review of past records and reports (Pelham, Fabiano, & Massetti, 2005).

Two important scales deserve primary focus. These are (1) the Child and Adolescent Functional Assessment Scale, a multidimensional assessment of impairment, and (2) the Behavioral And Emotional Rating Scale, which is based on strengths instead of deficits. Both measures show good temporal stability and interrater reliability, as well as both concurrent and convergent validity. While each of these scale ratings is effective in identifying impaired areas of functioning, they have not been frequently used as measures of treatment outcome.

The Brief Impairment Scale (BIS)

The Brief Impairment Scale (BIS) is a 23-item instrument that evaluates three domains of functioning: interpersonal relations, school/work functioning, and self-care/self-fulfillment. Researchers conclude that the BIS is psychometrically sound and useful in assessments, as well as an outcome measure, in both clinical practice and research. Its advantages over other global impairment instruments are that it is respondent based, quick to administer, and multidimensional.

Once the clinician arrives at a diagnosis, the critical question remains as to whether a functional impairment exists. Even though a child carries a specific diagnostic label (i.e., a *DSM-IV-TR* diagnostic number), this student may not show impairment in school or elsewhere. Impairment may be assessed with an instrument such as the BIS (Bird et al., 2005). The functional impairment score will reflect how well the student has adapted to the demands of school. It also points to the importance of considering which problematic behaviors are of prime concern and must be addressed in the school or classroom environment. Again, this approach would be consistent with a specific behavior problem orientation in the school setting.

MEDICATION MONITORING

In addition to providing ratings and observations of children who show characteristics of ADHD, teachers may also rate medication side effects. (To increase their awareness of medication side effects, teachers are encouraged to refer to the Medication Side Effects Rating Scale [Appendix C]). For example, some students may show side effects such as lethargy, reduced appetite, or increased tics. It is important for teachers to relay this information to parents (or perhaps directly to the physician, when a relationship has been established with the physician).

Remember that while medication may help improve the school performance of students with ADHD, it does not change the underlying physiological deficits. The child will still manifest characteristics of ADHD when off medication. Further, if a child has a learning disability (LD) or a behavioral disorder (BD), then medication will not change these conditions; the child will continue to manifest symptoms of a LD or BD whether on or off the medication. Also, since ADHD is so complex, additional comorbid conditions may not be affected by medication.

A BEHAVIORAL ALTERNATIVE

Behavioral interventions for ADHD and other behavioral problems have already been demonstrated to be effective. Teachers will need to follow a prescriptive plan to focus on specific target behaviors when general suggestions and accommodations are insufficient to deal with behavioral problems. The general sequence of decisions is represented graphically in Figure 3.1.

Figure 3.1   Flowchart of Decision Making for Behavioral Interventions

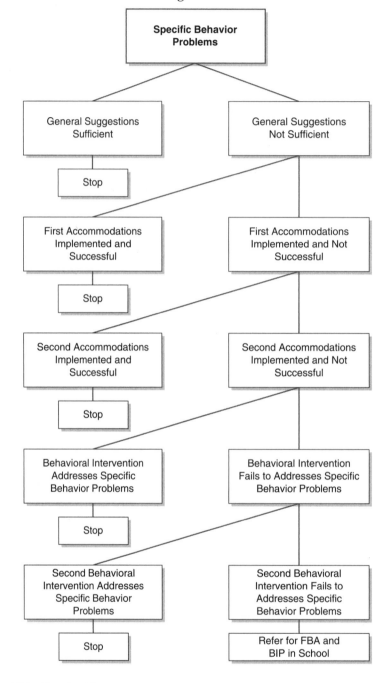

FBA = Functional Behavioral Assessment   BIP = Behavioral Intervention Plan

BEHAVIORAL OPERATIONS SEQUENCE

After implementing the general suggestions and accommodations, it is important for teachers to follow a basic sequence for each behavioral intervention. Of course, the first step is to define the problem. This means to list specific observable behaviors in order of their severity. Please note that the definition of *behavior* specifies that it be observable and countable. For example, "Mark hit John," would be a specific objective and observable behavior, in contrast to "Mark is aggressive." Another example would be "Mark is basically lazy"; a better description would be "Mark completes about 50 percent of his work (with variable results)."

Selection of Target Behaviors

A target behavior is one that is problematic; this behavior can be addressed by the behavioral intervention. See Figure 3.2 for a list of sample target behaviors. One should note that all of these behaviors are stated in a positive framework and all can be documented through observation.

Figure 3.2   Target Behaviors to Be Addressed by Teacher Programs

- Completes classwork.
- Completes chores.
- Plays appropriately with others.
- Plays by rules.
- Shows visual attention.
- Shows verbal attention.
- Puts desk in order (organizes).
- Puts room in order (cleans).
- Completes homework.
- Brings assignment book home.
- Maintains attention to task.
- Remembers things.
- Stays in seat.
- Engages in risky behavior.
- Relaxes quietly.
- Works quietly.
- Raises hand to ask/answer questions.

- Waits turn.
- Interrupts appropriately.
- Shows reduction of work errors.
- Displays appropriate behavior with peers.
- Follows directions.
- Checks work.
- Uses inside voice.
- Ignores teasing.
- Puts papers in binder.
- Participates in class.
- Asks for help.
- Improves handwriting.
- Knows class rules.
- Follows class rules.
- Knows bus rules.
- Follows bus rules.
- Uses appropriate language.
- Writes homework assignment.

- Maintains property.
- Shares with others.
- Cooperates with others.
- Gets along with peers.
- Makes positive comments.
- Speaks clearly.
- Accepts comments.
- Maintains eye contact.
- Talks respectfully to adults.
- Follows rules outside class.
- Walks in a line.
- Displays good table manners.
- Is responsible for belongings.
- Has needed class materials.
- Hangs up jacket/backpack.

Other Behaviors (Specify):

_____

_____

_____

_____

However, this list is not exhaustive and may not contain the target behavior for an individual child. In general, the child with ADHD may show off-task behavior, disorganization, failure to follow directions, incomplete or lost assignments, sloppy work, messy handwriting, disruptive behavior, and social skills problems. These problems may change with age. Some of the most common school difficulties associated with ADHD are found in the following box.

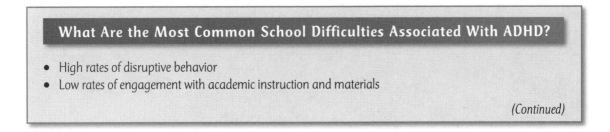

What Are the Most Common School Difficulties Associated With ADHD?

- High rates of disruptive behavior
- Low rates of engagement with academic instruction and materials

(Continued)

(Continued)

- High rates of disruptive behavior
- Low rates of engagement with academic instruction and materials
- Inconsistent completion of and accuracy on schoolwork
- Poor performance on homework, tests, and long-term assignments
- Difficulties getting along with peers and teachers

Adapted with permission from DuPaul & Stoner (2003).

The first step will therefore be to select a specific problem (target) behavior. Teachers may use the form Selecting Target Behaviors in Appendix D.

Choosing the Behavioral Intervention

The next step for the teacher is to select the behavioral intervention needed to address the problem (target) behavior. Although there are guidelines in the case studies and case examples, no concrete rules govern which intervention should be selected. Teachers must select any intervention that is *successful*. In short, if it doesn't work, something must be wrong.

If the intervention is successful, the program may be terminated after two weeks, and the behavior change can be maintained by positive behavioral supports (e.g., verbal praise).

The Behavioral Intervention Form may be used to plan the behavioral intervention. A blank Behavioral Intervention Form is in Appendix E.

Basic Behavioral Questions

Some basic behavioral questions must be answered before engaging any child in a behavioral intervention. These questions not only relate to the primary function of the behavior but also define the setting events, antecedents, and consequences for each behavioral intervention.

The primary function of the behavior problem may itself serve to indicate what needs to be done. For example, if the function of the problem (target) behavior is to escape or avoid a particular class, then one must question what about that class is difficult for the student. For example, perhaps the student avoids the class because it requires writing, or perhaps the class requires that the student read or be timed.

PRIMARY FUNCTIONS OF BEHAVIOR

Basically, there are two functions of behavior, and they are governed by positive or negative reinforcement. Positive reinforcement could involve positive outcomes for a problem behavior, such as attention from others, control of a situation, getting food or other tangible objects, as well as getting access to some individual(s), activities, or materials. Note, however, that reinforcement is highly individualized (i.e., what's punishing for one child may be reinforcing for another.) For example, a verbal reprimand may serve as a positive reinforcer (attention) for one child, while the same reprimand may punish the behavior of a second child.

Negative reinforcement occurs when the problem behavior results in the escape or avoidance of something that is unpleasant. For example, Michael learns that screaming or slamming his books on the desk will get him banished from a math class that he neither likes nor understands. Such misbehavior, which results in Michael being sent to the office, is exactly what he desires, thus reinforcing the problem behavior. Thus, it is more important to pay attention to the function of the behavior (getting out of math) than the form of the behavior (screaming/book slamming) when developing behavior interventions to control and replace the behavior.

Another function of behavior is sensory stimulation or sensory regulation. This function is especially important when working with children who have ADHD (Flick, 1998). It may also be a component of other disorders. In this case, the function of the child's behavior is to regulate (by increasing or decreasing) the level or type of sensory input in the environment.

This function could be subsumed either under positive or negative reinforcement. However, it could also be considered a separate function, since the child's behavior might result in an internal, nonobservable change. Problem behavior may be more understandable when considered as serving the function of increasing stimulation. The sensory regulation or sensory stimulation function might occur when there is a difference between the type or amount of sensory input in the environment and the child's internal sensory needs. Such a disparity may occur within any sensory system (e.g., tactile/touch, visual, olfactory/smell, auditory/hearing, gustatory/taste, proprioceptive and vestibular/sense of movement) (Emmons & Anderson, 2005).

For example, some children with ADHD may act out during quiet time or a quiet activity (e.g., reading). It would not be unusual for such a child to make vocal noises. This behavior would serve the function of increasing stimulation during an activity that is relatively passive and quiet. The sensory regulation or stimulation function might also occur when the child is unable to interpret correctly and respond to sensory input (O'Riordan & Passetti, 2006; Walker, Colvin, & Ramsey, 1995). Thus, when a child's behavior regulates sensory input or produces sensory stimulation, the interventions must address that child's sensory needs. No published studies have looked at combinations of variables (e.g., escape and attention) as opposed to separate functions.

Some time ago, Carr (1977) suggested that interventions should address the function of behavior by teaching students to communicate their needs, thus allowing them to achieve the same function through more appropriate behavior. In short, the child's problem behavior can be thought of as a form of communication, as well as a way to control the environment. Interventions that teach children more appropriate ways to communicate their needs has been called functional communication, and their goal is to teach functionally equivalent appropriate behavior in place of the problem behavior (Newcomer & Lewis, 2004).

Functional Behavioral Assessment prior to interventions has been well documented regarding replacing problem behavior with more appropriate behavior (Goldstein, 2002). It has also been used with children who have a variety of disabilities, as well as typical children (Kern & Dunlap, 1999). In fact, Horner, Carr, Strain, Todd, and Reed (2002) noted that the success of changing problem behavior was directly related to whether or not an FBA was conducted first, thus suggesting an intervention plan that matched the function of the behavior. It is important to be familiar with several possible functions of behavior and define the primary function of a problem behavior. Refer to the following box for a more complete listing of the primary functions of behavior:

> ## Primary Functions of Behavior
>
> - *Escape or avoidance*—avoiding a particular activity (e.g., a class), an interaction with a specific person or group, or an unpleasant situation
> - *Justice or revenge*—getting back at a person or group for a real or imagined slight, sometimes on behalf of a friend or family member
> - *Acceptance and affiliation*—belonging or gaining acceptance to a group; seeking to impress members of a peer group to gain admittance
> - *Power or control*—wishing to dominate, be in charge, control the environment; refusing to follow rules or directions; refusing to participate in some activities
> - *Expression of self*—seeking to announce independence and/or individuality to express the individual's vision of self
> - *Access to tangible rewards or personal gratification*—behaving so as to get tangible reinforcement (an item, money, or privilege); seeking to feel good or get immediate feedback or reward
> - *Sensory stimulation or sensory regulation*—wishing to increase or decrease level or type of sensory input to environment or produce sensory stimulation
> - *Play*—engaging in a play activity instead of the assigned task both to escape and to get stimulation, repeatedly with others or alone
> - *Seeking attention*—seeking either positive or negative attention from peers or the teacher (the most commonly identified function)
>
> *Remember*: A behavior can have a different function for different students. Know that many behaviors have attention as a secondary function in addition to some other function. Identifying attention too frequently may lead to an inaccurate hypothesis if it is the only function considered.
>
> Adapted with permission from http://dpi.wi.gov/sped/bul07-01.html (Wisconsin Department of Education).

Teachers must document the setting events, as well as the antecedents and consequences for the behavior problem and its alternative. The goal is to encourage and develop alternative behaviors (to the behavior problem) or to replace the behavior problem with a more desirable behavior.

TYPES OF REINFORCERS

Several types of reinforcers must be considered when establishing a behavioral intervention. There are basically three types of reinforcers:

1. *Primary reinforcers:* These are essentially the edibles. They should generally be avoided, but they can be used for an entire class (e.g., popcorn party).

2. *Activity reinforcers:* These are the essential activities that the child engages in at school. A good guideline for determining the strength of the reinforcer is how often the child engages in that activity.

3. *Social reinforcers:* These are the rewards that are given by teachers to students; they might be nonverbal (e.g., a pat on the back) or verbal (e.g., "Good work!"). Appendix F lists a sampling of nonverbal and verbal reinforcements.

Common Classroom Rewards

A list of common classroom rewards may be found in Appendix G. A list of reinforcers by age group for elementary, middle, and high school students can be found in the following box.

Suggested Reinforcers by Age Group

Elementary Students

- Listening to stories or music on a tape recorder or phonograph with earphones
- Working in an art corner with special paper scraps and pieces of art materials or working at the easel
- Audiotaping a story for the class to listen to
- Being first in line
- Leaving class early for lunch
- Taking charge of a variety of activities, such as attendance taking, passing papers
- Getting a drink at any time without asking permission
- Being allowed to clean the chalkboards and erasers
- Arranging the toys on the game shelf and being the first to pick a game to play
- Going to the library to work on a special project relating to a unit being studied
- Taking important messages to other teachers' rooms or to the office
- Tutoring a younger child in school
- Calling on students in the classroom (Turn to the student and say, "Your turn to pick a student.")
- Being able to look at magazines, special seasonal books, sports programs, etc. that are collected in a certain area in the room
- Being allowed to help the office secretary, custodian, cafeteria worker, or librarian for a 15-minute period

Middle School and High School Students

- Using a computer
- Doing extra-credit problems
- Having an opportunity to raise grades
- Making up questions to appear on an upcoming test
- Choosing the display to go on a bulletin board
- Challenging the teacher or another student to a mind game, such as Rack-O, chess, or a computer game
- Reading magazines in a corner of the room
- Listening to selected tapes on a tape recorder
- Appearing as a guest lecturer in other classes
- Doing special crossword puzzles that involve skills related to the content areas
- Solving mystery problems involving situations that require application of math skills
- Being dismissed early from class in order to work in the office
- Audiotaping a story for a student who is having difficulty reading

---

Of course, different children may be motivated by different reinforcers. To discover what motivates an individual child, teachers may use the Children's Classroom Reinforcement Survey in Appendix H and the Student Reinforcement Surveys #1 and #2 in Appendix I.

The teacher is now able to complete the questionnaire Basic Behavioral Questions in Appendix J.

ALTERNATE PLACEMENT

Should the teacher discover that the student does not respond to the interventions, the teacher may refer the child for more in-depth Functional Behavioral Assessment and Behavioral Intervention Plan. If the student still fails to respond, then the IEP team (that has conducted the FBA and BIP) may consider some alternate placements. Figure 3.3 may be used to make decisions so as to place the student at a level where he or she may be more successful and will not interfere with the ability of others to learn. The principle guiding this decision is to place the child in the least restrictive setting for the condition presented so that maximum learning occurs.

Figure 3.3   Consider Alternate Placement

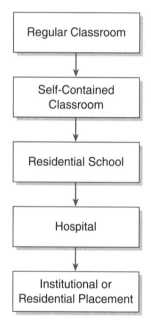

SUMMARY

This chapter covered the traditional assessment of ADHD with emphasis on the use of rating scales. A measure of functional impairment is essential for defining the disorder. Teachers often assume responsibility for medication monitoring as well as ratings of behavior functions. Most importantly, a behavioral alternative to traditional treatment may be employed. This behavioral alternative utilizes the primary foundations of behavior and knowledge of symptoms. Accommodations, general and specific suggestions, and behavioral interventions are discussed in this book. A symptomatic approach to behavioral intervention is proposed before a child is referred for the typical Functional Behavioral Assessment and Behavioral Intervention Plan. Should success not be forthcoming, alternate placement may be considered.

Education of Children With ADHD

Key Points

- ❖ General suggestions
- ❖ Academic suggestions
- ❖ Behavioral suggestions
- ❖ Accommodations/504 Plan
- ❖ Teaching children with ADHD

Marcus was a 14-year-old male who was classified as Other Health Impaired and had other behavioral problems. He was taking Vyvance. He was in a regular eighth-grade class functioning at grade level. Although Marcus was a bright child, he had trouble completing his work and was absent many days. He had been involved with a therapeutic program and showed a good response to this program. With medication, his therapeutic program was a success. He did show additional evidence of a conduct disorder, as he was arrested and placed in juvenile detention as a result of breaking and entering.

How would you address these problems?

There are three types of suggestions that may be used for students with ADHD:

1. *General suggestions*: These are helpful not only for students with ADHD but also for all students.

2. *Academic suggestions*: These deal with some of the specific deficits in academic work that the child with ADHD experiences.

3. *Behavioral suggestions:* These target the typical behavioral problems that many children with ADHD exhibit in the classroom.

Such suggestions are important in dealing with the characteristics of the child with ADHD in the classroom. Together with classroom accommodations, these suggestions may address some of the basic characteristics of ADHD. Teachers must remember that many of these students will not have a diagnosis but their problem behavior can still be addressed.

GENERAL SUGGESTIONS

These suggestions would be beneficial for all students in the classroom, including those with ADHD.

- The simplest behavioral technique is to praise the student whenever he or she displays appropriate behavior.
- Rules must be clearly understood. Simple rules (no more than five, stated positively) should be written down (i.e., posted) and reviewed periodically in the class. This helps to develop predictable routines.
- Exercise has many benefits. Teachers should try to incorporate some brief physical exercise, like stretching, into the academic routine. Standing for some academic activities (e.g., math facts, spelling bees) can also be helpful.
- Emphasize the quality of work, not the quantity. Understanding and accuracy are most important. Accept poor writing (if typical) but always praise improvement. Teach the self-instruction technique of verbalizing letter information or math processing while writing; this means that the child is taught self-talk as a slow-down technique to minimize careless errors. This technique uses both sides of the brain, the verbal left and the nonverbal right.
- Teachers should always keep parents informed and involved. Cooperative home and school programs can be very effective. In such cases, both parents and teachers must focus on positive information. Thus, the teacher may send notes home about the student's good behavior or improvements and even call parents to report on good behavior. Teachers should not contact parents only when there is a problem with behavior.
- Teachers must remember that learning should be fun for all students. Subjects may be made more interesting by varying the content of the subject and introducing some novelty.
- Offer more choices to complete activities. For example, students may write words on cards or write sentences with those words.
- Make sure that students comprehend the instructions before starting a task. In short, ask questions.
- Rules must be kept simple. Some examples might include "Work quietly," "Stay in your assigned seat," "Raise your hand to ask or answer questions," and "Complete task assignments."
- Teachers must use clear and specific commands. If the instruction is too complex, students need to know how to break it up into smaller units.
- Establish a classroom reward system where the entire class can earn a reward based either on how the class functions or the behavior of a specific student.

- Use rewards that any student can earn, whether disabled or not. This might be a class lottery, paper money, tickets, etc.
- Teachers need to establish goals for the class, as well as for individuals in that class.
- Transitions are difficult for any student but especially for the child with ADHD. Teachers must give advance warning when a subject (topic) will change or when an exam is nearing the end (e.g., warning at five minutes, then three minutes, then one minute).
- When giving directions, it's important for the teacher to have eye contact with the student. Watch the child's eyes and have the child repeat the instructions. Remember that the first step to remembering what to do involves attention.
- Make sure that each child understands the material. Many children will not say anything, so the teacher must query the student. Asking a child who is a good student and will likely know the answer about the material can provide a model of the material for another child.
- Ask questions of students. This engages their thinking (left brain) instead of always requiring that they "pay attention."

ACADEMIC SUGGESTIONS

These suggestions will help the child with ADHD with his or her achievement in various subjects.

- Monitor the student with ADHD to help maintain work activity, reinforcing the child for starting work, for continuing work, and for extending the work span (length of time before the child gets off-task). Continue monitoring until work is completed to reinforce work completion.
- Develop a private (nonintrusive) signal so that the child may be given this signal when not doing work (e.g., holding up a pen). When the child returns to work, you may give the student a pat on the shoulder or verbal praise. The child must also know how to signal the teacher when he or she needs help (e.g., by raising the hand).
- Use short work periods. This might involve breaking an assignment into shorter ones. Two 15-minute tasks may be more productive than one 30-minute task.
- Shorter assignments or alternate ways of doing the assignment (e.g., with a computer or a tape recorder) may be developed. Oral assignments would clearly help those children with ADHD who also have poor handwriting.

BEHAVIORAL SUGGESTIONS

These suggestions relate to some of the basic problems that are experienced by the student with ADHD. It should be emphasized, however, that students with ADHD are all different and not all suggestions will apply to every student with ADHD.

- Checklists are helpful for everyone but especially for children who are disorganized.
- Teachers may help children learn how to break down a project or assignment into smaller segments.

- It is best to seat the child with ADHD near the front of the class, as well as near others who can serve as positive role models.
- Children with ADHD should also be seated in locations that minimize distraction. Noisy air conditioners and high-traffic places, as well as doors and windows, should be avoided.
- Designate a study area or area for calming down (in the back of the classroom) for the child with ADHD and other children who may need to use it.
- In accordance with a shorter attention span, assignments should be brief, and feedback should be accurate and immediate.
- Instructions need to also be short, specific, and direct. It is helpful to teach a child with ADHD to repeat the instructions or paraphrase them in his or her own words. Teachers must also periodically check by asking questions of the student to determine if the message was received accurately.
- Students with ADHD may help the teacher by writing on the chalkboard or by assisting audiovisuals so that they are an active participant instead of merely staying seated.
- More lenient acceptance of handwriting or work output is important. Remember that quality is more important than quantity and that improvement should always be reinforced.

Specific ADHD Problems and Coping Strategies

Several of the problem behaviors commonly associated with ADHD may reflect underlying neurophysiological processes. For example, the child with ADHD generally has a lower level of alertness. Likewise, hyperactivity and poor fine-motor coordination associated with ADHD appear to be related to deficiencies in neurotransmitters. While some of these neurophysiologically based behaviors may be difficult to manage without medications, several other behavioral characteristics do respond to behavioral as well as other interventions. A discussion follows with specific steps a teacher can take to improve such behaviors in the school setting.

Excess Motor Activity/Hyperactivity

Children with ADHD and evidence of hyperactivity exhibit a lowered level of alertness; excess motor activity is believed to represent the child's attempt to maintain a more alert state (Flick, 1998). Without such motor activity, the child may become quite sleepy; in fact, many children do fall asleep in class. Generally such motor activity in girls tends to manifest as excessive talking (which has greater social acceptance), while boys may fidget, get out of their seats, or act out (which is less socially desirable behavior). While talking and moving around are not, of themselves, bad behaviors, they can become inappropriate and undesirable in the classroom setting. Such excessive actions tend to garner negative attention and often allow these children to avoid assignments that are perceived as difficult and "boring."

With children who have ADHD, some of this motor activity may always be going on, so the teacher must be somewhat flexible in this regard. Scheduling time for movement may be beneficial and should be incorporated into the class schedule. Problem behavior may vary with medication effects, diet, stress, and emotional factors—some of which may remain unknown. However, some improvement in the classroom may be obtained with the following steps:

Suggestions for Excess Motor Activity/Hyperactivity

- Establish the rules and limits for these activities, keeping in mind the physiological basis for the behavior.
- Develop predetermined signals that can cue students as to when to be quiet and when to talk (e.g., finger to lips; red light for quiet and green light for talking).
- Use movement as a reward for work completion. Assign short tasks and reward their completion with activity; then gradually increase the length of the tasks.
- Use students who obey the rules as models by reinforcing their quiet behavior with verbal praise. (Do not, however, compare children directly.)
- Practice using cognitive mediation by asking students who talk or who are out of their seats, "What should you be doing this moment?"
- Use many positive consequences for appropriate quiet behavior, fewer negative consequences for talking or being out of the seat.
- Use movement or talking as a positive consequence (i.e., privilege) for maintaining quiet or restricting movement at specified times or during certain activities. Also, other times for these behaviors may be prearranged (e.g., soft talking in designated areas allowed after work is completed).
- Use stretch breaks, exercise, or brief relaxation exercises to assist in self-control of motor movements.
- Integrate periods of active learning with seat work. Some teachers have students stand up for a review of math facts (e.g., multiplication tables) and randomly call on these students. This procedure will help to maintain attention, as well as allow for some movement.
- Allow students to become more aware of their need to move; then they can ask to move to a study carrel or to even work standing up.

Blurting Out/Impulsivity

Every teacher has at one time or another had problem children who blurt out answers instead of raising their hands and being called on to answer. This impulsive response style is one of the primary characteristics of ADHD. It is a basic lack of behavioral control. This characteristic also has physiological undercurrents and may only be controlled to a degree.

Suggestions for Blurting Out/Impulsivity

- Review and post rules regarding raising one's hand and being called on to obtain permissions (i.e., to answer a question, get assistance, go to the bathroom, etc.). In addition to posting written rules and/or verbalizing them, you may tape a card on the child's desk depicting the rule (see the example for "raising hand" in Appendix M).
- Ignore those who blurt out answers and fail to raise their hands.
- Praise those children who do raise their hands and use them as models. Remember, never compare one child with another; simply give the praise to the child who does the right thing. Make the praise specific, as in "Charles, you followed the rule and raised your hand to answer—very good. Now what is . . . ?"
- When a child who has blurted out before does raise a hand, direct attention to that student immediately.

(Continued)

(Continued)

- Monitor the number of times each day that the child with ADHD raises a hand to answer. Reward weekly improvement over the child's baseline levels and then over the previous week's performance. A simple count of the number of times the child raises a hand to answer may be kept from week to week. The count from the first week, before the problem is addressed, is used as the baseline. The intervention may start in the second week. In addition to counting the number of appropriate behaviors, give verbal praise and a backup reward when a specific goal is reached.

Off-Task Behavior: Distractibility or Inattention

Getting off-task may be related to many factors. For example, a novel stimulus (e.g., a siren) may attract attention. Children with ADHD satiate more rapidly than other children, even on interesting tasks. Boredom may turn these children to other interests, sometimes to things that they have brought with them to class in anticipation of experiencing boredom. Those with additional learning disabilities, commonly associated with ADHD, will likely experience frustration and difficulty in doing the work. As a result, a child may quickly lose motivation to continue working on an assignment.

Suggestions for Getting Off-Task Through Distractibility or Inattention

- Use preferential seating in the class so that cues/signals may be given and the student's work may more easily be monitored.
- Positively reinforce students who are on-task. A soft pat on the shoulder (nonverbal reinforcement) may be sufficient. Be aware also of those students who respond poorly to verbal praise while they are on-task. Elaborate verbal praise, in some cases, may actually cause students to get off-task.
- Reinforce completed work; this emphasizes the importance of continuing work to completion.
- Divide assigned work into smaller work components to help the child with ADHD. Knowing how long a child may maintain on-task work or about how many problems, sentences, and so on, the child can complete in one sitting will help the teacher divide up the work. The more the teacher knows about how to structure success for the child, the better the outcome will be for both student and teacher.
- Make it OK not to understand, to express frustration, and to ask for help. Many students get off-task when they hit a snag—perhaps a segment of the assignment they perceive as being too difficult or one they don't understand fully. The child must realize that he or she can communicate the difficulty to the teacher and then continue to work.
- Utilize some of the self-monitoring procedures described.
- A teacher might use privacy boards and allow the child to work in more isolated parts of the room or in study carrels.
- Plan for more active involvement in learning tasks to reduce distractibility.
- Cue the child to filter out excessive or distracting noise.
- As suggested by Dr. Mel Levine (1997), teachers may use reminder cards taped to the desk or notebooks. Messages might include verbal reminders such as "Am I turning out?" or "Am I listening to noise instead of the teacher?" Other reminder cards may simply have a nonverbal cue for appropriate behavior (e.g., cartoon picture of child doing work at desk).

Poor Attentional Skills: Visual/Auditory

Difficulty in listening, difficulty in following directions, and difficulty in paying attention are all common problems for children with ADHD. The basis for all of these difficulties is poor attention skills. Some children have the most difficulty with information that is presented visually; others—a minority—have difficulty with material that is presented through the auditory sense modality.

Suggestions for Poor Attentional Skills (Visual/Auditory)

- Keep all students actively involved in the learning process by calling out names randomly for answers. For example, when teaching multiplication tables, randomly name children to give answers.
- Use high-interest material and special projects related to concepts being taught to increase the student's interest.
- Use frequent questions to ensure that specific bits of information are learned, or simply rephrase questions to foster better involvement.
- Identify critical bits of information by specifically stating, "This is something that you will need to pay attention to." Another great attention getting device is to stop talking completely and pause; on most occasions, students will stop what they are doing and turn their focus on you.
- Repeat important information and present it in different sense modalities; for example, written (visual) and oral (auditory). Information is processed best with redundancy and repetition. In addition to your auditory and visual presentations, have the student write the material as well, to involve yet a third sense modality—kinesthetic.
- Print critical information in bright colors, write on the board with colored chalk, and use bright-colored paper or highlighters to help draw attention to material.
- Use prompts through your teacher's aides to help the child with ADHD get started and continue working. In class, prompt with questions such as "Joseph, what is it that you need to be doing right now?" to provide cognitive stimulation, which should cue the child to start (or continue) work. Initially, avoid direct requests, lest the child become dependent on your cue to begin work. It is far better for the idea to begin work to come from the child. Once this happens, you may say, "OK, you know what to do—now do it."
- Provide frequent reinforcement—praise or a soft touch on the shoulder—for those who pay attention. Use statements such as "Joe, you listened really well and you got the answer—good for you," or "I'm really proud of the way everyone started working right after I gave the directions," or "I really appreciate the way everyone looked at me while I gave directions."
- Use novelty to help elicit attention. Children with ADHD often respond and act like any other child in novel and challenging situations. In fact, novelties that might elicit mild anxiety in normal children may be beneficial to the child with ADHD. Of course, a delicate balance exists between choosing materials that are novel and stimulating and those that represent such a dramatic change that the child will have difficulty coping. Remember, the child with ADHD will have some difficulty adapting to drastic changes and transitions.
- Use an overhead projector, as suggested by Dr. Sandra Rief (1993); it will allow you to emphasize points of instruction visually, as with graphics. It will also allow you to reveal only those portions of the material you are discussing at the moment. This helps the child to focus on what is relevant.
- Use specific cues to denote where and when the child's attention is required. Rief (1993) terms these "point-and-go" signals.

Incomplete Work

This problem is intimately related to the problem of getting off-task. Put simply, if the child gets off-task to a significant degree, he or she will probably not complete the work assignment, whether it is classwork or homework. Once students develop poor work habits in class or at home, this pattern is likely to generalize to the other setting. To some extent, this problem may be resolved with the development of good class- and homework habits. Because of a poor sense of time, frustrations over the work, and various distractions, problems completing work may persist. However, establishing a consistent habit of appropriate work behavior will certainly be an important step toward successful task completion. Remember that children with ADHD have many problems with planning, organizing, and estimating time. Remember, also, that habits develop slowly. Don't expect the child "magically" to develop these learning habits overnight. If you have ever tried to develop a new habit, you know it can be a very slow process with many setbacks along the way.

Suggestions for Incomplete Work

- Monitor the input. Determine whether the child knows what to do by asking questions regarding class assignments or by enlisting the parents in using a homework-monitoring system.
- Teach the student how to self-monitor to plan and organize an assignment by modeling this behavior.
- Teach the student how to self-monitor progress toward a goal through using subgoals and a time schedule and to check if he or she is on course and on schedule. Use positive reinforcements as each subgoal is reached to provide incentive and motivation to continue.
- Provide periodic reminders, both visual and oral, so that the child is aware of the consequences both for incomplete work and for work completed.

Confusion Over Directions

This problem centers around attention. When attention falters during the presentation of task instructions, there is a breakdown of the information processed, which may result in confusion and a performance based on incomplete facts.

Suggestions for Confusion Over Directions

- For each task, provide simple, clear, and concise directions whenever possible.
- When directions are complex and require sequential planning, break them down and present the task step-by-step, providing reinforcement for completion of each step.
- Present directions both in writing (visual sense modality) and orally (auditory sense modality) and then post the written directions.
- Check to be sure "the message sent" was indeed "the message received." Sometimes it is best to call on someone who usually does get directions correct, then praise that student for giving accurate feedback on the assignment or tasks. This will demonstrate that knowing what to do is important, and that child gets a positive stroke. And when the correct answer is given, the child with ADHD is allowed to revise privately an initial misperception he or she might have had without the embarrassment of exposing that confusion aloud to the class.
- The teacher may find it beneficial to role-play and then rehearse what any child may do when he or she does not fully understand the directions for an assignment. Although this process might be obvious to most students, it well may not be obvious to the child with ADHD.

Disorganization

Many children who have ADHD are disorganized. Impulsivity, careless errors, and rushing through assignments lead to poorly organized work, confusion, and frequent forgetting of some part of the assignment. Such students may fail to complete all the work assigned because they have missed or misinterpreted what is needed to complete that assignment—or if they complete the work at home, they may forget to bring it back to school.

Suggestions for Disorganization

- Model organizational behavior patterns that are critical for the child to develop. These might include a neatly organized desk, planned lessons and activities, and an "everything in its own place" routine for materials, supplies, and books in the classroom.
- Post assignments and review them orally to aid the child in copying the assignment.
- Use a "study buddy" system so students can double-check homework assignments, due dates, and so forth, even after leaving school.
- If at all possible, enlist the active cooperation of the child's parents and use a homework assignment sheet (HAS) or planner.

  1. In the classroom, initial the HAS or planner to indicate that the child has written the correct assignment and has the needed books and other materials to complete it.

  2. Have the parent supervise completion of the work and initial the HAS or planner that the work was done and that it was filed in the appropriate place in the school bag.

  3. Failure to comply with a step in this sequence should result in a specific negative consequence (e.g., no privileges when materials are not brought home one day).

  By developing the kind of organizational routine illustrated on the HAS or planner, the child will learn a pattern of habits that forces him or her to self-monitor the steps in organizing work, using a checklist procedure. Using this type of monitoring system on the HAS or planner will also encourage the student to also mark a calendar with due dates for special projects.

- Focus on improvements in neatness and organization by giving compliments as often as possible.
- Follow up regularly with participating parents. (They need positive feedback, too!)

Poor Handwriting

Children with ADHD frequently have poor handwriting. This varies in degree from severe (dysgraphia) to mild (i.e., sloppy work at times, although the child has demonstrated being capable of better work). In the latter case, the child's work may be sloppy because he or she rushes through it with a generally impulsive style.

Suggestions for Poor Handwriting

- Provide each student with a sample of your rules for written work. This may include type of paper, the placement and sequence of identifying information (e.g., name, class, date), whether to use ink or pencil, whether proofreading is necessary, whether script or print is acceptable, as well as any other criteria you may have for this level of instruction.

(Continued)

(Continued)

- Use graph or computer paper to aid the child with fine-motor coordination problems. It may be especially helpful if the child starts with very large graph or computer pages; then gradually reduce the size of the squares or lines (using a copy machine with the enlargement-reduction feature). This approach will allow the teacher to reduce the size of the writing of letters or numbers gradually as coordination improves.
- Help the student use a cognitive mediation approach while writing. This use of self-talk forces the student to slow down and pay closer attention to the details of writing; it involves commenting on every movement involved in writing. While it is somewhat laborious at first, students who use this procedure do slow down and do generally produce neater work. Because the verbal component (self-talk) correlates with visual and kinesthetic cues, there is more whole-brain involvement in the graphic writing process.
- Of course, reinforce for those papers done neatly; also be alert for and reinforce noticeable improvements. In addition to giving verbal praise for better fine-motor control in handwriting, posting the student's better work will provide a model as well as a reinforcement.
- When a student has previously demonstrated better handwriting, sloppy papers may be returned to be redone.
- Be flexible with students exhibiting dysgraphia. Note that students with severe problems who show little variation in poor handwriting may function better using an alternative means to complete work, like a computer or a tape recorder. It may be necessary for a teacher to reduce drastically the amount of written work, and tests may best be administered orally. According to Dr. Mel Levine (1993), these techniques are called "bypass strategies" because they circumvent a child's dysfunctions.

Homework Problems

Though these problems primarily take place at home, it must be said again that solving the problems of students with ADHD requires the involvement of both teachers and parents.

Suggestions for Homework Problems

- As described above, coordinate with parents the use of a homework assignment sheet (HAS) or planner. This is checked at school and at home to monitor assignments given. Use of e-mail may also be considered.
- Assign a "study buddy" to help double-check accuracy of recording the assignments and to provide backup information when needed. Having several phone numbers may be more useful than having just one.
- Write assignments on the board and review each one orally.
- Develop an assignment sequence in advance and make it available to parents if needed.
- Teachers may need to modify assignments individually for those students who also have specific learning disabilities in reading, spelling, math, or writing. If the learning disability involves writing, a general reduction of written work is needed, and perhaps the teacher should allow that child to use a word processor to complete some assignments.
- Many teachers do not wish to continue to check homework assignments, especially when several students in the class are having problems writing down assignments. A general solution is to teach the students how to do this task through regular training exercises. An excellent resource for this is the Skills for School Success program by Archer and Gleason (1989).

Social Skills Problems

Although not all children with ADHD have problems with peer relationships, such difficulties are encountered with sufficient frequency to warrant their inclusion here. Considering the child's difficulty with controlling impulsive tendencies, problems with rule-governed behavior, and the often noted low frustration tolerance, it is not surprising that many have problems with aggression. In social play, their characteristic difficulty playing by the rules, taking turns, and simply listening and following directions may result in some upsets on the playground, in the lunchroom, and on the school bus. School problems related to ADHD behavior are not limited to the classroom; they are exhibited in other school-related activities as well.

Suggestions for Social Skills Problems

- Post and orally review rules for the school-related activity or situation just before the child goes into that social situation.
- Review the consequences for breaking those rules. Rules and consequences about social behavior should be reviewed daily at the beginning of the year and periodically thereafter.
- Incorporate a "behavior report card" for recess, lunchtime, or on the bus as part of an overall behavior program (either solely school based or home-school based). This "report card" covers both appropriate and inappropriate behavior.
- Generally focus positively on the more appropriate "alternative" behavior.
- Set up more structured play activities wherein appropriate behaviors are more likely to occur so that those behaviors may be encouraged more often.

ACCOMMODATIONS

Many children may have trouble with an academic subject; however, this does not mean that they cannot learn. Using accommodations for their specific problem, students may learn more easily and may be better able to communicate what they know. If the child has an Individualized Educational Program (IEP) and receives special education, accommodations may already be provided in the student's regular class. This student may also receive accommodations under Section 504, a federal law that prevents discrimination.

Many teachers routinely make accommodations in their regular classes for a child who is having problems. In planning or requesting accommodations, it is important to focus on the main needs of the child. Sometimes what worked for one parent or for another child may not be appropriate for the student in question. With the help of the child, two to five accommodations could be identified as helpful. Some of the suggestions below may also apply to the child at home. It is important for the child to agree to use the suggested accommodations if they are to work.

> ### The 504 Plan
>
> A 504 Plan is a legal document falling under the provisions of the Rehabilitation Act of 1973. It is designed to accommodate the unique needs of an individual with a disability and to assist those who have special needs but who are in a regular education setting. Students with ADHD often have a 504 Plan. A 504 Plan is not an Individual Education Program (IEP), which is required for special education students. However, a student moving from a special education to a regular education placement could be placed under a 504 Plan. Depending upon the student's individual needs, a school district may be required to provide the following: specialized instruction, modification to the curriculum, accommodations in nonacademic and extracurricular activities, adaptive equipment or assistive technology devices, an aide, assistance with health-related needs, school transportation or other related services, and other accommodations.

The Accommodation Process

The student's Section 504 team will need to review the suggested accommodations. This multidisciplinary team should consist of an administrator, the child's teacher, the parent, a special education teacher, other related service providers, and the student. The accommodations should be reviewed on an annual basis, preferably as part of the student's 504 Plan. All of the instructional accommodations that have been successful in the past, along with any additional accommodations, should be discussed. Any assessment-related accommodations should be based on the day-to-day instructional accommodations. Each accommodation must be justified and documented and all accommodations must be included in the student's 504 Plan.

List of Some Accommodations

Accommodations are things that the school or teacher does to make it easier to learn. These are adaptations or adjustments to what is being taught. Using accommodations is very much like the student using crutches for a broken ankle or having an arm in a sling. During that time, the temporarily disabled student may be given a modified form of exercise or perhaps no exercise at all. The student with ADHD may be excused from written assignments, or some alternate means of demonstrating learning may be allowed (e.g., oral tests or dictating responses into a tape recorder).

Appendix K lists some common and general accommodations. Appendix L lists 504 accommodations.

TEACHING CHILDREN WITH ADHD

Teachers of children with ADHD often encounter problem behaviors and situations quite similar to—and sometimes even more severe than—those faced by the parents. Additionally, teachers could encounter some ADHD behavior that is unique to the classroom. When a teacher reports such a behavior problem, a parent may confront the teacher with a statement like "Well, I don't have this kind of trouble with him at home. Why is he such a problem in your class?" The implication is that the teacher is structuring and handling the class and, specifically, interacting with the child incompetently. The teacher may resort to more drastic measures (i.e., punishing or ostracizing) to gain control, only to realize a continuing or worsening problem. Some teachers might then become defensive, feeling inadequate, overwhelmed, and overstressed.

Problem situations may result from a lack of understanding about ADHD and resultant behaviors, especially when the teacher has little or no knowledge of strategies to deal effectively with such behavior. Teachers who do not have such knowledge and skills may feel that their competency is threatened; they develop feelings of inadequacy, depression, and self-doubt and, ultimately, a sense of hopelessness and failure. After a teacher has a good understanding of ADHD along with the accompanying behaviors and has learned effective techniques for dealing with such behaviors, he or she can become more effective in interactions with the child who has ADHD and comorbid problems. The teacher will experience an enhanced sense of professional competence and a greater personal motivation for teaching children who manifest ADHD and related behaviors. Teachers are encouraged to read the *CHADD Educator's Manual* (Zeigler Dendy, 2006), which covers general concepts about ADHD, school assessment procedures and treatment recommendations, and some of the current legal issues around ADHD.

Teacher-Student Interactions

The three major factors regarding teachers that directly influence students with ADHD are (1) the teacher's knowledge of ADHD, (2) the teacher's individual characteristics, and (3) the teacher's teaching style.

Teacher Knowledge of ADHD

Teacher knowledge of ADHD is probably the most significant factor. Understanding ADHD behavior is essential to dealing with it effectively. Some common misunderstandings may unduly stress the child with ADHD and adversely affect his or her relationship with the teacher.

Inconsistency is a primary characteristic seen in the work performance of the child with ADHD; the child may do well with a given learning task one day and perform poorly on the same type of task the next day. Inconsistency in performance may set the child up for another problem: undue pressure. Teachers may say, "I know you can do this work because you did it quite well yesterday." Dr. Russell Barkley (2000) has eloquently reported that when the child with ADHD succeeds one time, we hold it against him for the rest of his life. However, when the teacher understands this characteristic and expects the child with ADHD to be inconsistent, then the teacher can take a more objective approach to change, applying less emotional pressure and stress and making fewer derogatory statements, such as "The child is just lazy—he can do better."

A general understanding of all of the basic characteristics of children with ADHD is critical to helping these children learn. For example, rather than criticize or embarrass the child who is disorganized, teachers may help the younger child develop skills and strategies to improve organization, such as the use of divided three-ring binders with subjects separated by color and a plastic pouch to keep pencils and other tools together. The teacher may also understand and recognize the child's need for stimulation by varying materials used for classroom tasks while keeping the content consistent; children with ADHD need the stability of routine but also variation within that routine to maintain greater interest. Likewise, slow-down tasks may be utilized for children with ADHD who have problems with impulsive responding. Use of self-talk and reminders to raise their hand to answer questions or to make comments communicates an understanding of the child's basic problems. Furthermore, addressing attention problems and distractibility through the use of self-monitoring procedures acknowledges the child's difficulties in a manner that accommodates the problem and considers potential emotional reactions.

Teacher Characteristics

A teacher's individual characteristics constitute another influential factor in dealing with the child who has ADHD. The most obvious such characteristic is teacher flexibility. A teacher who is open to adjusting for the problems experienced by a child with ADHD will have more success in dealing with these behaviors. On the other hand, if the teacher is rigid and inflexible, the child with ADHD will have greater difficulty, and so will the teacher.

Example: An inflexible teacher gives an assignment and insists that all students complete it in the same manner. A flexible teacher, in contrast, accommodates the child with ADHD with regard to her short work span and divides the assignment into two or three shorter assignments.

Another individual characteristic is teacher sensitivity. A child with ADHD is already aware of being somehow "different" from other students. Compounding this sense of being different, the child's self-esteem surely will suffer if the teacher also openly confronts the child about test grades or medication or embarrasses her over misbehavior. Any child's self-concept is seriously compromised by a history of ridicule and failure. A child with ADHD is a supersensitive child who needs a sensitive and caring teacher.

Teaching Style

A teacher's style of teaching is the third main factor affecting a student. Teachers who have problems teaching a child with ADHD often have a teaching style that is not well suited for such students. Such a style may reflect the following:

- A hurried method of teaching, speeding through lessons and assignments.
- A general lack of organization in presentation of lessons.
- A general lack of attention to those quiet students who don't stand out and, thus, attract the teacher's attention. (While a teacher certainly can't ignore disruptive students, he or she may often overlook the quiet, somewhat withdrawn student with primarily inattentive ADHD who mostly just daydreams.)
- An authoritarian approach, which may result in considerable conflict with students who have ADHD and who typically have difficulties with rule-governed behavior. (A teacher using a more relaxed approach may face far fewer conflicts, depending, of course, on how these conflicts are handled.)

Teacher Perceptions

How teachers perceive different interventions for children with ADHD was noted in a study by Pisecco, Huzinec, and Curtis (2001). The study looked at 159 elementary school teachers. Each teacher was given a short vignette describing the classroom behavior and the academic performance of a typical child with ADHD. A boy was described to half of the teachers; a girl to the other half. Following the vignette, teachers were provided brief descriptions of four interventions that could be used with a child: (1) daily report card (DRC), (2) response cost, (3) classroom lottery, and (4) stimulant medication. Teachers rated the daily report card as most acceptable; the classroom lottery least acceptable. In fact, the DRC received higher ratings than medication for both boys and girls. For girls, the response cost procedure also got higher ratings than medication. Overall, teachers rated stimulant medication as less acceptable for girls with ADHD than for boys with ADHD. Overall, teachers also believed that the DRC intervention would be as effective, in producing change, as would stimulant medication. Furthermore, they believed that the DRC would be more effective for girls than for boys, whereas stimulant medication would be more effective in boys than in girls. In general, teachers did not favor the use of stimulant medication for either boys or girls with ADHD. Of course, this study was based on a limited number of teachers; future research should survey a larger representative sample of teachers regarding a larger number of treatment interventions, including combinations of treatment.

ACADEMIC INSTRUCTION

The first major component of the most effective instruction for children with ADHD is effective academic instruction.* Teachers can help prepare their students with ADHD to achieve by applying the principles of effective teaching when they introduce, conduct, and conclude each lesson.

- Students with ADHD learn best with a carefully structured academic lesson—one where the teacher explains what he or she wants children to learn in the current lesson and places these skills and knowledge in the context of previous lessons. Effective teachers preview their expectations about what students will learn and how they should behave during the lesson.
- To conduct the most productive lessons for children with ADHD, effective teachers periodically question children's understanding of the material, probe for correct answers before calling on other students, and identify which students need additional assistance. Teachers should keep in mind that transitions from one lesson or class to another are particularly difficult for students with ADHD. When they are prepared for transitions, these children with ADHD are more likely to respond and to stay on task.
- Effective teachers conclude their lessons by providing advance warning that the lesson is about to end, checking the completed assignments of at least some of the students with ADHD, and instructing students how to begin preparing for the next activity.

In addition to the general strategies for introducing, conducting, and concluding their lessons, effective teachers of students with ADHD individualize their instructional practices in accordance with different academic subjects and the needs of their students within each area. Children with ADHD have different ways of learning and retaining

---

*Material in this section was adapted from U.S. Department of Education. (2006). *Teaching children with attention deficit hyperactivity disorder: Instructional strategies & practices,* retrieved from www.ed.gov/rschstat/research/pubs/adhd/adhd-teaching-2006.pdf.

information, not all of which involve traditional reading and listening. Effective teachers first identify areas in which each child requires extra assistance and then use special strategies to provide structured opportunities for the child to review and master an academic lesson that was previously presented to the entire class.

Many students with ADHD are easily distracted and have difficulty focusing their attention on assigned tasks. However, specific interventions can help children with ADHD improve their organization of homework and other daily assignments. In addition, children with ADHD often have difficulty in learning how to study effectively on their own. Some strategies may assist ADHD students in developing the study skills that are essential for academic success.

SUMMARY

This chapter begins with a review of general suggestions for students and suggestions for improving academic work and behavior. Also explored is the use of accommodations and modifications for the child with ADHD, together with a list of commonly used accommodations and accommodations employed with students who have a 504 Plan. Recommendations for teaching children with ADHD are offered. After the implementation of appropriate suggestions, accommodations, and teaching recommendations, students who continue to show behavioral problems may be addressed with symptomatic targeted interventions as described in this clinical manual. Those who still fail to respond (even with medication) may be referred for a more formal Functional Behavioral Assessment (FBA) and a Behavioral Intervention Plan (BIP). Those who fail to respond may also be considered for an alternate educational placement.

Basic Behavioral Techniques

Development of Appropriate Behavior

Key Points

- Premack principle
- Communication
- Verbal praise
- Modeling
- Differential reinforcement
- Behavioral plans
- Positive practices
- Point/token systems

- Home-school behavior chart
- Social skills
- Following instructions
- Sharing
- Cooperation
- Self-esteem
- Contingency contracting

Dylan is nine years old and in the third grade. He was diagnosed as having ADHD when he was in the first grade. He couldn't stay seated or keep from talking. He reportedly didn't finish his homework or his chores. Dylan also engaged in risky behaviors. For example, he climbed a tree to get onto the garage, and he ran across the street without looking on many occasions. He was not taking medication.

Dylan now does some of his work standing up; he also cleans the classroom and washes the chalkboard. Teachers have divided up his lessons, and they may give him only one part at a time. Each time he finishes short tasks, he is given praise.

Dylan's parents also give praise when he does something well. After a set number of small rewards (points), he selects something to do with his parents.

Would you do anything else to help Dylan learn?

In general, it's important to know that the best behavioral techniques are positive ones. This brief summary of behavior management procedures will emphasize positive techniques. Many other techniques are available for use, and the interested teacher may consult one of the resources listed at the back of this book.

BASELINE

Teachers must use some type of behavioral observation to have baseline data to compare with post-intervention data. These behavioral observations are typically recorded for at least one week—these are the baseline data. (Baseline recordings are shown for specific examples in Chapter 7.) Then, the effectiveness of the intervention can be determined. Such comparisons not only allow the teacher to state that intervening is better than doing nothing but may also allow for comparing the effectiveness of various interventions, should they be medical or behavioral.

PREMACK PRINCIPLE

This technique is a motivational procedure. This means getting the child to do something that he or she hasn't been doing. The basic procedure is also called "Grandma's Rule." Remember what grandma said: "When you eat your dinner, then you can have dessert." This can be put in a when-then format; for example, "*When* you finish your homework, *then* you can watch TV," or "*When* you do your chores, *then* you can go out and play." This procedure is so simple, it's the basis for most all behavior management.

There are a few conditions to consider:

- What you want the child to do must be developmentally appropriate and reasonable. For example, if a teacher asks the child to clean the whole classroom, this request might be unreasonable. If the teacher asks for something that the child has difficulty doing (e.g., math work), the child might resist. Ask this question: "What is so difficult about this task?" You must find out if there is a reason for the difficulty. For example, many children who have ADHD may have trouble remaining still, paying attention, or showing self-control. All of these problems may be physiological; that is, associated with differences in their nervous system.
- The payoff must be reasonable. For example, few children would clean their classroom for a penny. The payoff must be appropriate to the task expected. Perhaps it will be appropriate to talk to the child to come up with reasonable tasks and expected payoffs together.
- If the task is one that the child hasn't done, it may be necessary to model the behavior so that the child can imitate it. Remember, too, that the teacher can be lenient with the child's behavior at first, then expect more as the child shows that behavior more often (i.e., gets better at doing it). Cleaning one's desk is a good example. It is unlikely that the child will be able to do this very well the first time, but accept

improvement. Also, be sure to review what is meant by *clean your desk*; you might know, but the child may not. Furthermore, list what must be done to get the desk clean and be specific (e.g., books placed in desk neatly, all papers sorted in appropriate folders, trash thrown out).

Perhaps the most important thing about behavior management is to *be consistent*. This means to be consistent with (a) the behaviors you reinforce, (b) your expectations, and (c) the way things are done over time. Also, it is detrimental for one teacher to use positive behavior management techniques if other teachers do not. In fact, any difference can be confusing and may interfere with learning.

COMMUNICATION

This is the input in the system, so it's important to be clear about what a child should expect and what rules to follow. Rules should be few in number (maximum five), simple, clearly stated, and posted (i.e., on signs). They need to be reviewed periodically.

It's also best not to have to give many directives unless the behavior is a new one that is in development. Instead, it's best to ask questions. For example, at math time, instead of telling the older child what to do, say, "What are you supposed to do at this time?" If the child answers correctly, say, "That's right—do it." If he or she does not answer correctly, say what needs to be done and ask again, "Now, what is it you have to do?" This gives you a chance to give verbal praise when the child gets it right. After assignments are given, query the child about what needs to be done (e.g., "Now what was the assignment I gave you to do?"). If the child answers correctly, say, "Good, you were listening very well, and you got the assignment. Now go ahead and do it."

When giving specific instruction, it's best to do so when you are directly in front of the child and while you have eye contact. This allows you to reinforce the child for looking at you. If the child has trouble with this, you might gently hold his or her head (for younger children) so that the child is looking at you. You can then ask, "Now what did I just ask you to do?" Again, if the child's answer is correct, reinforce with verbal praise; if it is not correct, repeat the instruction and ask again. Each time the child gets it right, he or she deserves verbal praise. Say, "That's right—do it!"

If the child hesitates, count to three. Say, emphatically, "I'll give you to the count of *three* to do it!" If the child does what you ask before three, say, "Very good, I'm glad you decided to do [whatever]." Count slowly, one number per second. If the behavior is a new one under development, be sure to model that behavior and give the child a chance to imitate it. Reinforce any positive correct response.

Abide by the following basic rules of behavior management.

Teacher's 10 Rules of Behavior Management

1. Be *generous* (especially with verbal praise).

2. Be *watchful* (for any good behavior or any improvement).

3. Be *reasonable* (with expectation/rules and consequences).

(Continued)

(Continued)

4. Be *clear* (state rules/expectations and communications clearly).

5. Be *specific* (especially with verbal praise).

6. Be *consistent* (over time and across other teachers and parents).

7. Be *patient* (behavior change is a slow process).

8. Be *strong* (remember, bad behavior gets worse before it gets better).

9. Be *persistent* (behaviors are slow to change—reward improvement).

10. Be *smart* (use the positive approach wisely).

VERBAL PRAISE

Your verbal praise is reinforcing, but it's important to know how to give it.

* Be very specific and describe exactly what you like about the child's behavior. For example, "I really like the way you asked that question."
* Give praise immediately after the child shows the appropriate behavior. It's not very effective to say, "You know, that was very good the way you talked to me yesterday." That's not specific, and it's too late to be effective.
* Whenever you are trying to develop a behavior that is weak, be consistent about giving verbal praise each time you see the behavior. Once the behavior is developed, you can taper off reinforcement (i.e., give less verbal praise).

There are three occasions to give praise:

1. When the child shows any good appropriate behavior. Sometimes, many of these behaviors are taken for granted and not noticed. A child with a behavior disorder needs as much verbal praise as possible. *Focus on any good behavior.* Make a list so that you will be familiar with all of the child's good behavior. No matter how much inappropriate behavior is shown, the child will always show some appropriate behavior as well.

2. When the child shows an improvement in behavior. Again, this could be any behavior—academic or social. Examples would include improvement in handwriting, throwing a ball, language, grades, sitting still, etc. The list would be very long. When you see such improvement, note it by saying, "You know your handwriting has improved a great deal. Keep up the good work," or "I've noticed that you are dressing a lot better. You're looking good, and I'm proud of you!"

3. When you are trying to establish a new behavior. This means you are trying to teach the child an appropriate behavior, which may be a replacement for an undesirable behavior. Verbal praise should then be immediate and consistent (i.e., every time you see the behavior). For example, you may wish to teach the child appropriate social behaviors, such as saying *please* and *thank you*. First, model this behavior, and when the child imitates, say, "That's right—you got it!"

It's important to vary the reinforcement from time to time; for example, "I like to hear you say please," "You said please—that's very good," or "Saying please is a very grown-up thing to do." Alternate ways of giving praise could be established by first writing them down and then practicing them, perhaps rehearsing them in front of a mirror or using a tape recorder to hear how they sound. Praise should be honest and automatic—this means it should not sound like it was practiced. It's also important to use language that you feel comfortable with and to avoid just saying, "Good boy," or "Good girl." Remember that you must describe what you liked about the behavior (be very specific). "Good boy," or "Good girl," does not say anything about what you liked about the child's behavior.

All children must learn appropriate behaviors for school and in other situations. Whenever the child needs to develop a new behavior, consider the child's age and physical capabilities and whether there are any interfering behaviors. Behaviors that are inappropriate may be physiologically based or may be learned or acquired in association with behaviors that are physiologically based.

INDEPENDENT FUNCTIONING

When students receive direct instructions about their work, they can become dependent on the teacher. If the student does not have to think, he or she may simply wait to be told what to do. By asking questions, students must think about what they need to do. When the student shows good thinking and arrives at the correct answer, the teacher can reinforce this process by stating "Yes, that's correct," and then "Now do it." Here, the student arrives at the correct answer, gets reinforced with praise, and now does the task because he or she thought of it, not simply because the teacher said to do it. This approach obviously would not work for something that is needed for the first time, but it does apply to tasks that are done routinely, where the student should know what he or she is supposed to be doing. Asking questions will thus be an important part of teaching the student to "think for him- or herself."

DEVELOPING NEW BEHAVIORS

Listing Alternative Appropriate Behaviors

Evidence from clinical research indicates that behavioral programs that focus solely on punishing inappropriate behaviors may work only for a short time (Flick, 1998). Mild punishments may be necessary for some inappropriate behavior, but when the entire focus is on punishment (mild or severe) for inappropriate behaviors, that negative focus may backfire, bringing about results contrary to desired behaviors. Thus, teachers must focus on developing more appropriate behaviors through a positive orientation. The first step in this process is to list appropriate behaviors that are alternatives to the ADHD behaviors typically exhibited.

Exercise 5.1 focuses on listing behaviors that are alternatives to typical ADHD behaviors. When writing these alternative behaviors, teachers must think of the appropriate behavior that they would like to see in place of the typical ADHD behavior (e.g., if interrupting others is typical, then waiting one's turn to talk is desired). Teachers should try their hand at writing these, then check the example for feedback.

Exercise 5.1 Listing Alternative Behaviors

Characteristic of ADHD Behavior	Alternative (Opposite) Behavior
Has a short attention span.	
Has rapid shifts in attention.	
Gets off-task.	
Forgets to do tasks.	
Acts too quickly.	
Acts before thinking.	
Overactive—moves around.	
Talks excessively.	
Ignores peers/siblings.	
Shows anger to peers/siblings.	
Hogs toys.	
Acts out anger.	
Is defiant of authority—says no.	

Now, refer to the following example:

Example of Listing Alternative Behaviors

Characteristic of ADHD Behavior	Alternative (Opposite) Behavior
Has a short attention span.	Sustains attention.
Has rapid shifts in attention.	Focuses on one thing.
Gets off-task.	Stays on-task.
Forgets to do tasks.	Remembers to do tasks.
Acts too quickly.	Delays response (waits).
Acts before thinking.	Thinks before acting.
Overactive—moves around.	Remains still.
Talks excessively.	Remains quiet.
Ignores peers/siblings.	Greets peers/siblings.
Shows anger to peers/siblings.	Plays cooperatively with peers/siblings.
Hogs toys.	Shares toys.
Acts out anger.	Controls angry responses.
If defiant of authority—says no.	Is respectful to authority—says yes sir, no ma'am.

Exercise 5.1 has been adapted from Flick (1998).

Study the alternative, positive behaviors listed to see how they really are just the opposite of some of the undesirable ADHD characteristics. The objective of this exercise is twofold: (1) to provide some items for formal behavior programs (e.g., points/tokens) and informal behavior programs (e.g., verbal and nonverbal social rewards) and (2) to focus more on alternative, positive behaviors in general. This focus is extremely important in the development of a balanced behavioral program for the child with ADHD.

Note that for every inappropriate behavior in the example, there is an alternative appropriate behavior. Incorporating these will make for a more powerful behavioral program.

Generating More Appropriate Behaviors

Most children learn through imitation during some occasions in their life. Unfortunately, some role models demonstrate little appropriate behavior. For example, athletic role models sometimes exhibit bizarre, inappropriate, and crude social behaviors and often receive substantial media attention for such behavior. Recently, a six-year-old received a great deal of media attention following an incident at school where he head-butted another child; he was promptly handcuffed by a police officer who was on duty nearby. This is a good example of bad modeling. There was also much public outrage that a six-year-old (a child with ADHD who was on Ritalin) was handcuffed. It should also be noted that despite attempts to explain such behavior or to offer a reason for it, when such behavior is modeled, it—not the later verbal explanation—will have an influence on the child.

When teachers wish to develop an appropriate behavior that has not yet been exhibited by the child, modeling, imitation, and shaping may be involved. In Exercise 5.2, teachers write a brief descriptive statement to develop a modeling procedure for several behaviors. The statements should be as specific as possible because they will serve as a script, detailing the part teachers will play in training the child to exhibit certain behaviors.

Once teachers complete these descriptions, they should check their descriptions against the example. The 10 situations given will not cover every event where an appropriate behavior is needed, but the samples will provide guidelines for modeling other behaviors not on the list. When an appropriate behavior is modeled, the next step is to strengthen (i.e., reinforce) that behavior when the child imitates it.

Exercise 5.2   Modeling Behavior

What You Wish the Child to Do	How You Will Model This Behavior
Stick to a task.	
Sit quietly.	
Take turns.	
Play cooperatively.	
Ask questions of adults.	

(Continued)

Exercise 5.2   (Continued)

Share toys.	
Handle frustration.	
Be polite.	
Ask for things appropriately.	
Raise hand to answer.	

Now, refer to the following example:

Example of Modeling Behavior

What You Wish the Child to Do	*How You Will Model This Behavior*
Stick to a task.	Teacher works on project until complete.
Sit quietly.	Teacher sits without talking.
Take turns.	Teacher exchanges toy with child after brief play (10–15 minutes).
Play cooperatively.	Teacher plays with one child by the rules while another watches.
Ask questions of adults.	Teacher tells child, "OK, I'm going to show you how you can ask me a question." Explain how one waits for a break in conversation, then says name and asks question.
Share toys.	Teacher sets stage by saying what will be done; for example, "OK, after a short while [few seconds], I'm going to let you play with this toy." Teacher exchanges toys with the child.
Handle frustration.	Teacher explains, "If I'm having trouble doing something, then I'll need to take a break or take a deep breath before going back to it."
Be polite.	Teacher demonstrates asking for something by saying, "Please," saying, "Thank you," when getting it, and answering questions with "Yes sir/ma'am," or "No sir/ma'am."
Ask for things appropriately.	Teacher demonstrates by asking, "May I have another piece of pizza?" instead of "Can I" or the usual "Give me another piece of pizza!" or "I want another piece of that pizza!"
Raise hand to answer.	Teacher demonstrates how the child can ask questions or give answers by raising a hand first. (Use a routine question; for example, "May I be excused?")

Exercise 5.2 has been adapted from Flick (1998).

Note that it is important to show the child exactly what should be done in each situation; this is an example of modeling or role-playing. When the child imitates an appropriate behavior, teachers must reinforce it with statements such as "Good, that's exactly right—that's the way you need to raise your hand to answer a question in the classroom," or "That's right—that's just the way I showed you." Teachers should always be specific about what is liked; avoid saying, "Good boy," or "Good girl." If the child does not imitate the behavior exactly right, reinforce and encourage the attempt, saying, "Well, that was a good try. Let me show you again how to . . . ." After a second demonstration, say, "OK, now try it again."

If there is poor repetition over these trials, either the child is not ready to learn this behavior, or he or she is not in the appropriate state to learn (i.e., she may be tired, angry, too excited, or in a playful mood). Simply say, "OK, let's try this another time." As most people know, habits require repetitive practice to become established. It is also not unusual for those with ADHD to require more repetitive practice than most other children. Depending on the strength of the habit, the new behavior may need to be practiced daily or only occasionally. Remember that all learning takes time. Practicing a behavior several hundred times a day will not work; practicing for short periods of time over many days will be more effective and less stressful for everyone.

Differential Reinforcement

Differential reinforcement involves reinforcement of one behavior over another, specifically reinforcing the more desired behavior. When a behavior that is close to what is desired is either imitated or spontaneously emitted, it is important to pay attention to it, comment about it, and provide some social or tangible reward for the child. In most cases, the use of social praise, touch, and direct feedback on the appropriateness of the behavior is all that is needed. However, many younger children (e.g., preschool age) may need a tangible reward. Tangible rewards should always be paired with social praise.

Shaping occurs when the behavior exhibited gets closer and closer to the desired behavior. This is a slow process and goes like this: A child may exhibit cooperative play by taking turns playing with a toy. This change should be reinforced with touch (e.g., pat on the back or shoulder) and praise (e.g., "I like the way you are playing more cooperatively with your classmate"). However, the child may grab the toy away from the other child. Appropriate "taking of the toy" behavior may be modeled, or the teacher may wait for a positive variation in behavior and reinforce that behavior.

Modeling saves time and provides a basis for immediate learning to occur. Thus, when a child takes a toy appropriately, the teacher may say, "I like the way you guys are playing cooperatively, and I especially like the way you took the toy *easily* instead of *grabbing* it." This statement should also be given with touch, perhaps rubbing the child's back or shoulder while saying it. Brief, limited physical contact with the child can be effective; sustained or extended physical contact is best avoided. Additionally, some children may clearly find physical contact uncomfortable; in such cases, it is best to avoid it totally.

Exercise 5.3 is very general, but it is useful in thinking about how some behavior may be acceptable yet still not the most desirable. The intermediate step may have a component that is still a problem behavior. Again note the following examples.

It is important to reinforce each step of the child's progress with positive feedback that lets the child know he or she is on the right track. This reinforces the child for making a change, even though it may not be the most desirable change. Some reinforcement keeps the child responding; it provides motivation so that eventually, when the most desirable behavior is shown, the teacher can excitedly say, "Yes, that's exactly right! That's the appropriate way to ask permission for something." By the teacher's excitement and tone of voice, the child will know that he has pleased the teacher. It should again be noted that the child with ADHD generally seeks stimulation and excitement.

Exercise 5.3 Using Differential Reinforcement

Current Behavior	Some Improvement	Most Desirable (Goal)
Fighting over toy		
Fighting over seating (class, table, etc.)		
Asking permission rudely ("I wanna go out!")		

Examples of Using Differential Reinforcement

Current Behavior	Some Improvement	Most Desirable (Goal)
Fighting (physically) over a toy	Not hitting, but angry	Playing appropriately and cooperatively with toy
Fighting over seating (class, table, etc.)	Complaining about seating but complying	Taking turns for preferential seats
Asking permission rudely ("I wanna go out!")	Saying, "Can I go out?" in whining tone	Saying, "May I go out to play?" in a normal tone

Exercise 5.3 has been adapted from Flick (1998).

Thus, when consequences are provided in an excited tone of voice, the reception or communication of the feedback is enhanced, and the overall learning is more efficient. If the teacher appears excited, the child will be more alert, and the information will be processed better. Also, the child will more likely seek out this kind of excitement in the future.

A number of procedures can be used to promote and develop new and more appropriate behaviors. Teachers should avoid thinking only of punishing inappropriate behavior. When inappropriate behavior is frequently punished, the child may come to believe that getting punishment is the only way to get attention. Thus, inappropriate behavior may increase. What is needed is a balanced behavioral plan, involving both rewards and punishments with much more emphasis on the positive orientation.

Balanced Behavioral Plans With Rewards and Punishments

Simply stated, punishment alone is not effective for a number of reasons.

- It tells the child only what *not* to do.
- Punishment involves pain or unpleasantness and results in distancing in the relationship.
- The child is confused, never knowing exactly what he or she should do. For example, if a child is spanked for physical aggression towards another child, the message received is "Don't do to that child what I'm doing to you." The nonverbal

communication (spanking) is more powerful than the verbal message and informs the child, "This is the way we solve problems."

Extensive clinical research shows clearly that the most powerful behavioral program will result from a combination of mild punishment of the "bad" behavior and positive reinforcement for the "good" behavior. The "time-in" procedure described below illustrates the effects of a positive approach.

A Balanced Behavioral Plan: "Time-In"

The concept of "time-in" has been reviewed in the literature (Christophersen & VanScoyoc, 2007; Olmi, Sevier, & Nastasi, 1997). "The term 'time-in' refers to the circumstances outside of time-out when the child is getting a lot of positive attention from his caregivers for behavior" (Christophersen & VanScoyoc, "Time-Out Plus Time-In"). In an early study, Solnick, Rincover, and Peterson (1977) compared enriched time-in with impoverished time-in and found that the more enjoyable, or enriched, a child's environment, the more effective the use of time-out. Specifically, should a child's environment be boring and unrewarding (impoverished), it may not feel much different than being put in time-out. This would, of course, reduce the effectiveness of the time-out. Other research supports the importance of time-in (Marlow, Tingstrom, Olmi, & Edwards, 1997; Olmi et al., 1997).

The purpose of the following exercise is to show teachers the general effects of positive reinforcement alone. By itself, this positive approach can be very powerful; when later combined with mild punishment, it can be even more effective.

Time-In Instructions for Teachers

For three days, simply *observe* the child's activity during playtime at recess. Observe during the same period each day (e.g., 3:30–5:30 PM). Note for each half-hour segment whether the child was (a) playing appropriately or (b) playing inappropriately (see Exercise 5.4).

Over the next four days, approach the child at least three times during each half-hour period. If the child is playing inappropriately, turn around and walk away. If the child is playing appropriately—or at least is not doing anything inappropriate—go over and make physical contact (touching the shoulder); if there is some appropriate behavior to praise (e.g., sharing, cooperation), give descriptive verbal praise (i.e., clearly state which desirable behavior was observed).

For the next three days, return to the observation mode; simply observe and again record the number of times the child was (a) playing appropriately or (b) playing inappropriately during the half-hour observation times.

You might notice that the number of appropriate behaviors has increased and the number of inappropriate behaviors has decreased during this second observation period. The record in Exercise 5.4 shows general improvement in all five observation periods over a short period of time. The intervening four days of rewarding appropriate behaviors and not rewarding (ignoring) inappropriate behaviors had a dramatic impact in the child's overall behavior. During the second three-day period, there was improvement on 12 of the 15 observations, a satisfactory percentage of improvement. By adding a mild punishment (e.g., some type of "fine" for inappropriate behavior), this behavioral system could be made even stronger.

Exercise 5.4   Balanced Behavioral Plan: "Time-In"

Observation Times	3:30	4:00	4:30	5:00	5:30
First Three-Day Observation Period					
Appropriate	1	0	0	1	0
Inappropriate	2	3	3	2	3
Next Four Days of Positive Intervention					
Second Three-Day Observation Period					
Appropriate	2	1	3	3	3
Inappropriate	1	2	0	0	0
Net Results					
Appropriate	+1	+1	+3	+2	+3
Inappropriate	−1	−1	−3	−2	−3

Exercise 5.4 has been adapted from Flick (1998).

After completing Exercise 5.5, see the example for feedback on the behaviors listed. Note that this exercise can be used in the school setting by any teacher. Following the establishment of a combined reward for appropriate alternative behavior and punishment for the inappropriate behavior, it will be clear that *both* are needed for the punishment to be effective. When punishment is the sole approach, there is very little positive outlook for desired results, and depression, along with either "emotional shutdown" or acting out of anger, occurs. The balanced approach is especially important for the child with ADHD because some forms of punishment (e.g., physical punishment) are totally ineffective and often lead to a deprivation of positive feedback for appropriate behavior.

Exercise 5.5   Writing a Balanced Behavioral Plan: Positive Reinforcement and Punishment

For each of the inappropriate behaviors listed, write a positive reinforcement approach (reward) and a negative reinforcement approach (punishment).

Behavior	Punishment	Reward Alternative
Fighting		
Cursing		
Disrespectful talk		
Failure to do chore		
Temper tantrum when told no		

Example of Writing a Balanced Behavioral Plan:

Positive Reinforcement and Punishment

Behavior	Punishment	Reward Alternative
Fighting	Loses all privileges for one day.	Working/playing cooperatively—gets free time in school.
Cursing	Loses favorite activity (e.g., computer time) for one day.	Mark down good talk during occasion when child would have cursed; every three marks earn special reward (e.g., computer time or homework pass at school).
Disrespectful talk	Loses computer access for one day.	Record good talk to teachers; every five marks earn extra computer time in school.
Failure to do a chore	Must do extra chore (and original one) to restore privileges.	Praise when child performs chore and make contact (e.g., pat on shoulder/back).
Temper tantrum when told no	Ignore temper tantrum—if excessive, delay all privileges one hour.	Praise when child complies with requests first time. Keep record; after five marks, gets special treat.

Exercise 5.5 has been adapted from Flick (1998).

Positive Practice

One assumption often made when misbehavior occurs is that the "child simply doesn't know better." Thus, if a child slams a door closed when entering a room, a teacher may assume that the child doesn't know how to close the door. Although this is a very simple concept, it is really quite complex. For example, the child may be asked, "Do you know how to close the door?" (*note:* in private—not in front of the whole class). If the child says yes, the response may be "Well, show me the proper way to close the door." If the child does it correctly, the teacher might respond with "Yes, that's exactly right, but apparently you need a bit more practice doing this so that it will be automatic." Then the child is asked to go out and come in, closing the door appropriately for 5 to 10 practice trials. This is called "positive practice."

If the child does not initially demonstrate that he or she knows how to close the door, the teacher can model this behavior for the child, saying, "Let me show you the proper way to close the door." Following this private demonstration, the teacher and student can go through the practice steps, having the child close the door appropriately 5 to 10 times. If during one of those trials, the child slams the door, then three additional practice trials are added. These interactions may end with the teacher saying, "I don't know if we will have to practice this again. In the future, I'll be checking to see if you have learned to close the door correctly."

After modeling and reinforcement, it will be important for the teacher to "catch the child" showing this appropriate (changed) behavior. The teacher will watch the child and give verbal praise when the door is closed correctly, whether alone or in front of the whole class.

On some occasions, a child's misbehavior may be disrespectful to a teacher. In this case, he or she might go through the "positive practice" phase and then have to provide "restitution" for having spoken in a disrespectful manner. Restitution may involve having the child perform an added chore or some task for the teacher. This general procedure has been termed "overcorrection with positive practice and restitution." If the child requests something in a disrespectful manner, then following the overcorrection procedure, the child is allowed to ask for the requested item or favor in an appropriate manner. At this time, the proper response is "Yes, that is the appropriate way to ask. You may have. . . ."

Point and Token Systems

A behavioral system involving points or tokens is called a "token economy"; it sets specific behavioral goals to be met and uses well-defined rewards (points or tokens) and punishments (fines or loss of points or tokens). It is fairly objective, does not require a great deal of decision making for the teacher (once set up appropriately), and presents well-defined guidelines for the child who may previously have thought it impossible to get rewards and privileges on a consistent basis. Many children, both normal and those with ADHD, have worked successfully with such programs—particularly in school. However, children often become frustrated and angry or depressed if they never reach the desired goal. This can happen when children with ADHD are placed in competition with children without ADHD. Clearly, the child with ADHD is unlikely to be able to reach the same criteria set for most children without ADHD.

Point and token systems are excellent balanced behavioral programs, as many of them focus on both reward and punishment. It is also possible to deal with several behaviors (appropriate and inappropriate) at the same time, but teachers should *not* attempt to deal with too many behaviors at once. If this happens, the system becomes too complex, causing frustration for both parent or teacher and child, and the program is often dropped. The system also provides the child with opportunities to plan ahead (i.e., determine how many points are needed for some array of privileges) and to make decisions (i.e., with only so many available points, the child may have to choose which privileges are to be selected). Of course, these experiences provide an excellent introduction to events that will arise in adult life, where similar decisions must be made at higher and more complex levels. The point or token behavioral system may provide a wide range of experiences that have an impact on the child throughout life.

General Guidelines. First, let's look at a few age guidelines for these systems. Token systems are generally used with younger children, three to six years old. These guidelines may change with the child's estimated mental age. For example, a very bright two-year-old may be able to work with the system if simple communication skills are adequate, and a child older than six may still use the tokens up to perhaps eight or ten years of age if the child's mental age is lower. Second, consider some guidelines in the use of fines. With very young children, three to four years of age, there should be no loss of tokens (fines) for inappropriate behavior. Those in the five- to six-year range, whether mental or chronological, may be candidates for some limited fines. However, the general principle for younger children is to utilize a purely positive approach in developing new, more appropriate behavior; other techniques may be used to deal with that child's inappropriate behaviors. Of course, a purely positive approach may also be indicated for the child with ADHD.

Listing Behaviors. Basic to all point and token systems with older children are the following:

- Know the behaviors we wish to see *more of*—for the rewards.
- Know the behaviors we wish to see *less of*—for the punishments (fines).
- Know effective privileges and fines—the source of *motivation* for the program.

Exercise 5.6 helps to begin the process.

Exercise 5.6   Listing and Ranking of Behaviors

Desirable and Appropriate (1A) Behavior			Undesirable and Inappropriate (1B) Behavior		
Behavior	Frequency (Rating)	Importance (Rating)	Behavior	Frequency (Rating)	Importance (Rating)
1.			1.		
2.			2.		
3.			3.		

Exercise 5.6 has been adapted from Flick (1998).

This exercise is similar to one completed in Exercise 5.4. It provides a list of behaviors that may be used in setting up a program. However, it is important that these behaviors be ranked according to (1) how frequently the child exhibits the behavior and (2) how important it is that the behavior be developed. Teachers should rate each behavior by frequency on a 1–5 scale, with 1 being the lowest frequency and 5 the highest. The scale is developed as shown below:

Frequency Rating		Description
High	5	Seen most of the time—almost every day.
	4	Seen much of the time—every other day.
Medium	3	Seen a fair amount of time—once weekly.
Low	2	Seen a little of the time—once every other week.
	1	Seen very little of the time—once a month or less.

Importance Rating		Description
High	5	Very important
	4	Important
Medium	3	Somewhat important
Low	2	Of little importance
	1	Of very little importance

These two ratings—frequency and importance—are clearly important in determining which appropriate and inappropriate behaviors to select for the point or token system.

- A high frequency rating for an appropriate behavior means that there is little concern over that behavior and it may not even need to be included in the behavior program, except when there is a need to guarantee some success. "Don't mess with a good thing." However, a high frequency rating on an inappropriate behavior indicates that it should be included in the system.
- Likewise, a behavior that is inappropriate may be of relatively minor importance (with a rating of 1 or 2) compared with the child's other presenting behavior and, thus, not need to be included in the behavior program. An inappropriate behavior that is of high importance should be included.

These ratings provide an organized and systematic approach to the selection of behavior to work within the behavioral system. The table below shows one example of sorting and ranking behaviors.

Sample Listing and Ranking of Behaviors

Desirable and Appropriate (1A)			*Undesirable and Inappropriate (1B)*		
	Freq	*Imp*		*Freq*	*Imp*
1. Plays cooperatively with classmates.	1	5	1. Hits classmates.	5	5
2. Complies with requests.	2	5	2. Noncompliance.	4	5
3. Greets others.	3	3	3. Ignores others.	3	3
4. Completes tasks.	1	5	4. Leaves before completing tasks.	4	5
5. Raises hand.	1	2	5. Blurts out.	5	5

Adapted from Flick (1998).

You can use the rankings not only to select appropriate behaviors that you wish to improve through reward but also to decrease and remove inappropriate behaviors through punishment. As teachers get more experience in designating the behaviors they may wish to work with, some steps may be eliminated. For example, formal ratings may be eliminated if the teacher has a good subjective impression of the behavior to be included.

Following the selection of appropriate and inappropriate behaviors, the next step is to set the reward and fine values so the child knows what the payoff will be for exhibiting appropriate behaviors and what the punishment will be for inappropriate behavior.

Selecting Privileges. Privileges are the tangible rewards, social interactions, and specific activities and privileges that the child finds enjoyable and that serve to reinforce the designated behavior. Parents and teachers probably have a pretty good idea of what is reinforcing for a child, as the child will typically engage in that activity whenever possible.

Teachers already have an abundance of information obtained from several sources to indicate the things and activities that the child likes or dislikes. They can organize the child's likes and dislikes in lists. Of course, teachers must avoid those items on the "dislikes" list, but this list may be used to formulate extra chores for inappropriate behaviors that fall outside the structured behavioral system. The "likes" list of activities, things, and social interactions may be formulated as a final list of privileges (Exercise 5.7). Teachers should list these privileges and note their frequency and importance to the child alongside each one, using the same frequency and importance ratings used above to describe behaviors.

Exercise 5.7   Sample Selecting Privileges

Privilege	Unit of Time/ Money	Frequency Rating	Importance Rating	Composite Rating	Rank	Points
1.						
2.						
3.						
4.						
5.						
6.						
7.						
8.						

Sample Selecting Privileges

Privilege	Unit of Time/ Money	Frequency Rating	Importance Rating	Points
1. Computer time	Per ½ hour	5	5	5
2. Free time	Per ½ hour	4	3	3
3. Homework pass	Per 1 hour	5	4	4
4. Favorite book	Per 1 hour	1	3	15
5. Favorite magazine	Per 1 hour	2	3	15

Exercise 5.7 has been adapted from Flick (1998).

In addition to listing the privileges, teachers must also describe the unit of time or how much money may be involved in that privilege. This unit of time or money will also be important in determining the points required to earn the privilege. For extended events and for those things that cost money, we can only roughly estimate the number of points required.

Teachers must keep the points assigned to behaviors, fines, and privileges as low as possible to make running the program easy. Also, remember that these points assigned to privileges are only initial estimates. It will be important to determine how many points the child is generally able to earn and to make sure that the child can earn some of the privileges. The points assigned to behaviors, fines, and privileges can be revised once what the child can earn is known. It should also be remembered that some privileges are given daily, and it is most critical that the child be able to earn the daily privileges.

After listing the privileges, teachers might go back and rank each one with regard to how often the child wishes to engage in that activity or to have that thing and how important the privilege is to the child (as perceived by the teacher). Multiply these two rankings to get a composite rating. Then look through the list and rank order each privilege; for those privileges that have the same composite score, rank the one with a higher frequency ahead of the others. This process will produce a list of privileges rank ordered in a systematic way. It will, therefore, make sense to assign point values to privileges based on their rank. Several factors in addition to rank, however, will determine their point values.

While it may not be necessary to go into this much detail for many children, using the most powerful motivators of behaviors will be essential for the success of the program. Once teachers have done this exercise, these estimates may be used in future programs.

As others have noted (Boyajian, DuPaul, Handler, Eckert, & McGoey, 2001; DuPaul 1991; DuPaul & Stoner, 2003), it is important to use reinforcers that are viewed as "necessities" by the child (e.g., TV, playing video games, renting a movie), rather than relying on "luxury" items that he or she could live without (e.g., eating lobster at a fine restaurant or a trip to Disney World). It is recommended that money *not* be used as a general reinforcer. Also, any point system must be successful, or it should not exist; *success* is the major criterion for any behavioral program.

Systems for Different Ages. Programs are modified according to the child's chronological age or mental age.

Tokens: This system will be used primarily for preschool-aged children (ages 3–6). Teachers can use plastic poker chips in red, white, and blue. At ages 3–4 years, chips may be used interchangeably; at 5–6 years—assuming the child is able to discriminate colors—the red, white, and blue may assume different values, with blue representing good, white representing very good, and red standing for excellent.

A clear jar or bank will allow the child to see chips building up. Teachers can have a list of behaviors that will be reinforced with tokens and select one behavior from that list to start the program. The child is told that when the jar is full (small jar that can be filled with 10 chips), he or she will receive a privilege. It is very important that even young children begin to think about what is expected of them. It is, however, critical that the child be capable of performing the expected behavior. The payoff is defined for each occasion, and when the goal is met—the jar is full of chips—the child receives a small reward.

When using tokens or stickers, it is important that some basic rules be followed:

1. As soon as the child shows the appropriate behavior, he or she should be given the token or sticker.

2. When presenting the token or sticker, the teacher should say exactly what behavior was good and how pleased he or she is that the child showed the behavior;

for example, "Mark, I really liked the way you sat down while you worked. Here's a token."

3. The teacher should go to the jar with the child and put the token in the jar. The teacher might say, "Miranda, you're really doing well. You'll have that special treat very soon. Keep up the good behavior."

4. When the inappropriate behavior occurs, it is important for the teacher to (a) not attend to it, (b) select another specific privilege to withdraw, (c) withdraw a token (least desirable alternative), or (d) analyze the behavior to see if too much was expected of the child. If the child is determined capable of meeting the expectation, occasional inappropriate behavior may be ignored. If the inappropriate behavior continues, some revision of the program and the expectations may be made.

Points: A point system can be used with children ages 6 through 12 years. Again, keep in mind that these are simply rough guidelines. Some very difficult programs have been conducted with immature adolescents. Also, while children ages 6 to 8 may have only appropriate behaviors in the system (see Exercise 5.8a), children ages 9 to 12 may work with both appropriate and inappropriate behaviors (see Exercise 5.8b).

Exercise 5.8a Point System (Ages 6–8)

Behaviors	Points	Mon	Tues	Wed	Thurs	Fri	Sat	Sun
1.								
2.								
3.								
4.								
Total Points Earned								
Privileges	Points Used	Mon	Tues	Wed	Thurs	Fri	Sat	Sun
1.								
2.								
3.								
4.								
Total Points Used								
		Mon	Tues	Wed	Thurs	Fri	Sat	Sun
NET POINTS								

Exercise 5.8a has been adapted from Flick (1998).

Exercise 5.8b   Point System (Ages 9–12)

Behaviors	Points	Mon	Tues	Wed	Thurs	Fri	Sat	Sun
Followed Inst.	0-4/T	8	6	8	8	8		
Complete Work	0-4/T	8	8	8	8	8		
Obey Class Rules	0-4/T	6	4	8	6	8		
Got Along with Peers	0-4/T	4	6	8	8	8		
Ready by 7 AM	5	5	5	5	5	5		
Bring HAS/Ret. Home	5	5	5	5	5	5		
Complete Homework	10	10	10	1		10		
In bed by 9 PM	5	5	5	5	5	5		
Bonus	2	// (4)	/// (6)	////(8)	//////(10)	/// (6)	///////(12)	////////(14)
Total Points*		55	55	65	55	63	(163)+ 17 [180]	(120)+ 19 [139]
Points Used/Fines		45	35	10	20	20	60	100
Net Points/Day		10	20	55	35	43	120	(savings) + 39
Fines List	Points Lost	Mon	Tues	Wed	Thurs	Fri	Sat	Sun
Name Calls 5.6	10	/// (30)	/ (10)	—	—	/ (10)	/ (10)	—
Talks Back	5	/ (5)	/ (5)	—	—	—	—	—
Fail to Complete HW	20	—	—	—	20	—	—	—
Totals		35	15	0	20	10	10	0

* Savings in brackets.

Notice that there are no fines in Exercise 5.8a. As with younger children, fines are not recommended. In some cases, and especially where the child is very bright, some withdrawal of a privilege, time-out, or suspension of privileges for a short time (maximum one day) may be used. Once an attempt has been made to construct this program, refer to the example (Exercise 5.8a).

If the child is older (9–12 years of age), construct a behavioral program for that age level (see Exercise 5.8b). The major difference will be that of adding inappropriate behaviors to the lists; these older children will receive fines. Also, a few additional behaviors may be incorporated in the program; however, start with a fairly simple program, especially if you are a novice at setting up and managing such programs. Other behaviors can always be added later—still within limits.

On the Home/School Behavior Chart (see Exercise 5.16 in this chapter), notice that there are several places to put appropriate behaviors for development but only a few spaces for inappropriate behaviors that will be *fined*. The reason is simple; teachers should avoid emphasizing the negative, the inappropriate, and the undesirable behavior. Otherwise, a child might be burdened with so many fines that a negative balance of points is obtained—this should *never* be allowed to happen. A negative point balance might occur due to carelessness or other unusual circumstances, but this condition should not be allowed to continue. If it occurs, a runaway system will result, where a child may begin to feel hopeless, depressed, angry, and like a failure. This clearly affects self-concept and self-esteem. This type of mismanaged system is undoubtedly faulty in design; such a program should be terminated immediately.

If a child gets a number of fines, it is best to set a maximum number (e.g., five). If that number is exceeded, there is total loss of privileges for that day. It is essential, however, that everyone avoid negative point balances. If they occur, the program should be reassessed and started over with new point values assigned. If a teacher does not have success in three attempts, he or she should request professional consultation and cease all such behavioral programs.

Once the point system is set up, see an example of this type of program for home/school use (Exercise 5.8c). Use the suggestions provided to modify the behavioral program where needed. Remember: The only criterion is that the child be *successful* with the program.

Exercise 5.8c Point System (Ages 6–8)

Behaviors	Points Earned/ Hatch Mark	Mon	Tues	Wed	Thurs	Fri	Sat	Sun
Complies w/ requests	2	///	//	///	////	//	///	///
Dressed by 7:50 AM	5	/	/	/		/		

(Continued)

Exercise 5.8c (Continued)

Behaviors	Points Earned/ Hatch Mark	Mon	Tues	Wed	Thurs	Fri	Sat	Sun
Plays coop'ly w/sibs	3	//	///	//	/	///	//	//
Does chores	3	/		//	//	//	//	//
Points Earned		20	18	23	17	24	18+ 38 = 56	18+8=26
Privileges	Points Used/ Hatch Mark	Mon	Tues	Wed	Thurs	Fri	Sat	Sun
Riding bike ½ hr	5	//	//	/	/	//	///	//
Eating at pizza place	20						////	
Playing Nintendo	4	/		//	/	//	//	//
Points Used		14	10	13	9	18	48	18
		Mon	Tues	Wed	Thurs	Fri	Sat	Sun
NET POINTS		6	8	10	8	6	8	[8]*

* Savings in brackets.

Exercise 5.8d Point System (Ages 9–12)

Behaviors	Points Earned	Mon	Tues	Wed	Thurs	Fri	Sat	Sun
Playing coop'ly w/sibs	5 each	///(15)	//(10)	///(15)	//(10)	///(15)	//(10)	///(15)
Complying w/requests	5 each	/// (15)	///(15)	///(15)	////(20)	/(5)	/(5)	
Completing chores	2 each	// (4)	// (4)	// (4)	////(8)	////(8)	// (4)	////(8)
Putting dry clothes in hamper	5	5	5	5	5	5		
Home for supper by 6 PM	5		5	5	5	5	5	
Total Points Earned		39	39	44	48	38	53 + 24 = 77	13 + 43 = 56

Fines	Points Lost	Mon	Tues	Wed	Thurs	Fri	Sat	Sun
Hitting sibs	5 each	/(5)	/(5)		/(5)		///(15)	/(5)
Noncompliance	5 each	/(5)	/(5)		/(5)			/(5)
Late for supper (past 6 PM)	5	/(5)					/(5)	
Throws dirty clothes on floor	4						/(4)	
Total Points Lost		15	10	0	10	0	44	10
Points Available to Use		(24)	(29)	(44)	(38)	(38)	(33)	(46)
Privileges	Points Used	Mon	Tues	Wed	Thurs	Fri	Sat	Sun
Riding bike ½ hr	5	/(5)	//(10)	//(10)	///(15)	//(10)	/(5)	//(10)
Playing Nintendo (½ hr)	5	//(10)	//(10)	//(10)	///(15)	/(5)	/(5)	
Skating trip	15							
Movie selected (rent)	10						10	
Eating at pizza place	20			20				20
Special fishing trip	15							
Total Points Used		15	20	40	30	15	20	30
NET POINTS		9	9	4	8	23	13	[16]*

*Savings in brackets

Teachers can indicate with slash marks how many times a behavior was observed or how many events or privileges were used. At the end of the day, or at any time the child wishes to use privileges, the point totals may be calculated. Points used are subtracted from points earned to give net points for that day. The child starts each new day with zero points. However, the remaining net points from each day need to be stored (accumulated over time) and used when a sufficient number is reached.

Another possible way for the older child to earn extra points is the use of bonus points, awarded for special good behaviors. There should be sufficient incentives to motivate the child to earn more points. Any points left over at the end of the week will go into "savings." (See the bracketed points in Exercise 5.8d.) With young children, teachers must continuously provide guidance and cues to develop the idea of savings. Children with ADHD will resist delaying gratification and have a strong tendency to use the points *now*. At some point, the teacher may state, "Okay, you've worked hard for several weeks and you have x points in savings. I think it's time to use these points for something special." For example, a teacher can then arrange for a special trip (e.g., to McDonald's), a special activity (e.g., computer time), or anything that the child enjoys (e.g., a small toy), within some reasonable limit.

Duration of Token/Point System. How long should the program run? There are no exact rules, but in general, the program continues until there is at least 80 percent improvement; that is, when an appropriate behavior is shown 8 times in 10 possible situations. Remember that perfection is not the goal. A program continues to include other behaviors that were not originally addressed but now seem more important or to target a new behavior. When it is time to stop a program, teachers can throw a kind of "graduation party." This will emphasize again how well the child has done. Although the formal program may be stopped, continuing feedback on the child's behavior must be provided in the form of praise and touch. Providing verbal praise and appropriately touching the child (e.g., a pat on the shoulder or back) for the maintenance of appropriate behaviors will be crucial in ensuring a continuation of improvement.

Typically, during the beginning phase of the program, there is considerable variability; it may even seem as if some inappropriate behaviors are getting worse. The child will often test the system to see if parents or teachers mean what they say. This is especially evident when the child, faced with a low number of points, plans how he or she will earn a sufficient number to have access to desired privileges.

SOCIAL SKILLS

Fitting into today's society is a challenge for many children and especially so for those with ADHD. Being accepted by one's peers and classmates is vitally important, not only for older children and adolescents but also for preschool children. Children with ADHD often are rejected by their peers due to their impulsive and often aggressive style of interaction, along with their general difficulty in "playing by the rules." Children with ADHD often experience one or more of the following:

- Frustration
- Anger
- Feelings of inadequacy
- Helplessness over the lack of good coping skills
- Loneliness
- Depression because of frequent isolation from their peer group

Addressing Social Behaviors

Sometimes, some of the child's difficulties with ADHD seem to be made better by medication. However, though it takes the collaborative and persistent efforts of those working with the child, it is certainly desirable for him or her to learn and develop social and coping skills. Such skills help the child accept responsibility for social experiences, and these learned skills benefit the child in pervasive ways throughout life. Social graces (saying, "Yes, sir," offering a chair to an elder, etc.) are learned social skills.

Most of the essential social skills fall into one of these five categories:

1. Listening

2. Following instructions and rules

3. Sharing

4. Working and playing cooperatively

5. Problem solving and anger control

Today, our society faces many problems, and perhaps the most serious is the escalation of violence. It is not uncommon to hear of children physically hurting other children, their parents, or their teachers—an ineffective and destructive way of "problem solving" that relies upon hostility and aggression. Such violence is often matter-of-factly presented in the media, where it surely influences children.

What can teachers do to manage, control, and gradually eliminate undesirable social behaviors in children, while at the same time establishing, developing, and maintaining appropriate social behaviors? The following programs address these issues both generally and in more structured approaches. Some social skills discussed here will have ecological relevance and should receive priority in development; others may simply be desirable behaviors. In any case, teachers must emphasize and develop positive social skills, as the child cannot exhibit both appropriate and inappropriate behaviors at the same time.

Essentially, teachers will be most concerned about the development of more appropriate behavior that relates to the child's social acceptance, particularly behavior skills that enable the child to control aggressive styles of social interaction. The primary focus is necessarily on the development and maintenance of each social skill within the school context, but these learned social skills may also be generalized to the home context. The school situation is the ideal starting place, since teachers can structure the child's activities to include all the elements necessary to establish essential social skills. Also, the school setting typically involves the child's classmates or peers, thereby providing a "practice arena" for developing social skills. Tallmadge and Barkley (1983) originally suggested videotaping play interactions. When viewing the tape, one can then pick out the appropriate behaviors to reinforce and, at the same time, pick out one or two inappropriate behaviors that would be good candidates for replacing with alternative prosocial skills (e.g., listening, cooperation, sharing). This idea was supported by a more recent study (Welch, Fees, & Murrey, 2001).

Developing Listening Skills

A critical element of "paying attention" is *listening*—hearing and then processing auditory input from others. Listening skills are vital for academic work (gathering information, following directions, understanding assignments, etc.) and being able to listen actively contributes to effective social interactions as well. Often, when the child with ADHD misinterprets something said by another child and acts or responds based on an misinterpretation, the stage is set for negative interactions, conflict, and aggression. Such situations most often occur within a group context, not in a one-to-one situation. Peers often observe the child's inappropriate response and do not understand that the child with ADHD may have misinterpreted what was said. They see only the overt response— usually aggressive behavior—and quietly record this as yet another reason to "avoid that child." Following such an incident, even if the child with ADHD is told accurately what was initially said (as contrasted to what he or she "heard"), the child may still appear confused and may even develop the belief that others misunderstand him or her.

After listening skills have been learned and practiced, it's time to generalize these skills. The teacher can follow the same process to verify that communications were heard accurately. Thus, the teacher, too, might ask, "What did I just ask you to do?" The teacher gives immediate feedback (verbal praise) to the child for accurate responses and, on a daily or weekly basis, provides the parent with a record of the number of requests and the number of the child's accurate responses. This short-term record keeping is needed only for about two weeks; then it may be replaced by frequent praise from the teacher. When formal requests are given to a parent, these improving listening skills may become part of the child's behavioral (point system) programs. Alternatively, if the child's classroom listening performance remains at 90 percent correct or better, the child may receive some agreed-upon reward. The teacher's use of priming each morning, to remind the child of the potential reward, often results in faster learning of listening skills.

Following Instructions

Only after a child has well-established listening skills, can he or she be expected to follow instructions well (Enger, Russell, Setzer, & Walkanoff, 1998). Training in both listening and following directions can even be done together. Complying with requests or following directions is something a child is expected to "do," as compared with things the child "should not do." Thus, as prosocial skills become stronger and more frequent, there is a corresponding reduced probability of inappropriate behavior.

Teachers may use many tasks for such training. It is important to remember that any request given may bring about a reward for listening (i.e., knowing what to do) and for carrying out the request (i.e., doing it). Completing the task may, thus, result in additional positive reinforcement, such as verbal praise or a pat on the back. Both listening and following directions may also be included in a behavioral point system.

Including such behaviors on a home-school note (see the "Home-School Notes" section later in this chapter) will facilitate learning of the skill and enhance generalization of the skill. As the child is reinforced for compliance in more and more situations, such as in class, on the playground, in the lunchroom, and on the school bus, compliance becomes stronger and more generalized. Successfully generalizing compliance does, however, take cooperation among teacher, bus driver, and others. Consistency of consequences is required to strengthen the skill; inappropriate behaviors (e.g., breaking rules) may be reinforced if the child is able to manipulate attention from the bus driver or a teacher monitoring the lunchroom. Likewise, recording and relating of appropriate behavior (i.e., following the rules) must be consistent across caregivers. Keep in mind that it is far more important to teach the child a prosocial skill that emphasizes what he or she needs "to do" rather than what the child "should not do." Reminding the child of the rules in different situations and stating the consequences for adhering to or violating them (priming) will further improve the child's ability to be successful.

Sharing

At some point in life, everyone has had an experience of having to share with others. It is quite normal to share as part of developing friendship, and certainly siblings are often asked to share food, toys, and time. The child with ADHD may develop a sense of being the less favored child or even the "black sheep" of the family. Often feeling victimized, such a child may at times resent having to share, resent being second, and ultimately resent siblings. This situation generates conflict and leaves parents frustrated and frazzled when trying to seek peaceful solutions to hassles between and among their children. It can be quite difficult to know where to begin.

Since young children often feel competitive over sharing a toy and have difficulty doing so, teachers may begin training on this social skill with an exercise aimed at teaching the concept of sharing to one or more classmates. Conflict over a toy with subsequent fighting may, of course, result in placing the toy in time-out. However, this does not teach the child about sharing or playing cooperatively; it may only serve to discourage fighting. What is needed is the prosocial approach.

First, teachers might explain to both children that they have noticed difficulty in playing with this toy. Teachers then tell the children that they will be expected to share this toy, saying, "I would like to show you what I mean by sharing." The teacher will then model what is meant by sharing, saying, "I can play with the toy for a while, and then I can offer it to you." Depending on the age of the children, the time spent with the toy may vary, with briefer periods for younger children.

After modeling and sharing, the teacher might say, "OK, now I would like to see each of you share this toy. I'm going to use a timer; each of you will be able to play with this toy for one minute." Set the timer for one minute (time is subjective and depends on age of child). When the bell rings, say, "I liked the way you played with the toy," and to the other child, "I liked the way you played with something else while you were waiting for this toy." Allow the other child to play with the toy, again setting the timer for one minute. Repeat the praise for the second child.

If any hassle arises while the first child plays with the toy, warn the second child that fighting for the toy will result in the first child's having the toy for an additional minute. Any further hassles over the toy result in the toy's going into time-out, with the teacher saying, "We'll need to try this another time. This toy goes into time-out for [time]." The time may be estimated. For something really desirable, 15 minutes may be sufficient; an hour or a day may be used for other, less desirable toys. As with most programs, the really important factor is not the time-out but rather the opportunity to develop more appropriate, prosocial skills. Teachers should return to this training quickly and often for the most efficient learning to occur.

There are fewer opportunities at school than at home to observe and reinforce sharing or taking turns, but some occasions can be found, especially for younger children. Often, youngsters working on projects together at a table may be faced with the problem of taking turns with materials. This behavior may be monitored by the teacher and reported to the parent, as well as directly reinforced in the classroom. For example, on a Recording Sheet for Social Skills (Exercise 5.9), the teacher may demonstrate sharing and taking turns to the child and then say, "When I see you sharing and taking turns, I'm going to mark the paper so that your parent(s) at home can see how well you can do with this behavior." If fights break out in the classroom, the teacher may cue the child with the question, "What should you be doing instead of fighting over . . . ?" This allows the child to develop some cognitive awareness of the appropriate behavior. When the child changes the behavior and begins to share, the teacher may praise and give a pat on the back, saying, "I'm going to put that good mark on your report." As with other skill training, this information may be used equally well in the classroom and at home in a behavior (point) system. (Appendix N is a blank Recording Sheet for Social Skills.)

Exercise 5.9 Recording Sheet for Social Skills

Social Skill	M	T	W	Th	F	Totals
Listening						
Following rules						
Sharing						
Working/playing cooperatively						
Problem solving						
Anger control						
Totals						

Exercise 5.9 was adapted from Flick (1998).

Cooperation

This area has been of prime concern to both parents and teachers of children with ADHD. As with other appropriate behaviors, it is not possible for the child to play cooperatively and fight at the same time. Thus, more frequent reinforcement of cooperative behavior should result in a decrease in fighting or aggressive behavior. Teachers should have a plan for dealing with fighting. This may involve a time-out or a specific behavior penalty, and the child should be informed of this prior to the start of a game or task. Priming reminds the child of what to expect for appropriate as well as inappropriate behaviors. These reminders need not be directed toward one child (the child with ADHD); they may be quite general. Remember: It takes *two* to fight.

To develop such a social skill, suggest that the child with ADHD and the sibling or classmate play a game. To encourage this skill, pick a game where the child with ADHD will not be at a disadvantage. For example, a game like checkers should be avoided, as there are too many chances for the child with ADHD to make impulsive and poorly planned moves. Instead, choose a game where success depends upon chance (e.g., Candyland). Once the game is selected, tell both children, "You know that it has sometimes been difficult for you two to play together without fighting. I'm going to be looking for times when you two get along in play. When I see this, I'll let you know, but I'll also put a mark on this card [see Behavior Check Card, Exercise 5.10]. When you reach 10 marks, we will have a celebration by going somewhere (or doing something) that you both like."

In this structured situation, neither child will know when he or she will be observed; this kind of random check results in far greater consistency in exhibiting appropriate cooperative behavior. If necessary, the teacher can model cooperative behavior for a game (i.e., playing by the rules) and even show the child which behaviors would be inappropriate. Teachers can explain further what will happen if inappropriate behavior occurs and use a signal to warn the child when such behavior occurs. The signal may be holding out two fingers, communicating that the child has two choices: (1) change the inappropriate behavior or (2) accept the consequence for that behavior. Both children are told

Exercise 5.10 Behavior Check Card

Behavior	Mon	Tues	Wed	Thurs	Fri	Sat	Sun
Working cooperatively							
Playing cooperatively							
Cumulative totals							
Date	Point Total Goal This Week						

Exercise 5.10 was adapted from Flick (1998).

that if inappropriate behavior occurs (e.g., name-calling, hassling, fighting), the game will be stopped and put in time-out. However, by giving children a chance to change their behavior by themselves, the responsibility for the consequence is shifted onto the children. Remember: It is far better to promote positive, prosocial behavior than simply to punish an inappropriate behavior.

As the children get better at earning points for cooperative behavior and the point total increases, the teacher can set higher goals to get the same payoff. Some children will voice complaints over the increase in expectation, but their concerns may be lessened by stating, "Yes, you do need a greater number of points to get the reward, but you are getting so much better at cooperation that it's much easier for you to get the points. You know, I'm really proud of the progress you have made."

Social Graces

Children with ADHD who are also aggressive are clearly deficient in problem solving. Such children have difficulty in coming up with alternate solutions to their problems, fail to foresee the consequences of their behavior, and have difficulty addressing the complexities of conflict situations. Clearly, they have difficulty reflecting on behavioral alternatives. In fact, children with ADHD may have difficulty with all four basic steps of problem solving: (1) identifying the problem, (2) thinking of solutions, (3) foreseeing consequences, and (4) being able to develop a plan of action to achieve a goal (e.g., conflict resolution).

Teachers may approach this situation with firsthand knowledge of some of the past problems and conflict the child has experienced, or the child may be asked to report a recent problem encountered at home or at school. Say, "OK, let's take the time you hit a boy who teased you and called you a name, just because you got a short haircut." You can then model for the child how to go about problem solving.

Many children with ADHD fail to recognize the problem. Some might say the problem is "I got in trouble for hitting." A teacher can give feedback saying, "Well, you got in trouble because hitting is against the rules in school." The teacher might continue, saying, "It seems that the problem was that you got very angry over being teased and called names. It certainly wasn't appropriate for that boy to do what he did, but you got caught breaking a school rule." The teacher can then say, "Can you think of some other ways that you might have handled that situation other than hitting? Let's write them down." Teachers should develop a list of whatever the child says, allowing any and all solutions. After all items are listed, have the child go back through each one, saying, "OK, now let's look at what the consequences might be for each of these." Teachers may wish to offer some additional solutions if all of the child's solutions would result in poor consequences.

It is important to select problem-solving situations that do not arouse anger. For example, the teacher might say, "Remember when you saw that group of boys playing down the street? You weren't sure how to get invited to play. I remember that you just went over, introduced yourself, and asked if you could play a game with them. I remember that they told you no and you were really disappointed. I wonder what other approaches you might have taken in that situation? Let's go over that one because that's a situation that may come up again."

Where the child with ADHD has a problem with aggression, there are almost certainly poor peer relations. When impulsive children are quick to anger and respond in an explosive manner, they are often either shunned and avoided, or they are teased and prodded into acting out, often to see them "get in trouble."

To begin, parents and teachers should note that everyone gets angry sometimes but not everyone knows what anger looks or feels like. The first questions may be: What does anger look like? What are the outward signs of anger? Next, it can be pointed out that anger not only has outward signs but also inward signs. Teachers should see if the child can relate what it feels like inside to be angry. Lastly, it is helpful to explore some of the possible consequences to expressions of anger—what might happen when anger is acted out as aggression?

Teachers also need to identify some of the triggers for anger at school. At school, the child may be frustrated and angry over being rejected and left out of social groups and play activities. The child may also become angry over being teased and called names like "Spaz" because of being poorly coordinated

Each of these situations may then be explored. In the latter example, potential ways to handle teasing and name-calling can be developed in cooperation with the child. Second, it's important that the child be aware of internal cues, as feelings may intensify over time. Teachers and the child may role-play the situation. As the child assumes the role of the "teaser," he or she can reflect on feelings and thoughts. The child might comment, "I'm beginning to feel my muscles tensing up . . . my heart is beating faster . . . I need to relax . . . I need to just ignore him." Then ask, "What else could you do besides ignore him?" A list could be generated. The following might be suggested: counting to 10, looking at something else, and thinking about something else.

Robin, Schneider, and Dolnick (1976) described an interesting early development, called the "turtle technique," that can help control anger. Children with ADHD were taught to "play turtle" when teased and angered. "Going into their shells" was a protective strategy to ward off teasing and other forms of verbal aggression. This turtle technique was originally intended for use in the classroom, but it can be adapted for use by students in other environments. This technique has been more recently described by Bender (2007).

While those problem areas are critical for the child with ADHD to gain peer acceptance, the social niceties are also desirable for social relations in general. The Social Graces Checklist in Exercise 5.11 incorporates such behaviors as greeting others, saying thank you, introducing others, giving and receiving compliments, offering to help others, being sensitive to what others are feeling, and apologizing. A record of the frequency of each behavior may be kept for one week. Should the teacher determine that one or more of these behaviors would be useful to develop further, a behavior (point) system may be used. Through the use of modeling, imitation, shaping, and consistent reinforcement (especially at home), such behaviors may be developed and maintained.

Exercise 5.11   Social Graces Checklist

Date: _____

Name: _____

Social Skill	Mon	Tue	Wed	Thurs	Fri	Sat	Sun	Totals by Skill
Greet others.								
Say goodbye.								
Say thank you.								
Introduce others.								
Give compliments.								
Thank for compliments.								
Offer to help.								
Recognize others' feelings.								
Apologize.								
Be neat/clean in appearance.								
Totals by Day of Week								

Exercise 5.11 was adapted from Flick (1998).

SELF-CONCEPT/SELF-ESTEEM

The way a child perceives himself or herself constitutes self-concept; a child may have several differing views of that self. A child with ADHD may realize she has poor social skills and poor math skills, but she may also realize that she is an excellent soccer player. Such varying awareness is, indeed, fortunate; otherwise, the child with ADHD could be devastated by her many difficulties, making such comments as, "I'm really stupid in school," or "I really am a weirdo; I can't get along with anyone." Such a child exhibits a lack of understanding of the important fact that she is a person and, thus, distinct from what she does. The essential message for the teacher to convey to this child is, *You are not your behavior.* Adults should not criticize or put the child down—be aware of the child's internal dialogue regarding such a negative message. Over time, children can accumulate quite a number of negative messages; the effect is a progressive erosion of self-perception to the point of having a generally negative self-concept.

Self-esteem represents how the child feels about himself. It's a generalized feeling that develops over time and reflects the impact of life experiences. Often, this feeling state is based not only on what the child perceives but also on others' expectations. For example, a child with ADHD who is having a problem completing a task may be told, "I know you can do this work; you completed it yesterday." Such performance inconsistency (characteristic of the ADHD pattern) sets the child up to fail to meet the expectations of others, thereby creating another negative weight on the self-esteem scale. The greater the number of failure experiences, the lower the child's self-esteem. Despite putting forth effort in school, little is achieved. Despite a tremendous desire to be popular, other student treat the child as an annoying outcast. Although some children with ADHD do well in sports, others are banished to the sidelines and criticized when they do play.

Since the child with ADHD may encounter failures and disappointments in many areas of life besides the academic area, there is a general tendency for that child to develop a poor self-concept and to have low self-esteem. Teachers should remember, too, that most children with ADHD are exceptionally sensitive emotionally, as well as neurologically. When children with ADHD begin to believe that they are retarded, lazy, or losers, these beliefs may become associated with feelings of hopelessness and a belief that putting forth effort in school or in other situations does no good. When these feelings and beliefs lead to a pervasive sense of being "defeated," there may be significant loss of motivation. Positive strokes are clearly needed.

Giving Positive Strokes

It is most important that teachers of children with ADHD provide numerous and frequent positive strokes to counteract the many negative ones they receive. Exercise 5.12 will help develop an awareness of those things the child does well so this information can be used to provide positive strokes. If the teacher cannot list at least 10 things, he or she must go back to add those "parts of" things the child does well (even if the overall activity would not be described as done well). In other words, if only a single component of an activity is performed well, list that component; for example, "Child works very hard on tasks (once these have been organized and put into proper sequence)." This list will serve as a resource to provide positive strokes for the child.

Exercise 5.12   Positive Strokes

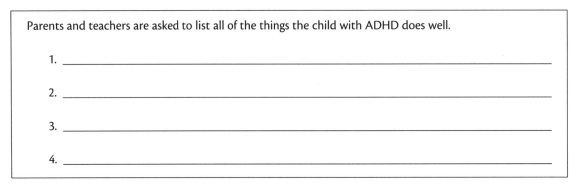

Parents and teachers are asked to list all of the things the child with ADHD does well.

1. _____

2. _____

3. _____

4. _____

5. _____

6. _____

7. _____

8. _____

9. _____

10. _____

The following is a list of sample positive strokes regarding what the child does well:

Examples of Positive Strokes

1. I really liked the birthday card you made for me—that was a very caring thing to do.

2. I appreciate the way you cleaned your desk.

3. You are really helpful to me in taking care of your classmates.

4. You know, you're very good at drawing those pictures of race cars.

5. I was really impressed by your play in the baseball game—two home runs—wow!

6. I really like the way you have organized your baseball card collection—it's really impressive and shows that you've put a lot of work into it.

7. I know that math isn't easy, but I am really impressed by the way you've accepted extra assignments to work on. It's really going to pay off.

Enhancing Self-Esteem

Parents and teachers of a child with ADHD need to be almost superhuman to remain positive and supportive in the presence of the child's difficulties and failures. However, parents, teachers, and others significant in the child's life provide a mirror that shows the child how he or she is appreciated; based on this, self-image is shaped. Therefore, to maintain adequate self-esteem, the significant people in the child's life must be aware of and constantly emphasize the positive for the child to enjoy success.

Teachers can affect self-esteem by their words and by how those words are used. Intonations of the voice reflecting disgust, lack of interest in activities, failure to listen to what the child says, backhanded compliments, and statements that question competence may all erode the child's self-esteem. Eventually, the teacher's perceived lack of interest may result in reduced or even closed communications with the child. Remember that the child with ADHD is quite sensitive to remarks of others. Accusations such as "You really annoy me," or "You're such a messy child," focus directly on the *child* and not on the *behavior*. It is not OK to focus your criticisms on the child. It is OK to state how you feel about his or her behavior; for example, "I really get upset when you interrupt my conversation." Sometimes a teacher, who is aware that the child has previously exhibited dangerous behavior and may simply want to "protect" the child, may, in the very act of being (over)protective, inadvertently say things that recall to the child his or her incompetency. For example: "Don't climb that tree. You know you always fall," or "Don't try to do that by yourself. You know you'll hurt yourself." Sometimes, it is very difficult to balance the need to protect the child with allowing the child to feel trusted in becoming more independent.

Teachers must be careful to avoid comparisons with other relatives and classmates. And when the child with ADHD shows improvement and does the best work ever, it's important to note that improvement and avoid finding fault. Don't give backhanded compliments.

> *Example of backhanded compliment:* "This is a really neat and organized math homework page. You are really improving. Maybe next time, you'll get all the answers right."

> *Example of sincere, reinforcing compliment:* "This is a really neat and organized math homework page. You are really improving. Look, you've even gotten more answers right this time than last."

The language used is most important. Critical comments and destructive words (like *dumb*, *stupid*, *pest*, and *worse*) can all depress the child's self-esteem. Everyone has negative qualities, but adults are allowed to promote their assets and hide their weaknesses; children with ADHD are often forced to expose their difficulties in front of a class or on the playing field. If these children are to feel good about themselves, they must receive more attention for what they do well now, for their effort, and for their improvement in all that they do. Teachers need to listen to this child, acknowledge what the child says, and be genuinely interested in the child's conversation.

Teachers should focus on any positive characteristics and emphasize improvements when they appear. For example, writing may be messy and words may be misspelled, but the child's story may have good content. It's important to point this out, saying, "I really like that story you wrote." These children must experience a sense of competency and be allowed to think and act in a more independent manner. Too often, in a need to get things done quickly, adults simply tell the child with ADHD what to do instead of allowing the child to think of what needs to be done. While this tactic seems to save time, it is at the expense of communicating to the child that he or she is competent; it says instead that the child must depend on others to tell him or her what to do. By not allowing the child to come up with the answer or do a task simply because it will take a little more time, the teacher may cause the child to feel inadequate, to perceive that he or she can't cope, and in general to develop a helpless, overly dependent attitude.

In the classroom, most teachers are aware that the child with ADHD needs more attention and is especially sensitive in situations where "differences" are made known. In fact, despite their sometimes rude and inappropriate behaviors, children with ADHD are quite sensitive to comments made in the classroom. If a child is misbehaving, it can be devastating for the teacher to say, "Johnny, did you take your medicine this morning?" or "Beth seems to act so smart at times. Let's see if she knows the answer to this question." Teachers need to offer many opportunities for small successes and praise, praise, praise! Teachers need to emphasize and bring out the "good stuff" for everyone to see.

Counteracting Negative Themes

To learn to pay attention to the "good stuff," teachers must use a reminder system to give more positive strokes. For example, teachers may be cued by a watch that beeps on the hour or, preferably, on the half-hour. Each time the beep sounds, the teacher should look for something the child has done that could be considered an occasion for a positive comment or token. (Tokens are especially effective for younger children; theater-type tickets [available from school supply houses] seem to work well with older students.) The teacher decides in advance on a specified number of tickets or tokens to give to the child each day. The child is told that these tokens or tickets may be traded in no later than the end of the week for some special privilege. The number of tokens or tickets may be increased as the teacher sees an increase in the overall number of times good behaviors appear. When any good, appropriate, or improved behavior is shown, it is rewarded, thus bringing about an increase in the number of these behaviors per day. This exercise is designed to counteract the generally negative themes that pervade most of the attention given to children with ADHD.

Lastly, there is the issue of the effect of grade retention on the self-concept and self-esteem of the child with ADHD. Mel Levine (1994) very early noted that retaining a child in a grade can cause significant setbacks to the child's pride, especially after the first grade. Moreover, he points out that grade retention has not been shown to help children succeed in the future. Children with a history of grade retention have a higher probability of leaving school without graduating and a propensity to engage in activities that are detrimental to them. Levine believed that there are effective alternatives to grade retention. These may include extra help at home or at school, summer school, or afterschool remedial programs. In short, there are many ways to counteract the negative impact of failure in school. The National Association of School Psychologists (NASP, 2003) recently supported Levine's position, and Levine continues to expound on this idea (Scherer, 2006).

INCLUDING HOME BEHAVIOR IN SCHOOL PROGRAMS

The child with ADHD appears to experience the most difficulty in the classroom setting; the demands of the classroom often elicit or generate ADHD behaviors. A brief analysis of the demands and expectations that are faced by any child in the classroom setting makes this assertion clear. During class, each student is expected to sit quietly, focus on the task at hand (i.e., seatwork assignment), and maintain attention (ignoring distractions) until the work is completed. Additionally, the child is expected to follow general class rules with regard to appropriate behavior with peers and with authority figures (e.g., teachers, aides, counselors, principal, and administrative staff).

In some cases, a parent may be quite surprised to discover that his or her child has exhibited behavioral problems in the school setting, as there may be few problems at home. This seemingly "split-personality" behavior is not uncommon. Once discovered, it may be handled in several different ways: (1) a behavioral contract between the student and teacher or parent may be written, (2) a home-school note system may be established, (3) combination behavior programs using a separate program at school and at home may be established, and (4) homework may be practiced in the same way that the child would be expected to complete school assignments (i.e., sitting quietly). The main criterion is that these programs at home not conflict with those in school.

CONTINGENCY CONTRACTING

Contingency contracting appears to be an effective way of improving academic performance and social behaviors for children with ADHD (Newstrom, McLaughlin, & Sweeny, 1999). The behavioral contract involves a written agreement between the student (who agrees to perform a certain task) and the teacher (who provides something the child wishes to have). Target behaviors must be clearly stated, and goals should be manageable. The contract should be signed by both student and teacher. The contingency contract has been replicated and is easily implemented for children with ADHD (Hubert, Weber, & McLaughlin, 2000; Swenson, Lolich, Williams, & McLaughlin, 2000).

The following guidelines (adapted from Koetz & Pittel, 2009) must be used for contingency contracts:

1. Develop a contract from negotiation between student and teacher (Kerr, 2002).

2. Select a behavior that is functionally and socially important to the student.

3. Write the contract clearly and use a positive orientation (i.e., specify what you wish the student to do) (Jackson, 2002).

4. List the reward(s) for successful completion of the contact. Students should participate in this phase to be sure that the reward is something that the student values.

5. Determine the frequency and source of the reward(s).

6. Specify any mild punishment that will immediately follow any inappropriate behavior (Cavalier & Bear, 2005).

7. Be sure to establish a timeline for the contract (e.g., contract will expire on [date]).

8. All parties sign the contract; a copy may also be given to the child's parents.

9. When successfully completed, the reward(s) should be given immediately.

10. Always use teacher praise along with the rewards for successful completion of the contract.

11. Stress that the student has assumed responsibility for one behavior, as outlined in the contract (Kerr, 2002).

12. Develop new contracts (upon successful completion of a contract) or renegotiate a change (when a contract is not successfully completed) (Cavalier & Bear, 2005).

A contingency contract (Exercise 5.13) is a written agreement between the teacher and the child wherein the teacher agrees to give the child something the child desires after the child fulfills some specified expectation of the teacher. It is also referred to as a "behavioral contract." While writing such a contract sounds simple enough, the teacher must be sure to determine whether the child is capable of meeting the expectation *and* whether the reward is appropriate for that accomplishment.

Generally, behavioral contracts are most appropriate for older children and adolescents (ages 10 to 15), yet such agreements may be used with some bright young children as young as age 8. While these contracts may be somewhat tricky to develop, they can serve as an effective motivation for the child to accomplish short-term goals. The word *tricky* is important, because teachers may expect too much of the child or perhaps have a payoff that is insufficient to maintain goal-oriented behavior. For example, it is not

Exercise 5.13   Behavioral Contract

I _____ (name of child), agree to

_____ (perform task or

behavioral goal as expected by parent/teacher). In return, I would like

_____

_____ (wished-for reward). I therefore

agree to the contract specified above.

_____   _____

(parent signature)   (child's signature)

---

uncommon for parents to offer something significant (e.g., a color TV) in return for all As on the next report card. While this may appear very attractive to the child at first, over a period of time, this reward may be perceived as quite distant and perhaps even impossible to achieve. If the expectation (all As) is too great or too far in the future, motivation will eventually be diminished. This type of motivational approach is insufficient to maintain the child's work effort until the goal is achieved, especially for the child with ADHD.

In a typical behavioral contract, the expectation may involve either academic behavior (e.g., completing homework) or other behaviors (e.g., keeping hands to self in class). The behavioral goal should be realistic and short-term. Parents and teachers are encouraged to write some examples of behavioral contracts and to compare these with the examples at the end of this chapter. Note these two points:

1. The teacher gives no punishment or negative feedback if the child does not uphold his or her part of the contract; the reward is simply not realized.

2. It is imperative that the teacher fulfill his or her part of the contract as agreed.

HOME-SCHOOL NOTES

A home-school note is a device used by teachers as part of a comprehensive home-school behavior management program. Simply stated, the school note describes (in varying detail) the child's academic performance and social behavior in the classroom on a regular basis. This critical communication between the teacher and the parents harnesses the most powerful motivations for the child to improve academic or other behaviors.

There are several general formats for the home-school note. The examples in Exercises 5.14 and 5.15 provide information on four problem areas for children with ADHD. These include (1) following instructions, (2) completing work, (3) obeying class rules, and (4) getting along with others. For ages 4 to 7, the note describes each area with a smiley, sad, or indifferent face to document whether the child did the appropriate thing, did not do the appropriate thing, or partially accomplished the goal in each area. The note for children ages 8 to 12 uses numerical ratings: 2 for yes, 1 for partially, and 0 for no. These numbers can then be used in a point system.

Exercise 5.14   School Note

| **Name:** _____ | **Date:** _____ |

Dear Teacher:

Please rate this child in each class period in the areas listed on the following scale: Excellent = 4, Good = 3, Fair = 2, Poor = 0, or NA (not applicable). Also indicate whether the class is in the morning or afternoon and initial at the bottom.

Note: IS = In-School Suspension, OS = Out-of-School Suspension

Area	Class Periods						
	1	2	3	4	5	6	7
Followed instructions.							
Completed work.							
Obeyed class rules.							
Got along with others.							
(write in)							
(write in)							
AM/PM class							
Time-outs							
Detentions							
Suspensions (IS/OS)							
Lunchroom behavior							
Recess behavior							

Positive Comments:

_____

_____

_____

_____

Teacher's Initials: _____

Exercise 5.15 shows a general and simplified form of the note. It describes both classwork and general behavior for the morning and afternoon sessions. Morning and afternoon behaviors are kept separate, because some children who have ADHD behave differently at different times.

Exercise 5.15   Weekly School Note

Name: _____   **Date:** _____

Dear Teacher:

Please rate this child in the areas listed on the following scale: Excellent = 4, Good = 3, Fair = 2, Poor = 0, or NA (not applicable) for each day of the week, mornings or afternoons.

Note: IS = In-School Suspension, OS = Out-of-School Suspension

	MON	TUE	WED	THUR	FRI
Morning					
Followed instructions.					
Completed work.					
Obeyed class rules.					
Got along with peers.					
(write in)					
(write in)					
Afternoon					
Followed instructions.					
Completed work.					
Obeyed class rules.					
Got along with peers.					
(write in)					
(write in)					
Time-outs					
Detentions					
Suspensions (IS/OS)					
Lunchroom Behavior					
Recess Behavior					

Positive Comments:

_____

_____

_____

_____

Teacher's Initials: _____

These notes are designed with speed and simplicity of recording in mind. Teachers need to keep the note system simple, clear, and concise while addressing the relevant problem area for the child. Some notes may record information and ratings from each of the child's teachers; others may simply represent a consensus report from one teacher (e.g., the homeroom teacher). The most desirable notes give sufficient information yet do not make excessive demands on a teacher's time. Teachers are encouraged to write some notes listing behavior that may be of concern in the classroom or in other school settings. Teachers should list *alternatives* to problem behaviors in a positive framework. Negative comments are generally to be suppressed, especially during the beginning phase of the behavioral program.

Variations on the home-school note are commonly found. Compare your proposed examples with those listed and reword those that don't meet the aforementioned criteria. As with all procedures discussed here, parent-teacher cooperation is of the utmost importance.

EFFECTIVE HOME-SCHOOL PROGRAMS

The behavioral chart (see Exercise 5.16) allows various behaviors that pertain to both home and school to be listed. Specifically, behaviors monitored in school may be reinforced with privileges provided by parents at home. Since more troublesome behaviors often occur in the school setting, the majority of the behaviors listed may pertain to school or the classroom. They may be fairly specific, or they may refer to the general categories of desired behavior—following directions, obeying class rules, and so on. More specific school-related behaviors might include (1) stays on task, (2) begins work without a cue, (3) controls acting out (temper), (4) stays in seat, (5) remains quiet, (6) inhibits blurting out and by raising hand to answer, (7) keeps hands to self, (8) shares with others, (9) takes turns, (10) plays/works cooperatively, (11) writes neatly, and (12) uses social graces (e.g., says please, thank you, good morning, yes sir).

Employing general behavioral categories is a good place to start; however, using more specific behavioral descriptions allows the child to get more accurate feedback on what is appropriate or inappropriate behavior. When the behavioral chart is initially established, the teacher lists four to six school-related behaviors. Problem behavior can be addressed at several different stages.

1. The teacher must communicate that bringing home the home-school note (or daily planner) is important. The child receives points for bringing home the note (whatever it reports), and no privileges are given for any day the note is not brought home (cooperation of parents needed here).

2. The teacher(s) monitor general behaviors in the morning and afternoon. These behaviors can be monitored separately to determine whether there is more difficulty in the morning or the afternoon (as is usually found). It is also possible to monitor these behaviors for each class to determine whether difficulty arises in some classes (e.g., math) but not others. If a child's behavior is a problem in just one class, this might reflect the child having difficulty with specific academic material in that class. Across each week, the teacher should total the number of points obtained for each program category. The teacher can then determine whether one or more problem areas need additional focus and other interventions.

3. The parent or teacher must review with the child the points obtained each day and give as much verbal praise as possible for any improvement, for generally good

behaviors, or when desired behaviors are maintained from one day to the next. Using a bonus point category, a teacher can also provide points for (a) improvements, (b) consistency, (c) positive comments from other teachers, or (d) when maximum points are recorded for either the morning or afternoon sessions or both (e.g., if four desirable behaviors are monitored, with ratings of 0 to 2, a total rating of 8 would deserve a bonus). It is a good idea for parents and teachers to provide bonus points liberally; remember that the child with ADHD typically has been frustrated and deprived of positive strokes when it comes to school-related activities. Teachers must encourage parents to do provide positive reinforcement.

Exercise 5.16   Home/School Behavior Chart

Behavior List	Points	Mon	Tues	Wed	Thurs	Fri	Sat	Sun
Total Points								
Points Used/Fines								
Net Points/Day								
Fines List	Points	Mon	Tues	Wed	Thurs	Fri	Sat	Sun
Totals								

Note: For behaviors, assign 1 point each; for fines, assign 2 points each. Keep points for privileges low (2–10 points each).

For decisions regarding changes in the program, such as fading to weekly or monthly monitoring and gradual termination of the program, follow the suggestions provided previously. The only difference may involve fading the program from daily monitoring to weekly or monthly monitoring. The general duration of the daily program may range from four to six weeks or up to nine weeks; however, much depends on how well the child does with the program. In general, the home-school program is not designed as a permanent program. However, some type of monitoring and feedback system (i.e., consequences) may be used for an entire school year, depending on the seriousness and pervasiveness of problem behavior. This recommendation is based on the typical clinical finding that results are generally maintained when learning continues and is reinforced for an extended period of time. Also, redundancy and "overlearning" might be needed for the successful development of positive habits in the child with ADHD. Teachers can continue to give positive feedback and positive reinforcement for any appropriate behavior beyond the life of the behavioral point system or specific behavioral program.

SUMMARY

Teachers must focus on removing inappropriate behavior and developing appropriate behavior. The latter task may involve replacing an inappropriate behavior or developing a new, appropriate behavior. Many basic procedures are covered. Lastly, there is a discussion about how to include home behavior in home-school programs. The behavioral strategies suggested are not only useful in developing more appropriate behaviors but may also help to encourage greater independent thinking and independent work habits.

Basic Behavioral Techniques

Removing Inappropriate Behavior

Key Points

- ❖ Development of ADHD
- ❖ Removing inappropriate behavior
- ❖ Ignoring
- ❖ Time-out
- ❖ Withdrawal of a privilege/behavior penalty
- ❖ Disciplining students with ADHD

Marvin is a 12-year-old boy in fifth grade in a public school. He is above average in abilities (WISE-III Full Scale IQ = 120). He is classified as Other Health Impaired with a diagnosis of ADHD and is taking Focalin XR. Marvin has little difficulty interacting with his peers. However, he is frequently off-task and rarely completes his work. When asked to turn in his work he often cries or expresses anger by having a temper tantrum.

How would you address these problems?

The following is a brief review of the basic behavioral techniques. It emphasizes the removal of inappropriate behavior typical of a child who has a disorder such as ADHD. However, most of these techniques will work with any child, with or without a disability.

DEVELOPMENT OF ADHD BEHAVIORS

It's important to realize that each child is different. While some behavioral tendencies are inherited, all behavior can be better managed with behavioral techniques. Note that problems can develop at any stage of the process in problem behavior development. It is most important that risk and protective factors be considered early within the child's first five years of life. Figure 6.1 illustrates these components over the first few years of life.

Figure 6.1 Problem Behavior Development, ADHD

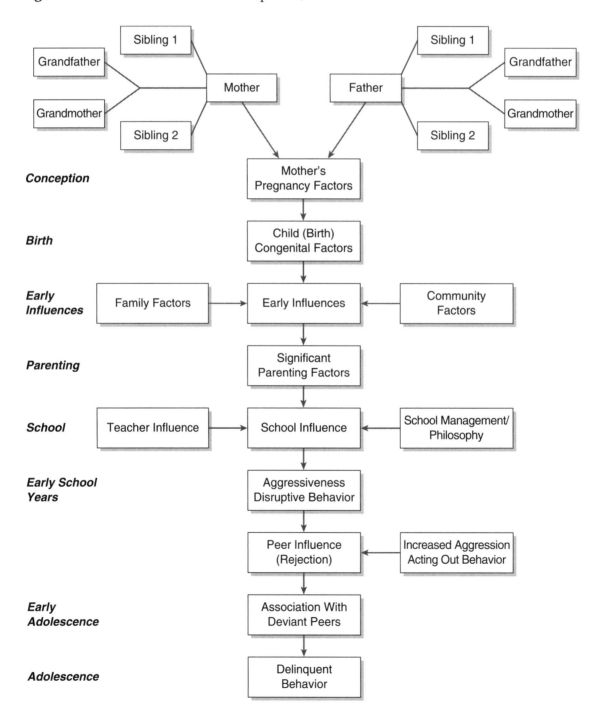

Maladaptive and dysfunctional behavior doesn't develop overnight. Rather, it develops over time and spills over into home and school environments, each affecting the other. Often, multiple factors lead to the current problem in the classroom (Stokes, 2002).

For example, all children inherit genes from their parents, who inherit genes from their parents; a good guide to some behavioral conditions may therefore lie in genetic influence. From conception, potential problems during the pregnancy must be considered (e.g., maternal smoking and/or drinking alcohol). Likewise, complications at birth have to be taken into account (e.g., anoxia at birth). Some early influences involve family and community factors; parenting factors may greatly influence the developing child at this stage.

When the child with ADHD enters school, he or she is influenced by the approach of teachers, as well as the philosophy of the school regarding the management of behavior problems. Should aggressive, disruptive behavior develop during the early school years, this may result in rejection by classmates (peers), poorly developed social skills, and increased aggression or other acting-out behaviors. It is well known that ADHD rarely occurs alone; it is most often frequently accompanied by comorbid conditions, such as oppositional defiant disorder, conduct disorder, or a learning disability, and other conditions. Children with ADHD who develop a comorbid behavior disorder tend to associate with other classmates who show like behavior. Eventually, such behavior may lead to delinquent status. However, not all ADHD behavior results in delinquency.

The first question a teacher might ask is, How did this behavior problem develop? Consider the flowchart for problem behavior development in Figure 6.1. It's important to realize that each child is different and that each child may develop a unique trajectory of problem behaviors. Any particular child might not progress to delinquent behavior if earlier behavior problems are resolved.

Problem behavior may certainly be influenced by many factors, but the main problem(s) appear to center around learning. Thus, many inappropriate behaviors are learned and reinforced through years of use because they continue to work for the child. These behaviors either get something or allow the child to get out of something. What most teachers want to do is (a) get rid of the inappropriate (undesirable) behavior and replace it with more appropriate (desirable) behavior or (b) simply develop more appropriate (desirable) behavior. Fortunately, since inappropriate behaviors are learned, they can be unlearned. Let's consider each component.

REMOVING INAPPROPRIATE BEHAVIOR

In many cases, the inappropriate behavior is just annoying or perhaps causes the teacher to become angry. The first thought might be "I've got to punish this behavior to stop it."

Corporal Punishment

Physical punishment does result in suppression of a behavior, but it does not get rid of it. When a teacher uses physical punishment, several things happen:

- The child stops the behavior but returns to it later.
- The child initially learns to exhibit the behavior *only* in the presence of the punishing agent.
- The agent often models the very behavior he or she wishes to remove. If the problem is aggression towards a classmate, for instance, the message is "Don't do to your classmate what I'm doing to you." Actions speak louder than words, however,

and the child receives the message that the way to handle problems like this is to use physical punishment (i.e., to hit someone).

- Physical punishment may also result in the child avoiding the punishing agent or perhaps tuning her or him out so that further socialization (and teaching) is limited.
- Over time, the child may develop a lack of sensitivity to physical punishment or even consider enduring it a "mark of toughness." Thus, physical punishment becomes even less effective and may even backfire; when the child is bigger, he or she may retaliate.

It is also important to note that physical punishment is often given long after the child exhibits the inappropriate behavior, whereas the most effective rewards and punishment are given as soon as possible after the behavior, preferably immediately afterward. The bottom line is *do not use physical punishment in school*. Basically, it is totally ineffective in dealing with behavior problems, and it is ineffective with ADHD. Instead, *use positive forms of reinforcement* and focus on developing more desirable and appropriate behaviors. Nevertheless, teachers will need to discourage some behaviors and eventually remove them.

Corporal punishment, striking with the hand or an implement, is the most severe form of physical punishment that can be used in school. It is estimated that 23 states still allow corporal punishment of their students, affecting almost 350,000 students per year (Finley, 2007). Both teachers and parents must remember that punishment (of any kind) does not teach the child what to do (i.e., the appropriate behavior). The research clearly shows undesirable side effects of using physical punishment, as reported early by Azrin and Haltz (1966). Those wishing to explore this issue in more detail may read resources relevant to ADHD (see Flick, 1998; Wright & Wright, 2009).

Verbal Reprimand

One form of punishment less severe than physical punishment is the verbal reprimand (Reid, 1999). This means that the child is "yelled at" or verbally scolded for exhibiting inappropriate behavior. This procedure is controversial, and intervention results are mixed, especially with students who have ADHD (Brown, 2009). Because of these mixed results and the fact that the reprimand is potentially harmful to the student, as well as other students, it is not a recommended procedure. Teachers may consult other resources for more in-depth discussions of this issue (see DuPaul & Stoner, 2003; Rosen, 2005).

Effective Punishment Techniques: Ignoring and Withdrawal of a Privilege

The emphasis should be on positive reinforcement for all behavior management. However, sometimes inappropriate behavior must be addressed with punishment techniques. Two techniques can be easily used in the school situation: ignoring and withdrawal of a privilege. Whether one or the other is used will often depend on the seriousness of the misbehavior. Ignoring can be used for less serious misbehavior; withdrawal of a privilege is used with more serious misbehavior. Both these techniques are addressed in depth in the next section.

Summary

Behavior that is annoying, disrespectful, or hurtful to the child, to another child, or to others is clearly inappropriate and unwanted. The problem for many teachers is to remove this inappropriate behavior in a manner that will be beneficial for the child and others. While this may sound simple, it is often complicated by misunderstandings, distortions in perceptions, and rigid, inflexible attitudes regarding discipline.

Behaviors become weaker when they are followed by (a) no consequence whatsoever or (b) an aversive consequence (i.e., punishment). Both research and clinical practice have documented quite well the notion that physical punishment is clearly not effective for most children and especially not for children with ADHD. However, many procedures do work well; these are classified as *mild punishments*. The first step for teachers is the selection of behaviors that they wish to change.

SELECTING BEHAVIORS AND IGNORING AND WITHDRAWING PRIVILEGES

Selecting Behavior(s) to Weaken or Remove

Teachers often agree on behaviors that need to change. First, it is clear that those behaviors that are dangerous to the child or others are of prime concern. They include aggressive behaviors, such as hitting, pushing, wielding dangerous objects (e.g., knives), and high-risk behaviors, such as running into the street, jumping from high places, or using dangerous objects inappropriately (e.g., trying to catch a sharp knife thrown in the air). Second, other behaviors, while not intrinsically dangerous in a physical sense, may be hurtful to others or simply annoying. These include throwing temper tantrums, making noises or inappropriate gestures, talking back disrespectfully, whining, making annoying verbal comments, and name-calling. Noncompliance may also be included in this category.

You probably already have in mind a list of all undesirable behaviors. However, it will be advantageous to review these in Exercise 6.1. List those behaviors that fall into

Exercise 6.1   Selection of Unwanted Behaviors to Change

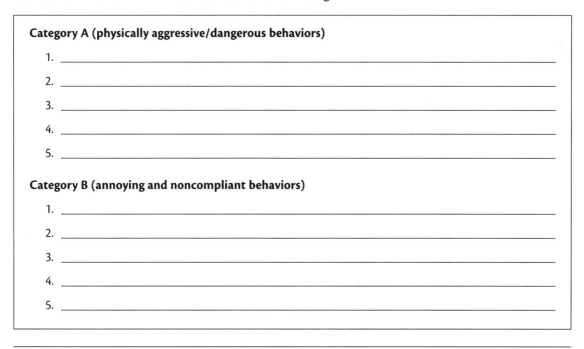

Category A (physically aggressive/dangerous behaviors)

1. _____
2. _____
3. _____
4. _____
5. _____

Category B (annoying and noncompliant behaviors)

1. _____
2. _____
3. _____
4. _____
5. _____

Exercise 6.1 has been adapted from Flick (1998).

Category A (physical aggression/dangerous behaviors) and those that belong in Category B (annoying and noncompliant behaviors). This will help sort out behaviors that vary in severity and make it easier to decide which techniques may be applied to change them. In general, the more significant ones are listed first in each category, with less serious ones following.

Ignoring

When a behavior is annoying or mildly disruptive, the first procedure to use is ignoring. The teacher will know quickly if this behavior is under attentional control, for it will initially get worse when ignored (though ignoring over the long term will extinguish the behavior). Paying attention to the behavior by saying, "Stop," or "No," or giving a lecture about the inappropriate behavior also only serves to make it worse.

When a teacher decides to ignore a behavior, it must be consistently ignored for as long as it continues. To pay attention to a behavior after initially ignoring it will do two things: (a) it will reinforce the behavior at a higher level of intensity, and (b) it will cause the child to become persistent. Thus, the unacceptable behavior will become worse, and persist longer. Essentially, the child does not know when the teacher will attend to it; frustration-tolerance is therefore built in. Teachers must be able to predict how strong the initial behavior is and how long it will last.

Many children will test teachers to see if they mean what they say or if they will pay attention to the inappropriate behavior. Of course, when this happens, the child will be more likely to show that behavior again. Therefore, consistently ignoring the behavior is important, for each time the behavior receives attention, it becomes stronger and more likely to occur.

Many behaviors respond to ignoring: yelling, temper outbursts, swearing, and demanding behaviors are just a few. This would be especially true for those behaviors that are elicited and maintained by *attention*. Again, a teacher will know if attention plays a part in a behavior if it gets worse when attention is withdrawn. For example, if the child says, "Get me that book!" and the teacher does not respond, the child might repeat the statement louder. The teacher might then let the child know that he or she must act appropriately in asking for the book while continuing to ignore the rude, demanding behavior. When the child changes the behavior and asks appropriately for the book, the teacher must reinforce this change, saying, "Now that's a lot better way of asking—you're using a normal tone of voice. Which book would you like?"

Teachers must be prepared for the inappropriate behavior to get worse before it gets better, and teachers must not assume that the child knows the appropriate behavior. The teacher could ask, "How do you ask for something that you want?" If the child correctly answers, reinforce that verbalization by saying, "That's right—now use it." If the child does not know, then model the correct verbal behavior and when the child imitates it, say, "Good, that's it—you said it just the way I showed you."

Sometimes teachers say they cannot ignore some inappropriate behavior, believing that if the misbehavior is ignored, the child has "gotten away with something." However, it is now well known that many children, especially children with ADHD, often perform behaviors that are certain to attract attention, "hook" the teacher, or create some desired effect (e.g., stir up some excitement). Often such behaviors are shocking behaviors that involve some taboo (e.g., sexual gesture or curse word). The child expects a response, and when there is one, albeit negative, it reinforces the preceding behavior; thus, giving attention to such misbehavior only serves to maintain it. Even a simple comment, such as

"That's a no-no," or "Stop that immediately," may inform the child that he or she has indeed "hooked the teacher," and though the behavior may stop at that time, it is likely to recur soon. The bottom line is that teachers should avoid giving attention to inappropriate behavior, even if that attention is to simply comment about it.

Attention from a teacher is extremely powerful and may be used to reinforce many behaviors. Some teachers state that they give equal attention to appropriate and inappropriate behaviors, which results in no change in the balance of these behaviors. Instead, a shift in the positive direction is needed; that is, withdraw attention to the annoying behavior and give more attention to a desired behavior that is opposite to the annoying behavior. This procedure will result in a balanced program.

Plan to Ignore Some Behaviors

Once the teacher has categorized the undesirable behaviors, one annoying behavior must be selected to ignore. The teacher should follow this sequence of steps:

Step 1: Be prepared. This old Scouting motto is good advice. Know what to expect when a (mis)behavior is ignored. For example, if whining is selected as the annoying behavior, the teacher might talk to herself (silently) about the child's reaction; that is, have an internal dialogue. The teacher might say, "I know that by withdrawing my attention, Sally is going to become increasingly more frustrated and angry, and her whining will become more intense. I will have to continue to talk to myself so that I don't make the mistake of giving in to her."

Step 2: Be consistent. The teacher might then say, "I know that once I choose to ignore a behavior, I'll have to continue ignoring it until it is under control. If I attend to Sally while she is engaged in whining, I know that whining will become more intense (because of her frustration and anger over being ignored). I will then reinforce her whining at a more intense level and reward her for persisting in misbehavior (continuing to whine for longer periods in the absence of getting attention for it). Teachers must continue to self-talk to avoid falling into the trap of attending to the misbehavior. Much will depend on how well teachers prepare for this stage of the process and their emotional state. If teachers are overstressed, drained, or too involved with personal problems, it will indeed be difficult to withstand the child's behavior. Remember that the child is usually quite skilled and experienced at getting attention, and the teacher is accustomed to giving attention to children. *Change will not come easily.*

Step 3: Reward yourself. Once success is achieved in riding out the child's behavior, self-reward and recognition can be provided for the way the child's behavior was handled. Teachers should continue self-talk, saying, "Good, I did a good job of controlling myself and the situation. I am in control." This self-talk is especially important for a teacher who also has a history of ADHD and who may exhibit a tendency to react impulsively with anger toward the child.

Any time behavior changes in an appropriate direction, it is important for that behavior to be rewarded, whether it comes from the child or the teacher. Most behavioral changes are quite difficult to realize, and ultimate success often comes in small steps. *Reward each of these steps.* Once the child's behavior changes and whining decreases, point out (more frequently and immediately after the change) that the child's behavior is now more appropriate. Reinforcement frequency may be tapered off as the behavior change becomes more stable and consistent. However, in the beginning stages of change, teachers should notice even subtle or minor improvements. For example, a teacher might say, "I really like the way you reacted when I said you couldn't have an extra piece of pizza in the lunchroom; you didn't even whine. I really like the grown-up way you handled that," or, "I really liked the way you waited for me to finish instructions before you started your work. That's a real improvement." Whatever is appropriate for the situation may receive a compliment.

Time-Out for Misbehavior

Much like ignoring, the time-out procedure removes the child from any potential positive reinforcement; in the case of ignoring, positive reinforcement is withheld from the child.* Time-out is very much like the old "go sit in the corner" punishment. Kids reportedly hate time-out, especially kids with ADHD. They say that it's boring; many ask for another punishment rather than be put in time-out. Also, the child with ADHD wishes to get the punishment over with quickly.

What is time-out like? If a child just hit his classmate, he might be told, "No hitting. Go to time-out—now!" He is then sent to a boring place—usually a time-out room. The time-out place should be devoid of all reinforcements. A kitchen timer is used and set for the child's age (i.e., one minute for each year). This and other criteria are in accordance with recommendations from Dr. Lynn Clark (1985). He also recommends that teachers use no more than 10 words or 10 seconds to get the child to time-out.

Once in time-out, the child is ignored until the timer rings. *This is important.* No one—another child, a teacher, or anyone else—should pay attention to, talk to, or otherwise provide reinforcement for the child in time-out. The child cannot take a toy to time-out, and you should not get hooked into attending to the behavior of a child in time-out. Some children are quite adept at getting into a hassle, particularly with a teacher, while in time-out. It is not surprising in such cases to hear the teacher say, "Time-out does not work; he misbehaves even more now." If time-out is used incorrectly, the misbehavior may become worse, as the child is actually getting rewarded, by attention, for getting into the time-out.

Immediately when the timer rings, time-out is over, and the child is asked, "Now Jimmy, tell me—why were you sent to time-out?" If the child says, "Because I hit my classmate," the teacher says, "That's right." If the child says, "I don't know," he is given the answer and allowed to resume his activities. It is best to avoid giving much attention just after time-out, and, of course, it is not recommended that the child receive a hug, kiss, treat, or anything special or he'll get the impression that time-out really pays off! The child also should not receive a lecture after time-out and should not be asked to promise never to exhibit that behavior again.

It is not unusual for child to engage in more appropriate behavior after time-out. When this occurs, it should not be ignored. Any time behavior changes in a more positive direction, it is best to point this out to the child. When the child shows an improvement in behavior after time-out, reinforce this change by pointing out that you are pleased to see this behavior. It is useful to be specific; for example, "You really have much better control over yourself now. I like the way you are sharing that toy with your classmate."

---

*Much of the material in this section was adapted from Flick (1998).

Behaviors to Address With Time-Out

Now that there is a general understanding of the time-out procedure, it is important to consider when to use time-out. It may depend on which behavior is shown. A list of specific acting-out behaviors follows:

Hitting others, threatening to hit	Cursing
Throwing objects at others	Kicking others
Throwing temper tantrums	Pushing others (hard)
Mistreating, hurting pets	Biting, threatening to bite
Hostile teasing	Damaging property
Obnoxious, loud crying	Hair pulling
Sassy talk, talking back	Mocking teachers
Slapping	Choking others
Angry screaming	Loud complaining, demanding
Pinching	Spitting, threatening to spit
Toy grabbing	Name-calling
Scratching	Disobeying a command to stop a behavior
Toy throwing	Persistent interrupting:
Acting dangerously	Of adult conversation
Destroying toys	After a warning

Time-out is best used for behaviors that would be classified as aggressive or acting-out behaviors. Whining, pouting, fearful, reclusive, timid, irritable, and grumpy behaviors, for example, would not be appropriate for time-out. Note that passive behavior, such as failing to perform some chore or forgetting to do something, is not an appropriate target for this procedure; not doing something is not an acting-out behavior.

Developing a Time-Out Plan

It is important to understand and practice time-out before actually using it. This means that teachers must review and make decisions regarding some critical issues. Also, they should make a plan to deal with any problems encountered in time-out. Now consider the following guidelines.

1. **Select target behavior(s).** It is important to use time-out for specific acting-out behaviors and to avoid using it for every misbehavior (see Exercise 6.2). Teachers who learn this procedure often use it for everything, which reduces its effectiveness, as there is a lack of balance such that punishment (time-out) may become a prime source of getting attention.

Exercise 6.2   Behaviors for Time-Out

Select *two* from your list to target for time-out (put a star next to these).

2. **Select a place for time-out.** Use any place that is boring, where the child will not receive attention from those passing by and where the child has no access to reinforcements. A corner will suffice. Do not lock the child in a room or use any place that may generate fear. The door should be left partly open, as it is important for the child to hear the timer ring. In the school setting, the ideal place is probably a corner. Seclusionary time-out—that is, separating or segregating the child—is not advisable. A special place in the classroom that is designated as a time-out zone can also be a place for calming down and regaining control.

3. **Determine the length of time-outs.** A specific number of minutes may be used (three minutes, five minutes, etc.). The total time for any time-out should not exceed five minutes.

4. **Measure the time.** Be consistent and use a kitchen timer. This avoids having the child continually yelling, "Can I come out now?" The timer cannot be manipulated, rushed, or avoided. The child needs to know that he or she can come out of time-out only when the bell rings. This structure allows the child to know what to expect and avoids troublesome situations; responsibility is not placed on the teacher or the child to decide when enough time is spent in time-out. Time-out is over only when the kitchen timer rings.

5. **Withdraw attention while the child is in time-out.** This cannot be emphasized enough. Teachers often make the mistake of lecturing or continuing a hassle with the child, which simply makes time-out ineffective. A child may yell, "This isn't going to work," or continue yelling, screaming, or crying; complain of pains; or even plead to use the bathroom. All of these behaviors should be *ignored*, unless a real physical danger is obvious. Any destructive behaviors engaged in during time-out may result in added punishment, such as a behavior penalty (described later in this section) and having the child "clean up" or "pay up" for any mess or damage incurred.

6. **Establish the connection after time-out.** Ask, "Why were you sent to time-out?" If the child answers incorrectly or doesn't know, inform the child of the behavior that precipitated the time-out. It is important to clarify the connection between the behavior and the time-out. It is especially important to make the child aware of the "cause-effect" sequence when the student lacks awareness and has weak internal cognitive recognition about which behaviors will bring about negative consequences. The child must know what the consequences will be for certain

misbehaviors. Students will learn consequences for the behaviors selected but only after much practice and review.

Again, there is no need for lecturing after time-out, nor should the child be forced to "promise never to do it again." Such promises do not result in improvement, and they entrap the child for any future transgressions. Spending an inordinate amount of time with a child immediately after time-out gives the child a message that certain behaviors can really get you upset or excited. Then when the child with ADHD needs to "stir up some excitement," the child will certainly know which buttons to push! Keep interaction after time-out to a minimum.

General Comments

It is important to note that time-out, like many other forms of punishment, is often overused by teachers. So much emphasis has been placed on dealing with behavior that is inappropriate, very little time is spent focusing on which behaviors a teacher wishes to see more often. Remember, punishment never tells the child what "to do," only what "not to do." *Balance reward and punishment techniques.* Note: This does not necessarily mean an equal number of rewards and punishments. Instead, focus on using positive reinforcements for appropriate behavior as much or even more than using negative (aversive) consequences for inappropriate behaviors. Skill development through reinforcement of appropriate behavior is crucial for the success of the child with ADHD.

Rehearse time-out before using it. Before time-out is used, a "dress rehearsal" will ensure there no surprises when time-out is actually employed and allow each participant—child and teacher—to review his or her role. This rehearsal can be conducted with just the identified child and not in front of the whole class. Time-out should be presented in the following way:

1. Say, "For some time now, we have had hassles over [the behavior problem]. This is not much fun for you or for me. So when you [misbehave], you will be sent to a time-out." Explain the sequence of events in time-out in a manner appropriate for the child's age.

2. Run through the procedure, saying, "OK, now let's suppose you have just name-called. That's a time-out for name-calling—go now!" The child knows where to go and that a timer will be set for a specific number of minutes; it will be placed where the child can hear it.

3. When the child comes out of time-out, you might ask, "Why were you sent to time-out?" If the child states the reason, say, "That is exactly right." If not, tell the child why.

This rehearsal is important; it ensures that the teacher and child are ready. Be aware that, as Goldstein, Harootunian, and Conoley (1994) have noted, the first few times that a child is placed in time-out, a "time-out burst," or a heightened degree of aggressiveness, may occur. These outbursts will usually subside, especially if the teacher adds the number of minutes of the outburst to the time-out.

Time-Out at Home and at School

In general, time-out will be used more frequently at home. There has been much controversy over its use in school, and it has generally been difficult to set up a time-out in the school setting. Because of these difficulties, time-out has not received as much emphasis in overall behavior management programs in schools. It can also backfire, as when the child is sent outside the classroom; the child often finds escaping the classroom *rewarding*, not *punishing*. Consider a child who is having difficulty doing a task, becomes easily distracted, and engages in an aggravating behavior with her neighbor (e.g., pinching his arm). Should this child be sent out of the room? This may actually take her out of an unrewarding and boring task; therefore, she is rewarded for acting out and will probably repeat the behavior in the future. In normal discipline programs, when this occurs a number of times, she may be suspended and forced to leave school, which she doesn't like. What a punishment! Suspension from school may work for normal children who would, for varying reasons, find it unpleasant to be sent out of the class or to be sent home. It would not, however, be effective for most children who experience the behavior problems associated with ADHD.

Typically, when time-out is used in the school, the child simply goes to a designated place and must still follow the lesson or continue working. A modified time-out is a time to "calm down," "refocus," or "redirect" activities to a different situation.

At home or at school, there may be different types of time-outs:

- *Time-Out for Two:* When classmates fight, rather than playing detective to discover "who started this," send both children to time-out. Either an average of their ages or a preset number of minutes (e.g., five minutes) may be chosen. When the questioning to "get to the bottom of this fight" is avoided, the effectiveness of time-out is enhanced. Remember that it is important to deliver consequences of behavior *immediately* following the behavior. If consequences are delayed, a teacher may get confused over what started the fight, and the classmates win. Punish both children by saying, "Both of you have a time-out for fighting—go now."

  When they come out of the time-out, ask both why they were sent to time-out. More importantly, ask them, "Now, can you think of another way you could have solved your problem without fighting?" Both children will compete for a "good answer," and this process will aid in the development of problem-solving concepts. Both children are now learning to develop cognitions that may mediate aggressive behavior in the future. When the child knows other options, and is reinforced for using them, coping skills can improve. The impulse-oriented child learns cognitive mediating techniques, which essentially involve "thinking before acting" as a means of controlling impulses.

- *Time-Out for Toys.* When a child misuses a toy or acts out destructively with it, or when the toy is a source of conflict between two young classmates, the toy may be placed in time-out for a specified time. The teacher may say, "You are not playing appropriately (or cooperatively) with this toy. It goes into time-out." For high-interest, frequently used toys, it is necessary to use only a short time-out. Other toys may be put in time-out for a day or two. Again, it is important to use reasonable time-outs. Many children with ADHD report that they have lost toys completely or that they have been thrown away. Excessive and cruel punishments are not only ineffective, they may create other problems, such as depression and hopelessness. Instead, reward good behavior by giving the toy back sooner. Thus, "time off for good behavior" may be used for any toy that would otherwise be in time-out for at least one hour.

- 3. *Time-Out for the Young Child.* For children less than two years of age, some special provisions can be made. Instead of sending the child to a time-out room, a straight-back chair may be used. Sometimes, even a time-out of very short duration (e.g., one minute) may be effective. Sometimes it may be necessary to hold the child to prevent him or her from escaping. No attention is given to the child in this situation other than to remind the child that once he or she complies, time-out will be over. So often, power struggles develop with the young child, and there is resistance to a change in control. However, it is important to win this power struggle if the teacher is to be effective with the child in other situations requiring discipline.

Problems With Time-Out

Some children comply immediately with time-out; others resist. The easiest way to deal with resistance to time-out is to add additional minutes. The young child may be held in the chair, *but no excessive force should be used*. Tell the child that when he or she calms down and the timer rings, the child can come out of time-out. It is important not to let the child out if there is a severe misbehavior. No lecturing or scolding need be given. It is also important to withdraw visual attention and not look at the child who is in time-out.

With an older child, simply add additional minutes to the time-out for each instance of resistance (i.e., failure to go), but this should not exceed three minutes. If the resistance continues, a behavior penalty may be given (i.e., withdrawal of a privilege).

Redirection

Redirection, as a substitute for time-out, may be especially useful for younger children (under age 8) and with older children whose mental age is within this range. Simply, redirection involves removing a child from one situation where acting out has started, or is about to occur, and placing that child in a different situation. If, for example, a child has become argumentative while participating in a classroom activity, he or she may be asked to join another group that is involved in a different activity. Very often, this change will interrupt the pattern of misbehavior. When more appropriate behavior appears in the alternate situation, this improved behavior may be reinforced with verbal praise and touch (e.g., a pat on the shoulder).

Time-Out in the Classroom Context

Time-out is a mild punishment and has been found to be quite effective with children who have ADHD. Time-out may be used primarily for the control of acting-out behaviors and persistent noncompliance. However, as Goldstein and Goldstein (1998) pointed out, teachers and parents must distinguish between *noncompliance* and *incompetence*. If the child with ADHD fails to comply with instructions in the classroom or in other school settings, teachers must look at how the instructions were given, whether the child received the entire message, or whether the child responded impulsively or was misguided by distractions. Teachers should check to see if the child knew what to do and just didn't do it (oppositional and noncompliant) or if he or she really "missed the message" (incompetent, but consistent with behavior characteristic of children with ADHD). Simply by asking, "[Name], what did I ask you to do?" you may be able to make this determination.

Another caution regarding use of time-out is that it is often overused and may become ineffective over time. Diminished effectiveness with time-out may also occur if the prime focus is on punishment, which never tells the child what "to do," only what "not to do." To maintain effective use of time-out, the procedure must be combined with a positive approach.

While factors such as the use of a timer, rehearsal of time-out, and follow-up after time-out are the same for a school setting as for the home, two possible variations may be applicable in the school setting. The first involves time. Since time-out in the classroom may be used for several students, the time may vary from three to five minutes and not depend solely on the child's age. Teachers must use their judgment to determine whether a short (three-minute) or long (five-minute) time-out period should be employed. This variation of time may depend upon the children's ages and the severity of the acting-out behavior.

Also, time-out will work only if there the child has something positive to return to. If a child has academic difficulty and continually experiences failure and criticism, he or she may actually come to enjoy longer and longer time-outs, because being removed from the classroom (where there is difficulty, failure, and constant criticism) becomes desirable. Continual misbehavior adds time to the time-out, as the child is expected to behave more appropriately before being released. However, if misbehavior continues, the child should be told, "That's an additional minute," only twice, and—importantly—there is no lecturing or discussion about the misbehavior while the child is in time-out. All behavior while in time-out should be ignored, unless it becomes a danger to the child or others or it makes it impossible for a teacher to continue teaching. Should that be the case, the child should quickly be removed from the classroom.

The second variation is the place selected for time-out. Typically, the child will remain in the class and simply face a wall (not a window or a door or anyplace where he or she might find interesting things to look at). Note that for time-out, it is best not to send the child to a partitioned carrel, since that place should be associated with positive things and should be reserved for use by any student who wishes to have a quieter place with fewer distractions.

Even though time-out is considered mildly punishing, it is perhaps best promoted as a time and place to "regain control" or "to bring oneself down" if emotionally upset or excited. If the child learns that when he or she becomes aware of a potential for acting out, the child can voluntarily go to such a designated place in the classroom—or briefly retreat to a mental "safe and quiet" place using a predetermined visualization—the time-out may be beneficial. Teachers must refrain from overusing time-out; excessive use may result in prolonged segregation of the child and may encroach upon this student's already fragile self-concept and diminished self-esteem. Overall, it is felt that time-out may be an intervention of "last resort," following implementation of generally more positive techniques.

Time-Out to Chill Out

Time-out is a very controversial procedure for students and teachers alike. It is best not used in a formal manner in the classroom. However, students can be taught how to use it for themselves, identifying it as a *chill-out* procedure. The teacher might say, "You can put yourself in a time-out. Whenever you are upset or angry, you can go to a specific place where there is a comfortable chair—sit down and calm down. After you get control of yourself, you can come back." Make available to students a place in the classroom (e.g., a beanbag chair in the back of the room) where they can go when upset. Perhaps a place can also be identified on the school grounds (e.g., a bench) where the student can go to calm down. However, being upset would be the *only* reason to go away to chill out.

This self-imposed self-control technique could be used by any student. Students can also be reinforced for using such a procedure when they are upset. The teacher might say, "I noticed that you were really upset about [situation], and I liked the way you handled it by giving yourself a chill-out. You must feel a lot better, and you look much calmer, too. I'm really proud of you for recognizing what you need and for doing it." Teachers must be cautioned, however, against students using this procedure (via negative reinforcement) to get out of a tough assignment. Teachers must therefore consider the function of the misbehavior. Students may not use their misbehavior to escape or avoid assigned tasks. In short, *the work still has to be completed.*

Withdrawing a Privilege

In a generally positive reinforcing environment, withdrawal of a privilege works quite well. However, if the teacher is more accustomed to focusing on problem behavior, then this procedure may not be as effective. In short, it will be important to focus on positive appropriate behaviors. This teaches the child what *to do* instead of what *not* to do. Many children simply to do not know what to do. They lack the skills needed to deal with different situations. Teach them what they need to know.

In some cases, it will be important to take something away from the child, indicating that the behavior is deemed unacceptable. The message is to *stop the behavior.* This is generally an appropriate response to more serious misbehaviors, such as violent acting-out behavior that can hurt either the child or someone else. Remember that too many rules may just be overwhelming and prompt a student to test out what teachers will do. Rules should be few in number and must be periodically reviewed. It may not be essential to query the child in question, but asking another (good) student what the rule is may serve to review the rule for all students.

Behavior is governed by consequences. While a behavior may be triggered by some situation or event, the consequence determines what will happen to the behavior. If the consequence is positive, the behavior will continue. If a negative consequence follows, the behavior may be weakened or suppressed. Suppression may not happen the first time; several occasions may be required to extinguish the behavior fully.

If the privilege that is withdrawn is important and if it is something the child likes, the withdrawal will be effective; if it is not something the child likes, the withdrawal may fail. So if a child hates to miss computer time, its withdrawal may be effective. However, if a child hates math and is not allowed to do it, the withdrawal may actually be reinforcing, resulting in more of the inappropriate behavior.

It is important to use only those things that are not involved in the child's social development or relaxation strategy. Thus, the child should not be deprived of recess or lunch or anything else that is given to all students. Computer time may be a special reward that is available to only a select few students. Each child is different, and each situation is different. The teacher must evaluate the consequence to see if it is effective. Remember that withdrawing the same privilege will not work for every child. Finally, the teacher should determine the function of the inappropriate behavior so that the same or similar function can be addressed by an appropriate behavior.

Following are guidelines for teachers to use when implementing the withdrawal of privileges in their classrooms:

1. Teachers must review with the child the consequences for the selected misbehaviors, as well as note the consequences for appropriate behavior. The child is informed

which privilege will be lost should the misbehavior occur and what the reward will be should the child show alternative appropriate behavior instead. This technique, called *priming*, will increase the effectiveness of the consequences and provide some cognitive link between past consequences and present behavioral control. The child will internalize what consequences will follow either misbehavior or appropriate behavior. It is also assumed that, given a choice, the child would prefer the positive consequence for appropriate behavior.

2. Teachers are wise to give the child some predetermined signal (preferably nonverbal) to serve as a warning and to allow the child to develop self-control, which may subsequently be rewarded. One signal might be to hold up two fingers for the child to see. This will serve as a signal for the child to decide either (a) to change the current misbehavior or (b) to accept the consequences. All of this is reviewed with the whole class prior to implementation, and the sequence can even be rehearsed.

3. Once the signal is given, teachers can say, "Mark, look here" (while holding up two fingers), and give Mark a few seconds to respond. Giving the child the opportunity to develop and gain control over his or her own behavior can be very effective.

4. If control is achieved, the teacher might say, "John, I'm very proud of the decision you made to stop teasing (annoying, hitting, etc.) your classmate. I like the way you are sitting quietly with her. For your good behavior, you can have extra computer time." If you have set up a point system, then points may be given instead of the reward. The teacher should, however, remind the child of the preference to see good behavior continue and that the teacher would be disappointed should the child lose the reward for any subsequent misbehavior. Remember, the last behavior prior to a reward is the one that is reinforced or strengthened. If the child were to misbehave prior to getting the reward, such behavior would then erroneously be rewarded.

5. Teachers should be consistent and follow through with the procedure. If not, the child will see that the teacher often says things he or she doesn't mean. It is also important for teachers to provide the reward as soon as possible (immediacy). Any significant delay may result in frustration and trigger angry, acting-out behavior.

Behavior Penalty

A behavior penalty involves taking a privilege or another kind of reinforcer away from the child for a short time. There are some advantages to the use of a behavior penalty: it does not require a special place, and it can be administered anywhere, anytime. The following are general guidelines for the use of a behavior penalty for teachers:

1. List those behaviors that may be difficult to deal with using other techniques (maximum of three).

2. Inform the child which behavior will result in a withdrawal of privilege.

3. Make a list of privileges in the school situation that can be taken away (e.g., computer time). Do not use activities that are essential for social skill development, such as recess time.

A Note on Recess

Both parents and teachers are aware that each child needs physical activity; research also supports the association between recess and better student learning (Jarrett, 2002). Jarrett reported that recess helped children keep their bodies still and their minds on-task while in the classroom. According to the Centers for Disease Control and Prevention (CDC, 2006), it was estimated that 96.8 percent of elementary schools had recess in at least one grade; on the average, the recess time was 30.2 minutes per day (Lee, Burgeson, Fulton, & Spain, 2007). According to the Center for Education Policy (CEP, 2008), recess time has decreased to only 29 minutes per day. The need for recess isn't being met after school either. Many children, and especially those with ADHD, spend time on video games or other passive activities (e.g., watching TV, surfing the Internet, or texting). According to Patte Barth (2008) of the Center for Public Education, children need (1) recess as unstructured play time when they get to choose their own play activity and (2) a minimum of one hour of physical activity per day (in school or out of school). Also, recess should not be withheld from students as a punishment or to make up work.

USING CLASS PROCEDURES TO FORESTALL PREDICTABLE SEQUENCES

In many cases, a teacher knows that a particular sequence of behaviors will escalate to disrespect and perhaps aggressive acting-out behavior. For example, let's assume that one child needs to develop behaviors that support his ability to think and prepare for class. In short, he will be responsible for coming to class prepared and ready to work. This might mean bringing a pencil or pen to complete his work. Another child might need to work on disrespectful behavior towards authority. If the first child fails to bring a pencil, the second might offer him one. This would obviate the first child's need to come to class prepared to work. The second child might become upset if the first is not allowed to take the pencil that she offers. She might think that the teacher is being unfair for not allowing her to offer the pencil. She may therefore get upset and argumentative with the teacher, engaging the teacher in an aversive interaction.

This scenario could be avoided by

- informing the class that help is not to be offered to any student;
- reminding the student by asking questions the day before (e.g., "Now, John, what will you need to bring to class tomorrow in order to be prepared?"); and
- commenting on occasions when the second student does not offer assistance when doing so was possible.

The issue is not whether the second student does or does not offer assistance; the issue concerns the first boy's need to come prepared for class. In fact, this would be a prerequisite for all students in the class. The second student should not receive attention for her improper behavior. It would be far better for the teacher to avoid the escalation by giving no comment to the second child. If the first child does not have what is needed to do the classwork, there should be an accepted procedure for getting it. An example might be for the teacher to say, "When you don't have what you need for class, raise your hand, and I will assist you." This would then apply to all students.

PREVENTION STRATEGIES

These intervention strategies are designed to ward off or prevent problems from occurring in the immediate or near future.

Employ Success-Oriented Programs

There is nothing better to promote future success than to focus on current success. The child with ADHD may experience so much failure that little is learned from yet another failure. About the only thing that occurs with failure is that self-esteem is further diminished, along with deterioration of self-concept. Given sufficient loss, there is often associated depression and diminished motivation to achieve. It is critical that you build on small successes and changes rather than expecting large gains in the short term. Teachers must continue goal setting, allowing the child to set the pace for improvement. Often, parents and teachers become discouraged when behavioral programs fail to produce the immediate and dramatic changes that might occur with medication. While these behavioral changes are generally smaller, take comfort in the knowledge that what is being taught and maintained will result in lifelong skills that will aid the child repeatedly as he or she grows up and is faced with increasingly more challenging situations. Medication effects rapidly dissipate, but when behavioral changes are maintained like other skills, the child's newly acquired adaptive behavior will become an asset for many years.

Review Expectations Regarding Transitional Situations

As previously mentioned, it is difficult for the child with ADHD to move from one situation to the next. Situations that have different rules may present problems. Stoner and Green (1992) found that less than 10 percent of all children in the first three grades could state or identify rules pertaining to their own classroom. Going from classroom to the playground or lunchroom may require a brief review of the primary rules that are appropriate to the new situation. Keep these rules simple, few in number, and posted for all to see during review. Likewise, the child must be prepared for any unexpected changes in routine. Cuing behavior to prepare for the new situation may be helpful. Mental rehearsal or role-playing what is required in the new situation will greatly benefit the child. As Goldstein and Goldstein (1998) have noted, it is unwise to allow the child with ADHD to unwind and have free time before going to an assigned task. Instead, the child should be prepared to approach the task, with free time becoming an appropriate consequence upon *completion* of the task.

DISCIPLINING STUDENTS WITH ADHD

Many students, and especially those with ADHD and/or OCC/CD, at one time or another may break the rules of conduct. Federal laws (e.g., Section 504 of the Rehabilitation Act of 1973 and Individuals with Disabilities Education Improvement Act [IDEA] of 2004) give specific procedural safeguards regarding misconduct. Section 504 includes laws that prohibit schools from discriminating against any student with a disability such as ADHD.

Federal law permits a school to suspend a student who receives special education services through an IEP under IDEA for as many as 10 consecutive days for violating the code of conduct of the school. The school must conduct a manifestation determination (MD).

The MD is the process of examining behaviors that have resulted in a disciplinary action to determine whether they are simply a manifestation of the student's disability. The manifestation determination should be considered if there is any change in placement.

If a student commits a weapons or drug offense or if the student causes bodily harm, the school may decide on an alternate placement (for up to 45 consecutive school days). The IEP team must consider whether the act was a manifestation of the child's disability (e.g., ADHD). In cases where the act is determined to be a manifestation of the disability, the school must keep the student in the same placement (without parental consent).

If the MD reveals that the act was a manifestation of the disability or if the school changes the placement (for 10 days or more), the school must conduct a Functional Behavioral Assessment (FBA). The FBA will need to ascertain the function of the student's behavior, examining its causes and/or purpose, and create a Behavioral Intervention Plan (BIP) to address the problem. An effective BIP modifies or reduces the unacceptable behavior and increases or develops acceptable replacements. The goal is to maximize learning and to reduce behavior problems so that the student with ADHD can function optimally.

SUMMARY

This chapter begins with a discussion about how ADHD behavior may develop. It is then concerned with the removal of inappropriate behavior. Techniques of ignoring, time-out, and behavior penalty (withdrawal of a privilege) are discussed. Because of the controversy around time-out and its difficulty in being implemented properly, it is reviewed but not encouraged. It would be far better to use alternate procedures to reduce inappropriate behavior that emphasize the development of appropriate behaviors (i.e., use of positive strategies).

Specific Behavioral Interventions for ADHD

Milton was a seventh-grade student who had ADHD and an LD. He was taking Focalin XR and was in a regular class. In response to directions in math, Milton would crumple up his paper and refused to complete the work. He was frequently verbally abusive to the teacher when asked to do certain assignments in math. Typical detentions and a couple of suspensions had not been effective in changing his behavior. Melton's handwriting was also poor.

How would you address these problems?

Most teachers spend a great deal of time dealing with inappropriate, disruptive, and otherwise problematic behaviors primarily associated with ADHD. Due to various factors, such as time constraints, inconsistencies in application, or a lack of understanding of behavioral principles, their attempts to modify behavior may often fail. Some of the basic principles of behavioral techniques have been reviewed in this book, but there has been no specific application of these techniques to date. While interventions for various diagnoses have been briefly discussed, there has been no focus on some of the common problematic behaviors that cut across diagnoses. It is these behavior problems, mostly associated with ADHD, that are the focus of this section. Basically, teachers ultimately have to deal with *problem behaviors*, not diagnoses. Some of these behaviors may relate directly to ADHD, but some may stem from other comorbid disorders associated with ADHD.

These problem behaviors might include (1) aggression, (2) social skills problems involving cooperation or sharing, (3) impulsivity, (4) hyperactivity, (5) inattention, (6) off-task behavior, (7) noncompliance, and (8) inappropriate verbalizations. In addition to providing general behavioral intervention strategies, this chapter includes a case study. Behavioral interventions will involve children who present the aforementioned behavioral problems in the classroom. These children will vary in age and types of problems; each will be described, and the strategies and/or programs addressing the problematic behaviors will be reviewed.

A few of the basic tenets of this approach should be emphasized.

Behaviors are controlled by their antecedents and consequences. These components need to be changed to change the behavior. The simple antecedents-behavior-consequence (ABC) model can be expanded to a four-term model by adding "setting events." The setting event changes the dynamics of the other three components (antecedents, behavior, consequence). For example, a student may not complete an assignment for a teacher who just gave extra homework, while the same student does complete an assignment given by a second teacher who gave only a small amount of homework (the two teachers differ in terms of setting events).

All behavior—appropriate or inappropriate—is learned. Proactive behavioral intervention involves teaching more appropriate skills through positive programming; aversive consequences are *always* avoided. Thus, if a teacher is attempting to remove an inappropriate behavior, he or she may teach an appropriate behavior as an alternative while ignoring the inappropriate behavior.

The least restrictive, least intrusive, and most parsimonious and effective intervention should be used. For example, it may be easier to employ verbal praise with the student than to implement a complex token economy.

These behavioral interventions are used only when the general and specific suggestions and accommodations are insufficient to deal with the problem behavior. Behavioral interventions may vary across a number of dimensions. Some of these dimensions are as follows:

- *Restrictiveness*—The extent to which the student has limited access to basic human freedoms like privacy, movement, and leisure (Cooper, Peterson, & Meier, 1987; Scott et al., 2002; Simonsen, Britton & Young, 2009).
- *Intrusiveness*—The extent to which behavioral interventions are obtrusive and affect bodily or personal rights (Erchul & Martens, 2002). Wolery, Bailey, and Sugai (1988) listed pain, discomfort, and social stigma as factors.
- *Effectiveness*—Wolery, Bailey and Sugai (1988) noted that the procedure should produce the least harm, assuming that the procedure is effective. Again, teachers should choose the least intrusive, least restrictive, and most effective procedure.

A student's problem behavior may be the only behavior that child learned to bring about a desired consequence (e.g., getting attention). Using a positive programming approach provides more options for the student so that he or she has more choices to obtain the same consequence.

Remember that the child's *behavior* is troubling, *not* the student. This orientation is consistent with "people first." An appropriate description of a child might be "a student with ADHD who exhibits defiance and verbal aggression," *not* "an aggressive ADHD student."

Not all problematic behavior is difficult to manage. Some of the cases presented here vary in age and type of problem, while covering some of the annoying and, sometimes, more serious behavior problems of students with different disabilities. Remember that these cases reflect problem behaviors, not diagnoses.

INATTENTION

A critical element of "paying attention" involves *listening*—hearing and then processing auditory input from others (i.e., auditory attention). Listening skills are vital for academic work (gathering information, following directions, understanding assignments, etc.). Really being able to listen contributes to effective social interactions as well. Recall that often, when a child misinterprets something said by another child and acts or responds based on that misinterpretation, the stage is set for negative interactions, conflict, and aggression. Such situations most often occur within a group (peer) context—not in a one-on-one situation. Peers see only the overt response—usually aggressive behavior—and quietly record this as another bit of evidence to "avoid the child." Following such an incident, even if the child is told accurately what was said (as contrasted to what the child "heard"), the student may still appear confused and may even develop the belief that he or she is misunderstood by others.

Listening

Following are examples of situations in which a child's ability to listen impact classroom behavior.

Young Child: Auditory Attention (Listening)

Zach was a six-year-old child who had trouble with the regular kindergarten program. Basically, he would not listen to oral instructions. The child was initially given some simple things to process. First, he was told to write letters of the alphabet, numbers, or his name. He was immediately asked to repeat what the teacher had said. He was reinforced with specific verbal praise or a pat on the shoulder each time he was able to recall what he was instructed to do. He was also read some simple stories and asked to repeat (in his own words) what was said. Zach showed general improvement over time.

Each day, Zach was asked to recall 10 items from those presented. Baseline data (see Figure 7.1) revealed that he could recall very few in the beginning.

Figure 7.1 Zach: Items Recalled

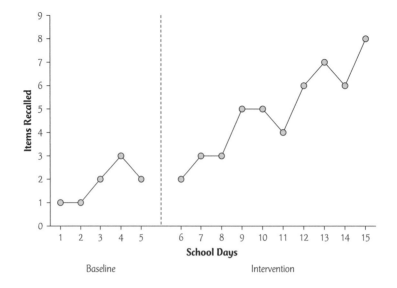

Over a two-week period, he recalled more items of the 10 presented. He was maintained by social rewards of specific praise and pats on the shoulder.

Older Child: Auditory Attention (Listening)

Branden was a eight-year-old male in second grade. Like Zach he had much difficulty with listening behavior. He was often lost while reading and failed to listen to his teacher when she gave relatively complex instructions. There were three components to instructions: (a) correctly responding to questions (e.g., "What should you be doing now?"), (b) correctly responding to complex instructions (e.g., "Put your books in your desk, take out a pencil and paper, open your book to page 17, and do the odd-numbered items"), and (c) correctly responding by rephrasing what is said in an orally read story. Each day, there were 20 items to be recalled. He was given specific praise and pats on the shoulder when he was correct. Figure 7.2 shows baseline and intervention data.

Figure 7.2 Branden: Items Recalled

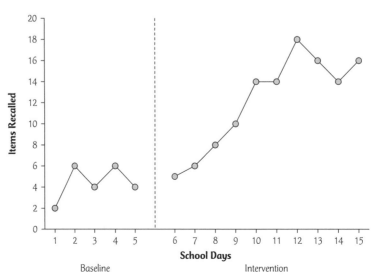

While Branden had a few poor days during the intervention, he generally improved and showed a higher percentage of items correctly recalled. He was maintained using special verbal praise and nonverbal pats on the shoulder.

After listening skills have been learned and practiced in a small-group setting, the teacher must work to generalize these skills to the classroom setting. The same process is used to verify that communications that were heard accurately. Thus, the teacher might ask, "What did I just ask you to do?" The teacher gives immediate feedback (verbal praise) to the child for accurate response statements. The teacher also provides the parent on a daily or weekly basis with a record of the number of requests and the number accurate responses. Of course, learning occurs much faster when parents at home follow the same procedures and reinforce their child for correct processing of information. The teacher might even suggest this positive approach for home use.

Remember that the child will make better progress when he or she knows what to do. The parent's or teacher's use of priming each morning, to remind the child of the potential reward, often results in faster learning of listening skills. Short-term record keeping may allow for back-up praise and reward at home and is needed only for about two weeks; this may be replaced by frequent praise from the teacher in the future. When formal reports are given to a parent, improving listening skills may be listed on the child's behavioral (point system) program, or—as the child's classroom listening performance stays at 90 percent correct or better—he or she will receive some agreed-upon reward from the teacher. It is extremely important to keep any feedback to parents very positive. Like the old saying, "If you can't say something nice, don't say anything at all."

Visual Attention

Young Child: Visual Attention

There is a limited number of applications for behavioral interventions for visual training with young children who have ADHD. Few applications have been discussed in the literature. In most cases, young children have received training on selective and/or sustained attention. The following is a simple application of behavioral techniques directly in the school situation.

Younger Children: Visual Attention

A preschool class of five students was taught by a teacher and an aide. Part of each day was spent listening to stories. None of the children in this class were able to engage in independent reading activities. However, two students, named Brittney (age 5½) and Michelle (age 5), had the most difficulty attending to stories. They engaged in distracting behavior and could not answer simple questions.

It was decided to train Brittney and Michelle in visual attention skills and then monitor their performance in the storytelling group. It was believed that becoming more visually attentive would assist them in hearing more of the stories and answering more of the questions. The teacher asked each girl five simple questions about each story. The procedure consisted of a baseline (where data was collected but no training initiated) and the intervention (where visual training was initiated with the students). These two students were called the Inattentive Group (IG); the remaining three students were labeled the Attentive Group (AG).

Visual training consisted of observational data—watching each student to see how long she would attend to a taped program. Similar procedures were used by Landau, Lorch, and Milich (1992) and Acevedo-Polakovich, Lorch, Milich, and Ashby (2006). Data were recorded as percent time spent watching the training video (*Sesame Street*) and the number of times each child looked away from the TV screen. Two observers recorded these two types of data. This intervention was thus relatively simple and straightforward.

The first step was to assess the class in terms of their performance on reading segments each day for one week to develop a baseline. A different story was read each day. Figure 7.3 shows the baseline data for the inattentive and the attentive students. The data are based on the number of questions answered for a week. If each student was asked one question per day, then the percentages will reflect differences in the students' ability to attend effectively to the stories. Baseline data were also collected regarding percent of time off-task and number of occasions of off-task behavior for each student (see Figure 7.4).

After one week of collecting baseline data, the intervention effects were recorded with regard to the percent of correct answers to questions. This intervention was conducted over a three-week period.

During the intervention, visual attention skills improved for the two inattentive girls, as shown in Figure 7.5.

Figure 7.3   Preschool Class: Baseline Story Responses

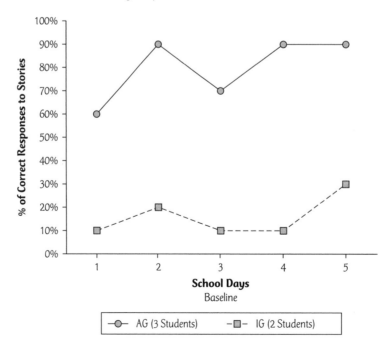

Figure 7.4 Preschool Class: Baseline Time Off-Task

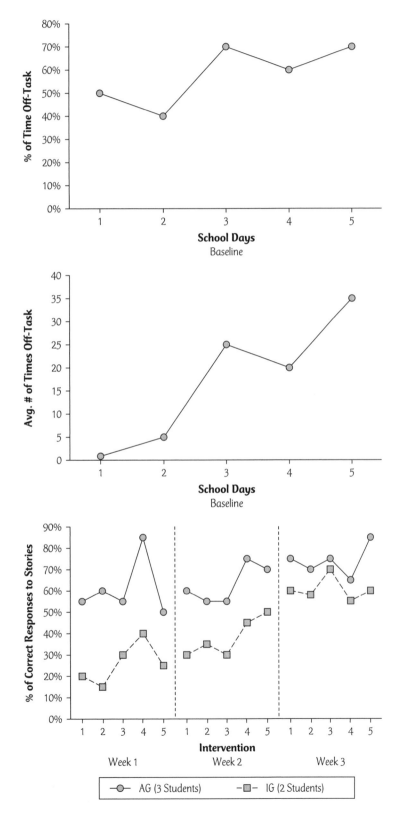

Figure 7.5 Preschool Class: Post-Intervention Story Responses

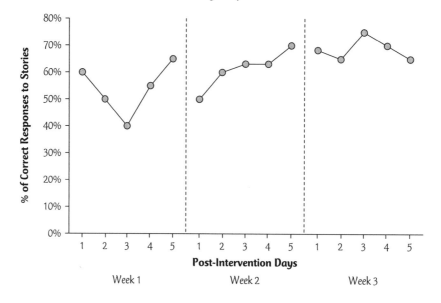

Similar findings were noted for the number of times that each student was off-task (i.e., not attending), as shown in Figure 7.6. The students above were also noted to remain on-task for three additional weeks.

Figure 7.6 Preschool Class: Post-Intervention Time Off-Task

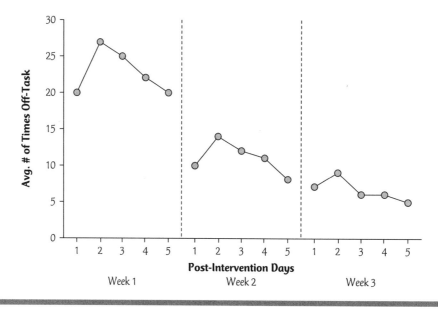

The following conclusions may be drawn:

- All children learned to answer questions better and seemed to improve their listening skills.
- The effect of improvement of visual attention on *listening* skills was noted as the intervention progressed.

- The inattentive group (IG) became more like the attentive group (AG) as the intervention progressed.
- In general, attentional skills were maintained for all students by noting when they appeared to be attending *and* by reinforcing, with praise, their correct responses to questions. Incorrect responses were simply not given attention; correct responses were praised.

Older Child: Visual Attention

Visual attention is important. It is very useful in maintaining on-task behavior, especially during written work. Following is an example of a student who was distractible and attended to things other than her work. She was often off-task, and this, of course, prevented her from completing many tasks.

Older Child: Visual Attention

Tiffany was a sixth-grade student who often failed to pay attention and often stared out the window. A simple intervention was planned, using a momentary time-sampling procedure of 15-second intervals. She was deemed to be on-task when she was oriented to the teacher and responding verbally, when she showed that she was following the teacher's instructions with evidence of attention to task, or when she raised her hand to ask for information. Data intervals of being on-task were then divided by the total number of intervals. She was observed two days per week for six weeks during math period using a multiple-baseline design.

During baseline of one week, teachers did not greet students at the door but followed their normal routine. During intervention, the teacher simply greeted Tiffany by name and gave some positive statement (e.g., "I really like your hairstyle," or "You really look good"). The teacher was allowed to vary the statement without specific instructions from day to day. Figure 7.7 illustrates the results.

Figure 7.7 Tiffany: Time On-Task

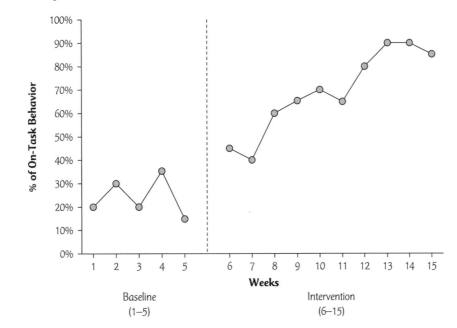

As a result of this simple teacher greeting at the door in the morning, attention to the teacher and on-task behavior improved significantly. Remaining on-task was maintained over time by giving periodic positive verbal praise for beginning a task, remaining on-task, and completing her work. Tiffany was also provided reinforcement when she was clearly paying attention to the teacher and was able to repeat directions or explain a procedure in math.

ON-TASK BEHAVIOR

Perhaps one of the most difficult behaviors to deal with is off-task behavior. It is important that children remain on-task so that assignments may be completed. A student may have trouble staying on-task for many reasons. Some factors may be physiological (e.g., ADHD), others may be simply learned, and some behaviors may be associated with another disorder. In any case, the behavior of remaining on-task may be shaped and developed. Following is an example of off-task behavior associated with ADHD. While some specific approaches may be used, the underlying behavior problem may respond to behavioral intervention.

On-Task Behavior

A general education kindergarten class had nine students. One was David, a seven-year-old boy with ADHD. He received pull-out services once a week along with special education services in class. He required a one-on-one aide to learn new skills. Ritalin was administered at home both morning and evening. David made bomb noises and would sometimes either put his head down, hit or push staff, and leave tasks before completing them. He also engaged in inappropriate talk, like yelling noises and making comments on television programs.

The behavioral interventions consisted of a token program with positive behavioral supports. The general instrumental format was *work* followed by *play*. During baseline, David completed work, then chose a play activity. Data were collected on (a) number of noises, (b) physical contact with staff, and (c) inappropriate talk. His rewards consisted of playtime, appropriate edibles (e.g., popcorn), and an adventure magazine. The plan was in effect for two weeks.

The results showed a decrease in his disruptive and inappropriate behaviors along with a significant increase in his productivity (see Figure 7.8).

As David's inappropriate behavior decreased, his work output increased. He was able to stay on-task longer to complete the work assigned. To complete more work, he was required to stay on-task for longer periods. Positive support was primarily used to increase his appropriate behavior; specific praise was delivered for completing his work partially or completely. He was given greater specific praise for completing all of his work. Of course, he was required to complete his work before engaging in play—a simple instrumental procedure. David could also earn tokens for suppressing his inappropriate behavior; in essence, tokens were given for appropriate behavior. He could trade in his tokens at the end of each day, or he could accumulate them and trade them in after a week. Reinforcers were primarily things he enjoyed, such as time on the computer, popcorn, or a McDonald's certificate.

Figure 7.8 David: Inappropriate Behavior and Work Completed

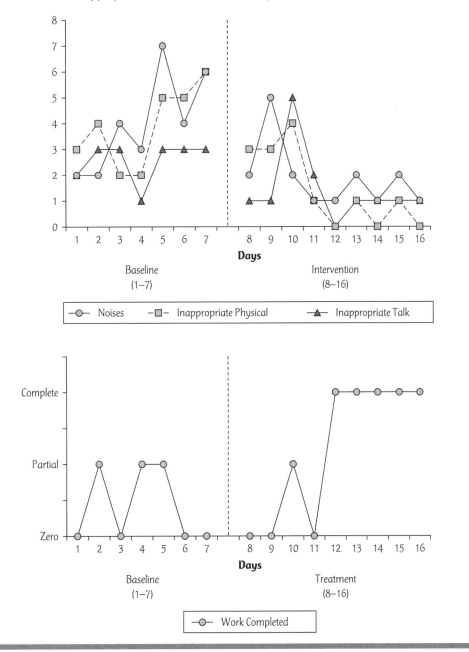

IMPULSIVITY

Impulsivity has several equivalent terms. It is often used interchangeably with *lack of self-control* or *behavioral disinhibition*. They all have about the same meaning, generally implying that "the child acts without thinking." Many possible situational contexts involve behavior that varies in severity and in the nature of consequences. For example, the impulsive child might blurt out answers or talk without permission. Such behavior may only be considered annoying, disturbing the class to a mild or moderate degree. On the other hand, when impulsivity is combined with other problems, such as aggression or depression, the results may have dire consequences. Acting out aggression with impulsivity may create many disruptive situations in and outside of the classroom (DuPaul & Stoner, 2003). Likewise, when impulsivity is combined with severe depression, consequences may also be disastrous, resulting in self-harm or even suicide.

Impulsivity can be of different types (Flick, 2000). Based on Robin (1998), it is reasonable to divide impulsivity into the following categories:

- *Behavioral impulsivity*: Poor judgment and acting rashly
- *Cognitive impulsivity*: Sloppily rushing through academic tasks making careless mistakes
- *Emotional impulsivity*: Exhibiting temper control problems and emotional overreactions

At present, however, no good data exist on the pattern of these types of impulsivity across various disorders, the nature of their respective developmental factors, whether such a breakdown would predict different outcomes for various disorders, or, most importantly, whether each type would be sensitive to different treatment effects. Nevertheless, such a breakdown appears heuristically useful. This scale would be especially useful for older children and young adolescents, and it could also be used in research with children who have ADHD.

Some relationship appears to exist among measures of impulsivity across situations, yet this has not been determined with research support. It will still behoove the classroom teacher to deal with the most frequent expressions of impulsivity, such as blurting out. The following general steps may be used to control blurting out (Flick, 1998):

1. Review and post rules regarding raising one's hand and being called on to obtain permissions (e.g., to answer a question, get assistance, go to the bathroom). In addition to posting written rules and verbalizing them, the teacher may tape a card on the child's desk depicting the rule. (See Flick, 1998, for examples of picture cards with hand raised to demonstrate the rule. These cards are also found in Appendix M.)

2. Ignore those who blurt out answers and fail to raise their hands.

3. Praise those children who do raise their hands and use them as models. Remember, *never* compare one child with another; simply give the praise to the child who does the right thing. Make the praise specific, as in "Charles, you followed the rule and raised your hand to answer—very good. Now what is . . . ?"

4. When a child who has blurted out before does raise a hand, direct attention to that child immediately.

5. Monitor the number of times each day that the child raises a hand to answer. Reward weekly improvement over each child's baseline levels and then over the previous week's performance. A simple count of the number of times the child raises a hand to answer may be kept from week to week. The count of inappropriate behavior during the first week, before the problem is addressed, is the baseline. The intervention may start in the second week. For example, the teacher may tape the card on the child's desk with a picture of a student raising a hand. In addition to counting the number of appropriate behaviors, the teacher should give verbal praise along with a backup reward when a specific goal is reached. Individual cards with varying rules are available in Appendix M.

As with most behavioral programs, a combination of (a) ignoring blurting out (extinction) and (b) positive reinforcement for the appropriate response (i.e., raising hand to answer) will result in a more powerful behavior change program. If this response is poorly developed in the child's behavioral repertoire, then the teacher may model the correct response for answering questions. This may be very important, especially for younger children who may have had more limited experience with this procedure. Remember that nonverbal modeling (a demonstration) can have a more powerful influence on a student's behavior than verbal explanations.

HYPERACTIVITY

Perhaps the most salient characteristic of ADHD is hyperactivity. Problematic hyperactivity may not be recognized as a real symptom until a child enters a situation where some self-control of movement is required. This may not occur until the child begins preschool or kindergarten. All young children are more active during the early years, but children with ADHD are most often noted to be restless and driven; they have much difficulty settling down for quiet activities, such as reading or nap time. Such hyperactive children seem easily bored and need more stimulation or movement activity. Enhanced self-stimulation, such as humming, drumming a pencil, or talking, may occur in place of overt motor activity. Older children and adolescents appear to show decreased overt motor activity but may still be restless or may still talk a lot; of course, the option for these students is to succumb to boredom and go to sleep in class.

When talking excessively in situations where talking is "against the rule," the student may be exhibiting a combination of (a) a lack of self-control and (b) a need to engage in excess vocal-motor activity. The suggestions that apply to excessive talking (a form of vocal-motor hyperactivity) include the following:

- Reviewing the rules about which situations and which times are appropriate for talking.
- Ignoring, when talking is minimal.
- Giving *praise and attention* to those who remain quiet at the appropriate time.
- Pointing out occasions when a student remains quiet in those situations where he or she would have talked and praising this behavior change immediately.
- Asking the student or the class, "What should you be doing now?" and reinforcing a correct answer, whether from the identified child or another student.
- Implementing a random variable schedule of recording/monitoring whether or not the child is talking during the recording interval. Any regular recording schedule allows the child to know when he or she is being recorded and, thus, may inhibit talking. Should every incident of talking be noted, however, the student may actually receive attention each time, thus reinforcing the talking.

Like other behavior problems, excess talking may reflect an academic problem. If the student has difficulty with some academic material, he or she may talk to escape from or avoid doing the task. If such a child were sent out of the room, this would be exactly what the student desired. Again, this is called negative reinforcement. While excess talking may originate in an underlying physiological need (e.g., vocal-motor stimulation or a focus of neurologically based hyperactivity), repeated experience of being sent out of the room may add a learned component. Therefore, it is important for the teacher to explore the function of the behavioral problem.

Hyperactivity

Johnny was a nine-year-old in a third-grade classroom. His pediatrician had diagnosed him with ADHD. He was given a special education classification of Other Health Impaired. His BIP indicated special tutoring in reading and math and a daily behavioral report. Johnny was not taking any medication. This child showed poor academic work, out-of-seat behavior, interrupting, and talking back to his teachers. He rarely completed his work. Classmates generally rejected him, so there was social impairment as well as academic impairment. Johnny's talking was so excessive, it interfered with his and others' academic work.

The teachers decided to concentrate on his excessive talking in their behavioral intervention. Johnny's talking behavior (or lack of it) was recorded during 15-second intervals twice during both the morning and afternoon periods. He was coded as being on-task when he worked quietly by himself. All observations were recorded by an aide working in two classrooms. There was one week for baseline recording and two weeks for recording the effects of the behavioral intervention. The consequence for working quietly was extra time on a computer game; each day, he was able to play a second game if he had earned 25 points or more. A class party was contingent on his acquiring 100 points during the first week and 200 points during the second week during intervention. The criterion for success was gradually increased as he improved. Figure 7.9 shows his results.

Figure 7.9 Johnny: Time Working Quietly

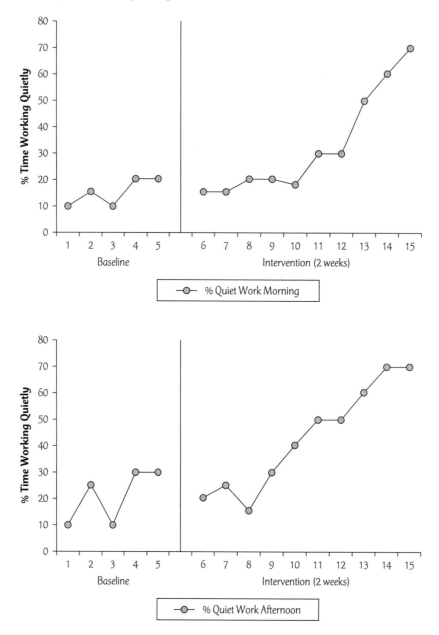

Clearly, little work was done during baseline, either morning or afternoon. At most, Johnny completed only 30 percent of his work. He was able to play the computer game twice during the first week post-intervention and four times during the second week. He continued the program for three additional weeks. Johnny was also given much verbal praise when successful, and all of his appropriate behaviors received attention during and after the intervention.

REINFORCEMENT

Size of Reinforcer

A progressive-delay reinforcement schedule may be used to increase self-control and decrease disruptive behavior in children with ADHD. When initially given a choice between an immediate smaller reinforcer and a larger delayed reinforcer, most children choose the smaller but immediate reinforcer. However, when access to the larger reinforcer requires either no activity or involvement in a concurrent task during the delay, most children demonstrate self-control; disruptive behavior decreases during delays that require a concurrent task compared to sessions without an activity requirement (e.g., Dixon, Horner, & Guercio, 2003).

Immediacy and Quality of Reinforcer

In a study by Neef, Bicard, Endo, Coury, and Aman (2005), children with ADHD were most influenced by the immediacy and the quality of a reinforcer, and least by its rate and the effort required to get it, suggesting impulsivity. Children of typical development were most influenced only by the quality of the reinforcer; the influence of immediacy relative to other factors was not statistically significant. Other studies support this finding (Cooper et al., 1999; Hoch, McComas, Johnson, Faranda, & Guenther, 2002).

Reinforcement

Ms. Locke was generally considered to be a good teacher. Her second-grade classroom was well organized, and she had posted just a few class rules that were important. Most children knew the rules from daily review. However, two students, both eight years old, routinely had trouble with "raising their hand to answer." Instead, Bryan and Lemar would blurt out answers, typically in math class. They knew the rules, but both were diagnosed with ADHD and both were on medication. In addition to blurting out, both boys showed much evidence of hyperactive behavior: tapping their pencils, humming, walking around the room, talking to other kids, and sometimes tapping others on the shoulder or head. Other kids were clearly annoyed, and some reacted aggressively to these annoyances.

When blurting out answers, Bryan and Lemar would act very competitively, trying to be the first one to get the answers correct. Both boys were getting Cs in math, and both scored within the average range with regard to math facts. They basically knew the material, but they just responded impulsively—they had trouble with that one rule.

Ms. Locke decided to use a behavioral intervention with both boys. She first proceeded to get baseline data. A 30-minute period each day was devoted to "math facts." Impulsive behaviors would be counted during this time. Both boys received a review of the rule prior to each 30-minute session. The results of the baseline data appear in Figure 7.10. Data was obtained for one week; Bryan averaged

5.4 for raising his hand, while Lemar averaged 7.4. The number of math facts reviewed was kept constant, with Ms. Locke asking 50 math fact questions each day.

Figure 7.10   Bryan and Lemar: Raising Hand to Respond—Baseline

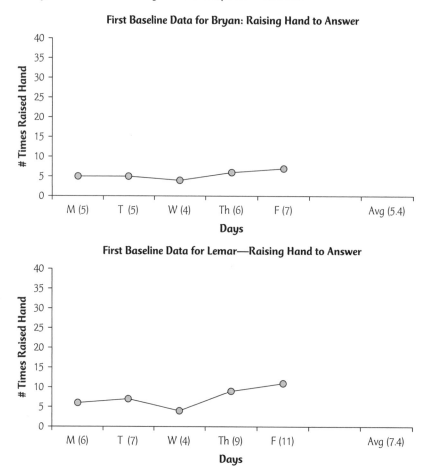

The intervention would consist of two parts: (1) a cue or visual reminder of the rule and (2) reinforcement of correct responses. A response was considered correct when the student raised his hand to answer without blurting out. This rule was always reviewed prior to the 30-minute session. The cue or visual reminder was a cartoonlike picture of a boy raising his hand. This picture was attached to a stick so that it could be held up easily before each question. Both boys sat in the front row but apart from each other.

A differential reinforcement of lower rates of responding (DR-LR) was used. The targets were 10 percent below baseline data. In the beginning, this was considered to be 10 percent below the average determined at baseline. Each student knew his own target behavior each day. When a student reached the target behavior, he was given a mark on a card that was taped to his desk. He was also given verbal praise at that point; Ms. Locke might say, "Very good, Bryan, you reached your target raising your hand, so you get a mark." This was said while the mark was given. Figure 7.11 shows the accumulation of points for each boy. Bryan averaged 10.6 (exceeding the criterion target), while Lemar averaged 29.7 during the intervention phase.

Figure 7.11   Bryan and Lemar: Raising Hand to Respond—Post-Intervention

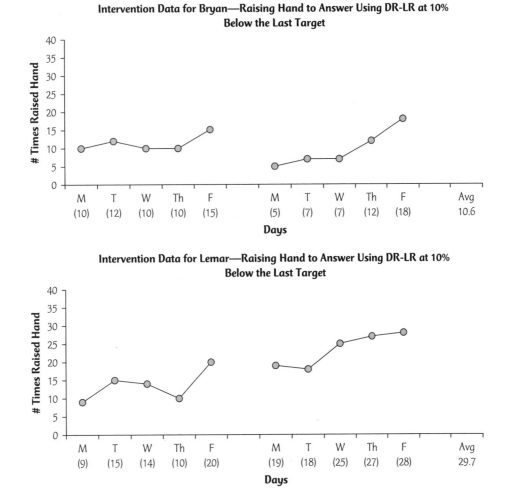

Both boys had preselected some backup reinforcers to get when they accumulated a sufficient number of points. These reinforcers were either tangible rewards (e.g., a small toy car) or extra computer time. When both boys accumulated a sufficient number of marks, the class would have a popcorn party. The experimental period lasted for two weeks.

In addition to making progress, each boy showed some improvements in other areas as well. For example, the amount of time on-task, completion of work, and in-seat behavior all improved, although these were not officially monitored. After completing the intervention, each boy seemed to maintain his appropriate behaviors with continued verbal praise, with only minor increases in blurting out. Ms. Locke was satisfied with the results and intended to continue the use of verbal praise for correct behavior and periodically use the visual reminder. Both Bryan and Lemar were visibly satisfied with their newly developed behavior, and it seemed to generalize to other subject sessions (e.g., reading).

At the end of the intervention, Ms. Locke wished to record a second baseline to see how much had changed. Refer to Figure 7.12 for these data. While Bryan improved some (post-intervention average = 6.7), Lemar improved more (average = 8.0) compared to the first baseline.

Figure 7.12 Bryan and Lemar: Raising Hand to Respond—Second Baseline

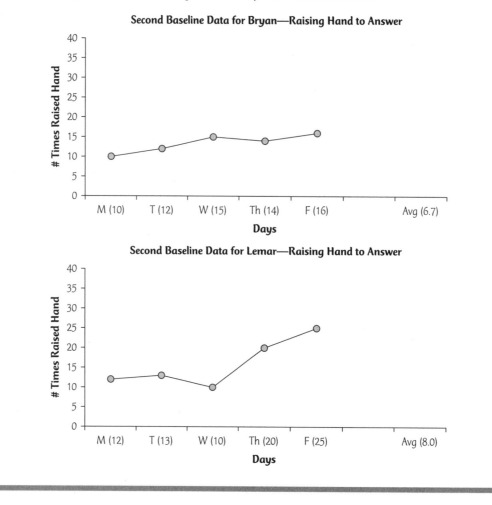

Second Baseline Data for Bryan—Raising Hand to Answer

 # Times Raised Hand

M (10)   T (12)   W (15)   Th (14)   F (16)   Avg (6.7)

Days

Second Baseline Data for Lemar—Raising Hand to Answer

 # Times Raised Hand

M (12)   T (13)   W (10)   Th (20)   F (25)   Avg (8.0)

Days

FOLLOWING INSTRUCTIONS

Only after a child has well-established listening skills can he or she be expected to follow instructions well (DuPaul, 1991; Enger et al., 1998). Training in these two skill areas (listening and following directions) can even be done together. Complying with requests or following directions is something a child is expected "to do" as opposed to "not to do." As prosocial skills become stronger and more frequently used, inappropriate behavior is correspondingly reduced. When the child is doing what he or she is supposed to—following directions or rules—the child cannot be doing what he or she is not supposed to do.

Following Instructions

The study participants were five kindergarten girls (ages 4.8 to 6 years). In the daily routine, 10 simple instructions were given: (1) pick up the toys, (2) sit down, (3) come and get a pencil and paper, (4) write your name on the paper, (5) fold your paper, (6) bring the pencil and paper to the teacher's desk, (7) put the student's chair on the table, (8) get the student's mat out, (9) lie down, and (10) be quiet. This multiple-baseline design used the typical routine during the day; teacher attention in the form of specific praise was the single consequence. Data were recorded on a sheet indicating who correctly followed instructions. Figure 7.13 shows the daily mean percent of instructions followed each day; correct responses were checked if the child did what was requested within 15 seconds.

Figure 7.13 Kindergarten Girls: Instructions Followed

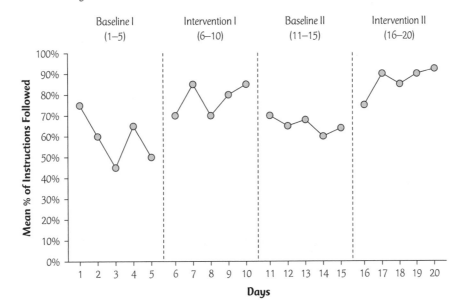

A number of obervations are apparent. First, there is much variability in the first baseline. Second, there is general improvement from baseline to the second intervention. Third, when attention and specific praise are not forthcoming for each task, the percent of correct appropriate behavior (i.e., following instructions) is lower. Each child did improve with appropriate attention but regressed without it. Thus, attention in the form of specific praise (e.g., "I like the way you picked up your toys as soon as I said to do it") was essential. Of course, timing each student would help, but timing was done in baseline II (where correct responding dropped). The most important factor was the specific verbal praise given by the teacher for those who did the requested behavior. (Adapted from Friedberg & McClure, 2002; Power, Karustis, & Habboushe, 2001; Schutte & Hopkins, 1970; Watson & Gresham, 1998)

The teacher may use many other tasks for this type of exercise. Remember, any request given may bring about a reward for listening (i.e., knowing what to do) and for carrying out the request (i.e., doing it). Completing the task may thus result in additional praise and touch. Both skills (listening and following directions) may also be included in a behavioral point system.

Behaviors rated on a home-school note will facilitate learning of the skill and enhance generalization of the skill. As the child is reinforced for compliance in more and more situations, compliance becomes stronger and more "generalized," including to situations such as in class, on the playground, in the lunchroom, and on the school bus. Successfully generalizing this compliance behavior does, however, take cooperation among teacher, bus driver, and others, along with the use of consistent consequences to strengthen the skill. Inappropriate behaviors (e.g., breaking rules) may be reinforced when the child is able to manipulate attention from the bus driver or the person monitoring the lunchroom. Misbehavior must incur predictable consequences, just as recording and relating of appropriate behavior must be consistent. Keep in mind that it is far more important to teach the child a prosocial skill that emphasizes what he or she needs "to do" rather than "not to do." Reminding the child of what the rules are in different situations and stating the consequences for adhering to or violating them (priming) will further improve the child's ability to be successful.

NONCOMPLIANCE

Compliance is a key goal of healthy early childhood development and is linked to children's social and emotional competence (Hamre & Pianta, 2001). Compliance that is invariant is neither expected nor desired. Using direct observation, studies across 12 cultures showed that compliance to parental requests ranged from 72 percent for children two to three years old, to 79 percent for children four to five years old, and up to 82 percent for children six to eight years old (Weiss, Caspe, & Lopez, 2006). Some noncompliance is, therefore, normal and may even promote the development of autonomy and prosocial independence (Boyd & Richardson, 1985). However, *excessive* noncompliance appears as the most frequent reason for psychiatric referral of young children (Forehand & McMahon, 1981; Kalb & Loeber, 2003; McCartney & Phillips, 2006; Walker, Ramsey, & Gresham, 2004). Longitudinal investigations showed a progression from noncompliance to tantrums to physical attacks on up to stealing and conduct problems (Chamberlain & Patterson, 1995; Eddy, Reid, & Curry, 2002; Loeber & Farrington, 2001; Martinez & Forgatch, 2001). Such data suggest that excessive noncompliance can be a precursor to more serious behavior problems (Kalb & Loeber, 2003).

Teachers complain more about what some children fail to do than about what they do. Although some of these children are bright, they come to class unprepared and often resist doing homework. They might be heard to say, "I thought that assignment was due next Monday." Many of these children promise to "do better" but continue not to comply. Anger often underlies such oppositional behavior; noncompliance over assignments, chores (at home), and direct requests suggests a passive form of anger. These problems are in contrast to children who do "forget" or become confused over instructions, fail to write them down, or just misinterpret them, as in some cases of children with ADHD. Some of the earliest behaviorists to work with children and families, Patterson and Guillon (1968), noted that noncompliance was an underlying problem that must be addressed in working with difficult to manage children.

Research with aggressive children and children seen in clinics has emphasized the dysfunctional nature of noncompliance (Patterson, 1982). Early on, Patterson conceptualized noncompliance as a coercive response that is maintained by parental mismanagement of a child's behavior. He proposed that the early appearance of noncompliance puts children at risk for a series of events, including coercive family interactions, poor peer relations, impaired academic performance, possible delinquency, and more problems in later life (Patterson, DeBaryshe, & Ramsey, 1989; see also Campbell, 2006; Shaw et al., 1998; Slough & McMahon, 2007; Smith & Lerman, 1999; Webster-Stratton, 1998). Patterson's view then was that addressing noncompliance would facilitate working with other aspects of behavior disorders.

Noncompliance to Requests: Elementary School

Tommy was a seven-year-old who frequently ignored requests and directions. His passive-aggressive, oppositional behavior made it difficult to maintain continuity in teaching. An analysis and review of academic records and functions of behavior indicated that (a) Tommy did not lack the ability to perform the tasks requested and (b) his resistance did not appear to be an attempt to escape or avoid tasks. He did not seem to respond to requests that prompted cognitive mediation (e.g., "What are you supposed to be doing now?" or "What did I just ask you to do?") Generally, Tommy was capable of answering these questions, but he appeared to enjoy the control aspects of these situations, as well as some of the attention received as a result of noncompliance.

The compliance of children like Tommy, who exhibit challenging oppositional behavior, may be increased by making easily achievable, high-probability requests initially. Before making a request that the child has been known to deny and/or act out because of, make three to five high-probability requests and give positive reinforcement (e.g., praise) after each. For example, Tommy was asked to take something to the office for his teacher. Upon his return, he was told, "I'm glad I can count on you to take care of important matters." Such praise initiates the momentum of positive behavior. Five seconds after giving the positive reinforcement for the last high-probability request, make a low-probability request. If it is unsuccessful, give another higher-probability request rather than a reprimand.

Figure 7.14 Graph of Response to Requests

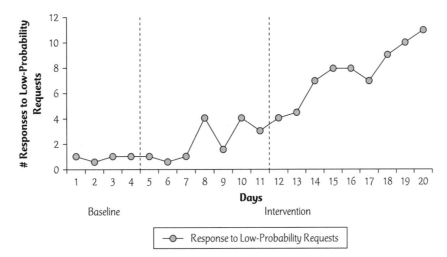

Figure 7.14 shows Tommy's responses to low-probability requests. During days 1–4, Tommy's responses to low-probability requests were consistently low. On days 5–11, he showed a steady increase in positive responses to low-probability requests when these came after a high-probability request. Tommy's response to low-probability requests steadily increased on days 12–20 to a point of over 85 percent compliance.

Most parents and teachers have found that ignoring, pleading, and attempts at negotiations do not work; get-tough approaches and physical discipline may only make the problems worse. While behavioral interventions are essential to changing noncompliance, they are not the only tools available to teachers. Following are some other approaches:

- *Encourage assertiveness:* For example, when a difficult assignment is to be completed within a limited amount of time, some students will comment on the difficulty and ask for extended time. A teacher may praise such students for being assertive, making them models for other students.
- *Offer choices:* When children can choose from two or three options, they are more likely to complete the chosen assignment. This procedure not only empowers the child in making decisions, it may also allow the child to choose a topic that holds more interest for him or her.
- *Structure homework:* While homework assignments are complex and may require a comprehensive approach to dealing with problematic behavior (Flick, 2001), it will be important to structure this process. Begin with the assignments: parents will need to know what assignments are given, and teachers need to know that the covered assignments got home along with materials needed to complete them. Parents will need to structure a time and place for homework as well. Finally, assignments completed will need to be checked by the teacher. This structure must be developed and reinforced at every step until homework becomes automatic (Flick, 2001).
- *Adjust expectations:* If a teacher expects too much of the child, the child may resist work completion. Many children will avoid some tasks, saying that the work is too much or too difficult. Giving more reasonable work assignments and reinforcing their completion can be helpful.
- *Reinforce compliance:* Reinforcement may be given at three points: (a) when the child *begins* the task, (b) while the child is *working* on a task, and (c) when the child *completes* the task. It is most effective when all three events are reinforced. A child may signal avoidance of a task when he gets up to sharpen a pencil each day that a specific task is scheduled. He may even talk, disturb others, and eventually be sent out to the office—reinforcing exactly what he desires, task avoidance.

  The teacher may adjust the task difficulty and announce that all students who are "caught" working on the assigned task when a bell rings will earn a bubble gum break. Most likely, the child will be in his seat working to earn the reward. The teacher may also keep a record of the number of times a child complies on assignments. After the teacher has recorded a week of baseline information, he or she may tell the child that he will first earn a ticket for each instance of compliance. After one week, this may be reduced to getting a ticket for every other instance of compliance, and then every third time. In other words, the child will be asked to complete the assignments but get fewer tickets. Basically, as the child gets better at completing tasks, fewer reinforcements are needed. Of course, tickets (rewarding in themselves) may sometimes be traded for some other desirable reward (e.g., no homework or computer time).
- *Reinforce improvement:* This is a variation on the above. It will be important for any teacher to give positive feedback when the child complies in a situation where

there was previous noncompliance. Any improvement in compliance, whether a change in frequency of compliance or a substitution of compliance for prior noncompliance, should be reinforced. Nordquist and McEvoy (1983) used a combination of differential attention (to compliance) and time-out (for noncompliance) in two four-year-olds who were highly oppositional to instructions from adults (parents, teachers, and other service personnel). More recently, this approach was supported by McNeill, Watson, Henington, and Meeks (2002) and Steele, Elkin, and Roberts (2007).

- *Repeated request:* A request may be repeated over and over until that request is recognized and completed by the student. This is a variant of the "broken record" procedure used to deny a request by the student. In this case, a positive request is made by the teacher until compliance is achieved.

- *High-probability requests*: Some requests may carry a high probability of compliance, even in a child who is predominately noncompliant with most requests. For example, it would be most unlikely for a child to refuse to go get a box of candy so that a teacher can give her one. Similarly, it may be easy for a teacher to get compliance on a simple task (e.g., "Go get that roll of tickets so I can give one to you to place in the jar. We'll draw one later to pick a winner of Pokémon cards [or whatever is popular at the time]").

Many oppositional behaviors are learned and developed very early within teacher-child interactions. Such behaviors must also be addressed through teacher training, as well as in-school programs, to be maximally effective.

The following case studies involve more complex problems.

Group Program

Three boys in Ms. X's class, all eight years old, created most of the disturbances because of their problem behaviors. Their names were Dylan, Chris, and Roger. Dylan had the most difficulty with anger, engaging in frequent name-calling, making disruptive noises, and occasionally displaying a full temper tantrum. Chris had difficulty raising his hand to answer and would often blurt out answers; he would also talk loudly and laugh out loud with little control. Roger also had trouble with self-control and would often yell out answers, make inappropriate noises, and hit others.

Some of these disruptive behaviors were related to the inability of all three boys to perform an assigned task or their difficulty in doing so. Most of the tasks that precipitated disruptive behaviors were written. In fact, some of the boys were now accustomed to getting out of the tasks by being sent to the office for inappropriate aggressive behavior. The length of the task was evidently a factor as well, as most acting-out behaviors occurred when lengthy written assignments were given. Adjusting assignment expectations reduced acting-out behaviors just slightly. It was as if they had developed a life of their own.

- Some behavioral interventions were initiated on an individual and a group basis. Any temper tantrum was ignored. The teacher would completely ignore it (turn away), and the class would be instructed to ignore it (i.e., not to look at or say anything about the temper outburst). When the child exhibited self-control (i.e., stopped the tantrum) or if the child coped with a situation differently (i.e., did not show a tantrum in a situation where tantrums were previously shown), then verbal praise and recognition were given.

- Individual point systems were established for Dylan, Chris, and Roger.
  - Dylan would receive points for talking to others appropriately, remaining quiet during work activity, and coping with frustration without temper outbursts. He lost points for name-calling, making noises, and having temper outbursts. With net points, he would be eligible for a small toy from the reward menu.
  - Chris would receive points for raising his hand to answer, talking in an appropriate voice, and controlling his laughter. He would lose points for the opposite inappropriate behaviors. Like Dylan, he could get a small toy with a specified number of net points.
  - Roger also got points for raising his hand, remaining quiet, and controlling aggression; he would likewise lose points for his inappropriate behaviors. Net points would allow for the selection of a small toy.

It is important to remember that the one major criterion in setting up such programs is that they be successful. At first, there must be liberal distribution of points and conservative fines (loss of points). A simple signal system is used to convey (+) or (–) points; for example, Dylan (+1) or Dylan (–1) cards. This system may be used to convey information on the child's behavior that is (a) immediate, (b) least intrusive on others, and (c) least embarrassing. The teacher keeps the record at his or her desk. The system begins with daily point exchanges; later, points are exchanged every two days, then only once per week. However, praise is also delivered along with each positive reinforcement and when the points are exchanged. During the day, verbal praise may also be given to let a child know how he or she is doing—providing such praise also serves as a model for others regarding what appropriate behaviors pay off. In general, a positive approach to managing behavior is emphasized.

Based on the total net points earned by all three boys, group (class) reinforcement was also made available. Thus, the three boys were able to earn special privileges for their class by their behavior. This group program improved compliance overall by (a) motivating other kids not to respond to a child's inappropriate behavior, (b) having other classmates encourage and help the identified boys to engage in more appropriate behaviors, (c) improving the acceptance and peer-status of the boys with a history of acting-out behaviors, and (d) generally enhancing the personal self-concept of the identified boys.

Figure 7.15 shows some of the data plates for three behaviors. Note the dramatic reduction of each following the interventions. It is possible to plot the progress of each behavior over time to see its rate of improvemen. Doing so can be quite rewarding for the child and gives the teacher an opportunity to praise the child while giving feedback (e.g., "I've really been impressed by the way you have developed better control over name-calling. Look at how that behavior has decreased. I'm really proud of you!").

It is also possible to plot the improvement of total net points for the three boys over a period of time, as in Figure 7.16.

Figure 7.15 Individual Behavior Data

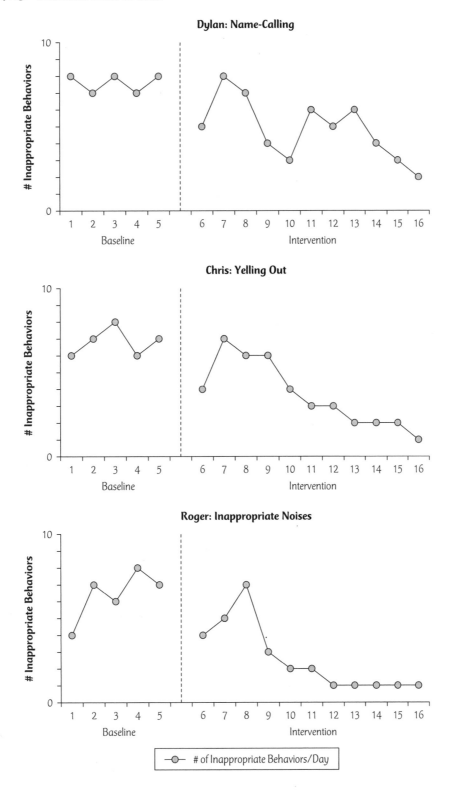

Figure 7.16   *Aggregate Behavior Data*

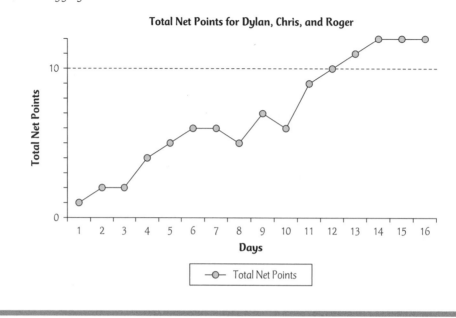

SOCIAL SKILLS PROBLEMS

Fitting into today's society is a challenge for many children and especially for those with behavioral and emotional disabilities. Many children may show aggressive behavior when they do not know how to deal with a situation (Fox & Boulton, 2005). This section will focus on two important social skills that are especially important for all children—sharing and cooperation.

Sharing

At some point in life, everyone has had the experience of having to share with others. Since young children often feel competitive about sharing a toy or materials, begin training on this social skill with an exercise aimed at teaching the concept of sharing to one or more playmates in class. Materials may be crayons, construction paper, or whatever the children are using at the time. One option is to place the toy in time-out. However, this approach may only stop conflict. To enact a prosocial approach, first explain to both children that you have noticed difficulty in playing with this item. Tell them that you expect them to share. Then model sharing. After modeling sharing, have the children practice sharing for a preset time; set a kitchen timer. Praise each child in turn for sharing. Deal with hassles by warning the child that fighting will result in the other child's having the item for an additional minute. Any further hassles result in the toy or materials going into time-out.

As with most programs, the really important factor is not the time-out but rather the opportunity to develop more appropriate prosocial skills. Return to this training quickly and often for the most efficient learning to occur. Of course, when the children learn the appropriate social behavior, the formal procedure (i.e., modeling and playing for one minute) may be faded. The teacher will then focus on normal play interactions; when appropriate, comments may be made to both children: "I really like the way you are sharing that toy." See Chapter 5, particularly Exercise 5.9, for more discussion of teaching sharing; A blank Recording Sheet for Social Skills is in Appendix N.

Cooperation

This area has been of prime concern to parents of children with various disabilities (Dunn & Bruner, 2004; Phillips, Schuen, & Saklofske, 1997; Prout & Brown, 2007; Shonkoff & Phillips, 2000). As with other appropriate behaviors, it is not possible for the child to play cooperatively and fight at the exact same time. Thus, more frequent reinforcement of cooperative behavior should result in a decrease in fighting or other aggressive behavior.

Have a plan for dealing with fighting. Priming reminds the child of what to expect for appropriate as well as inappropriate behaviors. State in advance of a situation developing the consequences for appropriate behavior (e.g., a token or a ticket for your cooperation) and for inappropriate behavior (e.g., loss of time with a toy). These reminders need not be directed toward one child; they may be quite general. This procedure is technically *not* bribing; the teacher simply reminds the students what consequences will be forthcoming. *Always remember, it takes two to fight.*

To develop such a social skill, a teacher might suggest that the identified child and her classmate play a game. Pick a game where success depends on luck so that neither child is at an advantage. Tell both children, "When I see you playing well together and not fighting, I'll let you know, and I'll put a mark on this card [see Appendix N]. When you two reach 10 marks, we will have a celebration."

Random checks result in far greater consistency of cooperative behavior. For behaviors that are weak or just beginning to develop, reinforce the child positively for nearly every instance of the appropriate behavior at first. Modeling cooperative and uncooperative behavior for a game can be helpful, as can giving the child a nonverbal signal when misbehavior occurs. Then the child can either change the inappropriate behavior or accept the consequence, thus taking on responsibility for the outcome.

As the children get better at earning points for cooperative behavior, you can set higher goals for the same payoff. Conditions are never raised to some prearranged expectation or to a point where the child consistently fails. Failure, especially continual failure, teaches nothing. Remember, teachers must avoid having preset expectations about what each child can do. Children with ADHD are generally immature. If expectations are high (but developmentally appropriate), such children will certainly fail. Some children will voice complaints over the increase in expectation, but you might lessen their concerns by stating, "Yes, you do need a greater number of points to get the reward, but you are getting so much *better* at cooperation that it's much easier for you to get the points. You know, I'm really proud of the progress you have made."

See Chapter 5 for more discussion of teaching cooperation.

AGGRESSION

Four types of aggression are discussed below: (a) defiance and verbal aggression, (b) hostile-aggressive behavior, (c) behaviors that may require physical restraint, and (d) passive-aggressive behavior.

Defiance and Verbal Aggression

Students who are verbally aggressive use words to get what they want, to gain attention or to avoid doing some task. To address this problem, it is essential that the purpose or function of behavior be established before a proactive behavioral intervention is selected. As noted by Wolfgang and Glickman (1986) and Cole, Cole, and Lightfoot

(2004), such students attempt to control or manipulate others through their actions and words. This behavior, listed by Wolfgang and Glickman and, more recently, by the Center for Mental Health in Schools at UCLA (UCLA, 1999), includes making fun of or teasing others, swearing, yelling out, joking or laughing (especially when others are reprimanded), and being sarcastic (and disrespectful) toward the teacher (Jimerson & Brock, 2004). Rarely does this student engage in physically aggressive behavior.

The first step is to avoid confrontations with the student. Basically, ignoring or not attending or responding to the outburst may prevent further escalation. It is usually nonproductive to attempt dealing with such a student who is upset. Teachers must ignore by withdrawing attention, not responding, or even turning away from the student. If the behavior is short-lived or weak, this procedure may be sufficient; if it reoccurs consistently, then other interventions would be warranted.

It is important to determine the purpose or function that the aggressive behavior serves and what circumstances may trigger it. For example, Marcus, Vollmer, Swanson, Roane, and Ringdahl (2001) found that some children's self-injurious aggressive behavior was maintained by positive or negative reinforcement. For one child, aggression was found to be sensitive to peer attention. If the annoying behavior is designed to gain attention, the following steps are needed:

- Weaken the inappropriate behavior by not attending to it.
- Develop the more appropriate behavioral response through positive reinforcement when it is exhibited (i.e., direct attention and verbal comment, such as "[name], I like the way you controlled yourself—not yelling out"). It is especially important to note any improvement with the child (e.g., "You handled that situation better than in the past—that shows much better self-control").
- Sometimes the student will not have the appropriate response in his or her behavioral repertoire, and it will be necessary to model the appropriate response. This kind of training might best occur in private to avoid any embarrassment to the student. Then when it is time for the student to use the behavior, the teacher may provide a signal or cue (e.g., tapping one's finger to the head may be the prearranged signal to "use your head—think of what you need to do"). Of course, this is a learning paradigm, and mastery may require several training sessions along with constant differential reinforcement in the classroom. *Differential reinforcement* involves praise of the appropriate behavior. The student is praised for not exhibiting the target inappropriate behavior and for exhibiting any appropriate behavior in situations that previously triggered the inappropriate behavior.

Defiance and Verbal Aggression

Chad was a nine-year-old student in the third grade. Chad was diagnosed with ADHD and was placed on Vyvance medication. However, he was not completely controlled and acted out on a daily basis by hitting other students, not completing his work, and occasionally even trying to hit the teacher when asked to complete his work. He had been previously tested and functioned above average in ability and achievements. He was later given the diagnosis of oppositional defiant disorder as well as ADHD. Other than his behavioral problems, Chad was deemed to be a good student.

Records were kept on his hitting behavior, and after one week, a series of behavioral contracts were begun. The contracts were flexible so that they could be modified weekly, depending upon his success or failure. The initial behavioral control specified that (a) Chad needed to complete his assigned work in the classroom and (b) he was to follow the rules of "keeping hands and feet to himself." One thing Chad disliked was doing homework on the weekend; in fact, he detested such assignments. It was felt that Chad was quite motivated to avoid doing homework on weekends. Figure 7.17 shows his results from baseline to intervention.

Figure 7.17   Chad: Incidence of Aggressive Behavior

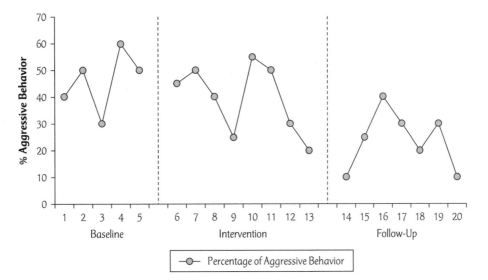

Chad was able to become increasingly more controlled and not only improved with regard to his work output but also reduced his aggressive acting-out behaviors. He was able to earn a no-homework pass each week of the intervention. He also earned a no-homework pass during the fourth week of follow-up. In future weeks, the contracts became increasingly more difficult to complete. However, the criteria were increased gradually so that Chad could continue to be successful. Of course, much verbal praise was given when he was successful. He was also given verbal praise for other desirable behaviors that were not part of the criteria in his behavioral contract. After several weeks, Chad was able to continue his productive work output while still retaining control over aggressive tendencies.

Hostile-Aggressive Behavior

Students who display this type of aggressive behavior are certainly dreaded by teachers (Bushman & Anderson, 2001). Capable of dominating and controlling others, their actions are often explosive. Such behaviors have the intent to do harm, whether it be physical or emotional. Physical aggression involves kicking, hitting, spitting, throwing materials at a person or at property, and biting (Bohnert, Crnic, & Lim, 2003).

Typically, such behavior is triggered by frustration. However, when this behavior is exhibited, the student gains much negative attention from others, including the teacher. A typical reprimand may lead to an escalation of defensiveness and verbal lashing out toward the teacher with comments such as "You always pick on me, leave me alone, I didn't do anything!" This may create anger and confusion on the part of the teacher, who only wishes to re-establish control. Typically, this interchange may escalate until the teacher ends the cycle, usually by sending the child out of the room to the principal's office. When the exchange ends, the teacher is often left with feelings of failure and confusion and negative feelings toward the student. This situation will probably sensitize the teacher to respond more angrily and quickly in the future, while labeling the student a "troublemaker" (Spoth, Redmond, & Shin, 2000).

Typically, teachers may attempt to deal with hostile-aggressive behaviors either by acting as an authoritarian (giving ultimatums) or by attempting to reason with the student. In the former case, the student might adopt a position of "You can't make me do anything," resulting in ineffective management. In the latter case, much time is wasted talking with the student, who is generally unable to explain the reasons for getting upset or losing control. Again the teacher may feel frustrated and confused and like a failure.

Using a behavioral approach, it is essential first to identify the problematic behavior(s) and then determine its function. This assessment will help to identify the specific situations that can trigger outbursts. It will also be helpful to meet with the student (and parents) to discuss which behaviors are acceptable and which ones are not. Of course, it will also be essential to identify whatever consequences the student might receive for problematic behavior. It is always possible that the student's behavior may be triggered by academic work or tasks that are beyond his or her capabilities or are difficult to perform (e.g., labored handwriting may slow down academic work). If the student receives much attention for the outburst (positive reinforcement) and then is allowed to escape from the unpleasant work assignment, these consequences may reinforce the behavior problem. In addition, if the student is sent to the principal's office, a number of interesting events there may further reinforce the whole sequence of inappropriate behavior (Miller, Tansy, & Hughes, 1998; Shapiro & Kratochwill, 2000).

In developing a proactive plan, the teacher may use a signal or other cue to let the student know when his or her behavior is escalating (for example, holding up a fist may signal that the student needs to get control or close up). When the student stops the escalation, he or she can receive positive feedback; when the student then goes on to exhibit further appropriate behavior, he or she may receive additional positive feedback. Remember that the student's unacceptable behavior did not develop overnight; likewise, it will take some time to establish an alternate replacement behavior. It will also be important to use backup reinforcers for those times when the student changes behavior. This might mean giving the student a special job as a reward for improved control.

It is, of course, not only important that the student learn an appropriate replacement behavior but also that he or she learn some problem-solving procedures centering around what to do when frustrated and angry. This not only provides some options regarding the replacement behavior but may also help the student generalize improved self-control to other situations. In short, it is important that the student be able to demonstrate the alternate replacement behavior(s) in all classrooms and other settings, with all teachers and other authority figures. The generalization and maintenance phase will require the cooperation of other teachers as well as parents. Change will be more rapid and more extensive when all authority figures handle the problem behavior in the same manner. As suggested by Flick (1998, 2000, 2002) and Petermann and Petermann (1997), school behavior programs must also involve parents (e.g., in a token economy) to be more effective.

When aggression is multiply determined, treatment may need to be more complex. Lalli and Casey (1996) reported that the aggression of a young boy with developmental delays occurred more frequently when he was asked to pick up his toys. The request ended a period of play and social interaction. Treatment consisted of praise, a break, and access to his toys, all contingent on compliance. These researchers found that aggression decreased only when social interaction was added to the break. More recent support for this study was provided by Owen Blakemore, Berenbaum, and Liben (2009) and Ollendick and Schroeder (2003). This child needed more reinforced compliance-type behaviors. High-probability compliance behaviors might be more easily established for such a child and be a gateway to low-probability compliance.

To develop a long-term proactive behavioral intervention plan, the teacher needs to make some changes in the classroom.

- It is essential that the teacher feel a sense of competency in dealing with problem behaviors. The use of self-talk and affirmations will help. The teacher might say to him- or herself, "I know what this student is doing, and it's not a personal attack. I can remain calm and help the student by doing what was planned." Many students with such problematic hostile-type behaviors are not aware either (a) that frustration and anger are escalating or (b) that the escalation occurs so quickly. They are unable to react appropriately in time. In either of these conditions, it will be important for the student to be able to access quickly the appropriate alternate replacement behavior by overlearning it. This means that the teacher will need to continue reinforcing the appropriate behavior and to avoid giving attention to the inappropriate behavior.
- Teachers should remain close to the child who frequently shows misbehavior. Proximity control involves decreasing unwanted behavior by the teacher positioning him- or herself next to the student (Zirpoli & Mellow, 2001). This would also certainly help in "catching the child being good" so as to give positive reinforcement (Allen & Cowdery, 2004).
- Teachers should establish a quiet spot in the classroom where students can go to calm down and get control. In essence, this type of "chill-out" or "calm-down" place is simply a variation of time-out. While time-out is technically a withdrawal from all positive reinforcement, it also allows children to calm down and get control before they are released from time-out (an important requirement). Teachers must be careful not to allow a child to escape or temporarily avoid work; after calming down, the student needs to return to work. (See Chapter 6 for further discussion of time-out.)
- It is essential that teachers prevent conflicts from escalating to the point of losing control. If two students are in the process of escalating conflict, they must be separated. Remember: *It takes two to have a fight*. It is thus appropriate to communicate that when one student is inappropriately threatened, a fight can be avoided. When a student escalates but then exhibits self-control, the teacher should give positive reinforcement for that self-control behavior. However, the teacher may need to deal with a second phase of defensiveness. Here, a simple redirection procedure may be appropriate (Reimers & Brunger, 1999). Avoid confrontation and giving attention to the second-line defensive behavior. Instead, simply focus on what needs to be done (using redirection), saying, "What do you need to be doing now?" Questions such as this allow the student to shift from a feeling mode to a thinking mode; the latter, of course, will facilitate greater cognitive control.

Two teacher reactions are *not* advised:

1. Do not corner a student who is emotionally out of control. Leave sufficient personal space for the student to be taken out of the classroom.

2. Do not argue with a student. Give choices to the student for the present situation and the option to discuss it (for older children) at some later time. Any attempt to

discuss the student's behavior during an emotional upheaval may simply reinforce the escalation process.

Hostile-Aggressive Behavior

Corey was an eight-year-old in the second grade. He was diagnosed with ADHD and took Adderall-XR, which did help him in the classroom. However, he continued to show aggressive behavior, such as hitting and cursing, and he even bit one student. He was disrespectful to his teacher and rarely completed his work prior to taking medication. Some of his other disruptive behavior included being out of his seat, walking around the room, and tapping his pencil on the desk.

Corey was a bright student who failed to make academic progress mainly because of his behavior. His teacher decided to focus on his main behavior problem and primarily to reward appropriate behavior, since use of reprimands as well as suspensions had been ineffective. Corey loved to collect football cards; his parents supplied these cards for him to earn in school. They also reinforced his good productive days with backup reinforcements (i.e., football cards) at home. Teachers were to communicate by e-mail regarding his good behavior each day, also noted by tokens. It was determined that initially he would be able to earn 25 points each week; later this would increase to 50 points per week. Corey would receive one football card for each 25 tokens he earned. He would also receive one card at home for each one earned in school. In addition to the cards, Corey received much verbal praise for his appropriate desirable behavior. Figure 7.18 shows his results.

Figure 7.18   Corey: Aggressive Behavior—Intervention I

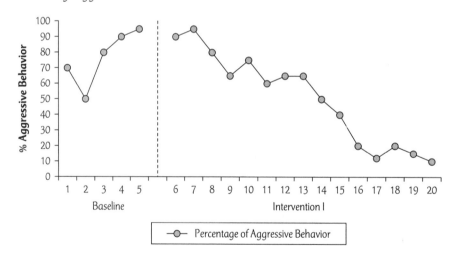

Corey's program was carried out for three weeks, with some modifications after that. Follow-up programs continued to reveal some aggressive behavior. Corey was also taught appropriate social skills (especially sharing and cooperation). These skills were modeled by the teacher and then requested of the student. Subsequently, they were reinforced whenever Corey exhibited them in the classroom or on the school grounds. The follow-up and behavioral interventions were continued into the fourth through the sixth week. Figure 7.19 shows the results:

Figure 7.19 Corey: Aggressive Behavior—Intervention II

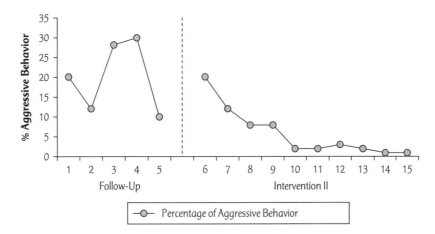

After the fifth week, Corey did not show aggressive behavior on any day. His classwork output increased, and his inappropriate behavior in class decreased. Corey continued to receive verbal praise for any appropriate behavior. His behavioral interventions were discontinued.

Behaviors That May Require Physical Restraint

Physical restraint is a procedure where a teacher uses his or her body to immobilize a student to protect the safety of staff or other students. Since this procedure has been misused, it has led to lawsuits over violation of the student's constitutional rights. Thus, it is important to evaluate the risk and to use the procedure judiciously (McAfee, Schwilk, & Mitruski, 2006). This procedure should be used only as a last resort to protect the student from self-injury or hurting others or damaging property.

This is clearly a controversial procedure. In 2006, a seven-year-old girl with ADHD and an emotional disorder died after being pinned down at a state-licensed day treatment center (Samuels, 2009). Ron Hager, a senior lawyer for the National Disability Rights Network, stated, "We want to promote the use of positive-behavioral intervention supports school wide" and "the more that you can mindfully create an environment where things don't escalate, the less that restraint will occur" (as cited in Samuels, 2009). Its use is thus discouraged; instead, a positive reinforcement framework is suggested.

Passive-Aggressive Behavior

A student might show passive-aggressive behavior either to get attention or to express anger (Shapiro & Kratochwill, 2002). Typical passive-aggressive behaviors include hearing only what one wants, moving slowly when asked to do something, purposefully forgetting, being accidentally destructive, complaining, and turning in incomplete work. Such a student may deal with anger and frustration by eliciting similar feelings in others. Of course, there can be other reasons for the above behaviors, but the frequency and pervasiveness of these characteristics make them stand out.

It may appear that the student is attempting to avoid or escape from some activity, but it is the manipulation or conflict that results from such behaviors that drives the student. Such a student generally receives much attention for manipulative behaviors. Once the behaviors are reinforced by attention, a cycle begins that periodically reinforces the behaviors and prevents the student from shifting to engage in more appropriate behaviors. These students also lack self-esteem, since their complex manipulative behaviors often prevent them from realizing any success with task completion. These students are also deficient in their ability to express feelings of frustration and anger, leading them to vent their feelings indirectly by manipulating and controlling others' emotions.

The first step in dealing with this type of student's behavior is again to determine the function of the problem behavior. If attention does not appear to maintain the behavior, it is questionable as to whether the student really displays passive-aggressive behaviors. Secondly, the teacher must examine how he or she has been dealing with the behavior. The teacher's feeling state must be appraised after confrontation with the student. If the teacher feels helplessness and anger, then the methods used are not working.

The teacher should make a list of three to five behaviors that are most annoying and then find alternate behaviors for each one. What is most important is for the teacher to withdraw attention from the student's inappropriate manipulative behaviors. Next, the teacher should reinforce any spontaneous exhibition of alternate behaviors. If the student is not showing any of the alternate behaviors, then these can be modeled for the student. The student can then be engaged in a role-play where the alternate behaviors are exhibited in place of the inappropriate behaviors. When these alternate behaviors are exhibited in the natural environment of the classroom, they can be reinforced either by verbal praise or perhaps through the use of a token or point system. Cooperative learning, where the student works with another student who already shows these appropriate alternate behaviors, is yet another behavioral intervention.

The student will also need to learn more acceptable ways of expressing anger. Using a problem-solving approach, the student may be queried, "What else could you do when you feel frustrated and angry?" The teacher might then list all the appropriate and inappropriate behaviors given by the student. In fact, this may be an excellent exercise to conduct with the entire class so that through observation, the identified student may learn other options to replace the problematic behavior.

Additionally, it is important to build up the student's self-esteem by giving tasks that the student is entirely capable of performing and by reinforcing them as they are completed. The teacher might say, "You did an excellent job on that project I gave you—I'm really proud of you." Of course, an underlying problem with the completion of some academic tasks may represent some type of learning impairment, attentional problem, or even a neurologically based dysfunction (e.g., handwriting disorder due to impaired fine-motor or visual-spatial functions); thus, such conditions must be ruled out.

Passive-Aggressive Behavior

John is a 10-year-old student with ADHD who had problems fighting with other students, primarily during morning sessions that involved partner activity. As previously noted, fighting is generally more likely to occur when attempts to gain teacher attention fail. However, fighting also occurred when this student was provoked by his peers. Fighting seemed to serve the function of a need to control his peers. Although there was a hierarchy of disciplinary actions, behavioral interventions were used to avoid moving up to suspension and to reduce further escalation of his problems.

The following functions were attributed to this student's behavior:

- *Attention seeking*: John was frustrated when the teacher did not attend to him. Frustration led to anger and increased the likelihood of a fight. Fighting then brought attention, albeit negative attention.
- *The need to control peers*: This need seemed directly related to John's deficit in social skills, especially his ability to work cooperatively with others.

Behavioral Intervention Plan

The following intervention strategies were developed:

- Focusing attention on John prior to his becoming emotionally upset. This could be to clarify any problems with the work or to specify the role of each student in a cooperative effort.
- Developing a signal that John could give if a misunderstanding or a question about the work arose. This signal could be as simple as raising a hand to get the teacher's attention.
- Providing John with training in social skills, with special emphasis on interactive cooperative behavior.
- Monitoring John on the following behaviors: (a) following instructions, (b) completing assignments, (c) making requests for assistance, and (d) engaging in cooperative peer relations. A token (point) system was used to monitor these components, and John would work to earn additional computer time. John's behavioral program had a positive orientation.

Baseline

Behavior	Pts	M	T	W	Th	F	Total
Follow Instruction	1	//	/	///	/	/	8
Complete Assignment	1	/		/		/	3
Request Assistance	1	/		/	//		4
Cooperative Peer Relations	1	/	//	/	/	///	8
Total		5	3	6	4	5	

Sample Token (Point) System

Behavior	Pts	M	T	W	Th	F	Total
Follow Instruction	1	/////	///	////////	////	booking /////////	29
Complete Assignment	1	//	///	/	//	////	12
Request Assistance	1	//	//	/	/////	//	12
Cooperative Peer Relations	1	/////	/////	///	////////	////	25
Total		14	13	13	19	19	

As indicated by the slash marks, John showed significant improvement in all positive appropriate behaviors. His episodes of verbal aggression also significantly decreased. Over the course of two weeks, John's verbal aggression decreased from baseline average of about four outbursts to about three outbursts during the first week and about one during the second week. This program needs to continue until the verbal outbursts are down to zero. During this time, John will do the following:

- Continue in the social skills program.

- Work with those students who serve as excellent models and are instructed to withdraw attention from John when he escalates emotional behavior.

- Continue to signal the teacher when questions about the work arise or some difficulty is encountered.

INAPPROPRIATE VERBALIZATIONS

This category of problems consists of several inappropriate behaviors. These may include cursing, gestures, disrespectful talk, name-calling, and any other inappropriate verbalization directed towards the teacher, some other adult, or peers. Many teachers report this as a common problem. It can be addressed by a self-monitoring approach.

Inappropriate Verbalizations

Chris is a 14-year-old boy who was originally diagnosed with ADHD and a conduct disorder. He often engaged in uttering obscenities, talking in a disrespectful manner, and making obscene gestures. These behaviors were becoming more frequent, such that he was referred for a behavioral intervention. A self-monitoring, self-management approach was designed.

Chris received reinforcements for any appropriate verbalization. This included any positive response to directions or conversations where positive words or appropriate tone of voice and facial expression were exhibited. During baseline, episodes of these appropriate verbalizations were counted with a counter recorder (i.e., one that clicks each time it is pressed). Events were recorded during random 15-minute periods each day, in each class or activity (including lunchroom, gym, and recess). Each day, ten 15-minute periods contributed to Chris's score.

During intervention, Chris was instructed to make a slash mark on a card each time he engaged in an appropriate verbalization. All of the appropriate verbalizations were noted on the card as a reminder. In addition, a review was conducted each morning to determine how familiar he was with the appropriate verbalizations. Each one remembered correctly received verbal praise. He was then given the card. At the same time, either the teacher or an aide tallied the number of appropriate verbalizations during each 15-minute recording period. Chris was not directly aware of when these random periods occurred—only that there were ten 15-minute periods each day. If at the end of the day, there was 90 percent or better agreement between his and the teacher or aide's recordings, he was allowed to leave school five minutes earlier than normal. Each day, his self-monitoring was recorded and compared to baseline. Figure 7.20 shows the results.

During intervention, Chris received a no-homework pass when his total number of appropriate verbalizations exceeded the previous day's by 5 points. His performance was plotted on a graph, and he was given verbal praise for success (e.g., "You really did well today. You've exceeded your previous day's points by 5—congratulations! You get a homework pass for one subject"). After two weeks of intervention, Chris showed success on 7 out of 10 days.

Figure 7.20   Chris: Appropriate Verbalizations

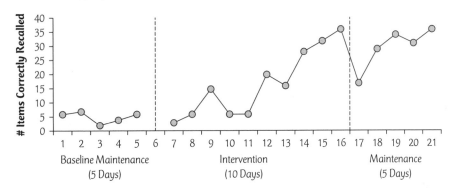

During the maintenance phase, he continued to receive verbal praise but no longer earned the homework pass. On three out of five days, his performance equaled that of his best performance during the intervention phase. Overall, his teacher commented that the program was a success and Chris continued to give appropriate verbalizations. These appropriate verbalizations were maintained with verbal praise by the teacher.

Name: _____				**Date:** _____					
Target behaviors: (a) Positive response to directions, (b) positive words used in conversation, (c) appropriate tone of voice, (d) appropriate facial expression									
(1)	*(2)*	*(3)*	*(4)*	*(5)*	*(6)*	*(7)*	*(8)*	*(9)*	*(10)*
TOTALS									

The above box displays the recording card used with Chris. Each of the target behaviors were reviewed with Chris each day of intervention. He was given examples of each and might be asked to role-play them. Correct role-plays were praised; incorrect role-plays received comments, and appropriate ones were modeled.

SELF-MONITORING

Self-monitoring is the process of having students record data about their own behavior to change its rate (Coleman & Webber, 2002). Self-monitoring has been used with children who vary in age (Agran et al., 2005) and who show a wide array of handicapping conditions. There has been considerable variation in procedure, which may account for its underutilization by teachers (Agran et al., 2005). Self-monitoring has been used for both academic and nonacademic behavior problems (Shapiro & Cole, 1994). One of the easiest programs to use is the Listen, Look, and Think (a self-regulation program) by Parker (1992) for both individual students and the whole class.

Self-Monitoring

Justin was a 12-year-old sixth grader who was diagnosed with LD and ADHD. He had difficulty attending to instruction, following rules, and completing assigned tasks (mostly because he would get off-task). When Justin stayed on-task, he was more likely to complete an assignment. A self-monitoring program was set up for Justin with three components: baseline, intervention, and maintenance.

During baseline, the teacher kept a record of the number of times Justin was on-task or off-task during a 20-minute work period. Justin also kept a record during each of these periods every day during math. A page was marked with either a (+) for being on-task, or a (−) for being off-task each time a tone sounded. The tone, played on an endless loop tape, was given at varying intervals. The baseline period was in operation over five days. The percent agreement between student and teacher was low.

During intervention, Justin was told that he would receive a point each time he was on-task when the beep sounded, but *only* when his mark agreed with that of the teacher. There were 20 possible marks during each work period. When there was agreement between his mark and the teacher's mark, he got a bonus. Thus, Justin got double points for being on-task and an additional point if his mark agreed with the teacher's. His score for each work period could, thus, range from 20 to 40 points. He was also given positive verbal feedback when his score matched that of the teacher. His reward was arranged with his mother as a trip to McDonald's. He received this after earning 200 points. His mother also agreed not to allow him to go to McDonald's at any other time.

During the maintenance phase, Justin was still given verbal praise when his ratings matched those of the teacher, but he was not earning trips to McDonald's. Such trips were now random and not always linked to his performance in school. Thus, he had to do well in school to go to McDonald's (reward), but he was not rewarded for not doing well in school (being off-task). Data is presented in Figure 7.21 for the three periods of this program; the number of sessions appears at the bottom. Justin's rating agreement with the teacher varied from 20 percent in baseline to 95 percent during the intervention phase and 83 percent during maintenance. The form used in the program was provided for each work period; it, too, is found in Figure 7.21.

Justin's on-task behavior improved significantly. In a follow-up assessment, he was found to have maintained his ability to stay on-task, as he completed 90 percent of his work and his teacher's rating was at an average of 36 over a three-day period. Also, Justin's work improved in other subject areas as well, as he learned to stay on-task. Because of his LD in reading, he did require special remedial tutoring in that area, and he continued to have problems with reading assignments.

Figure 7.21   Justin: Points for On-Task Behavior

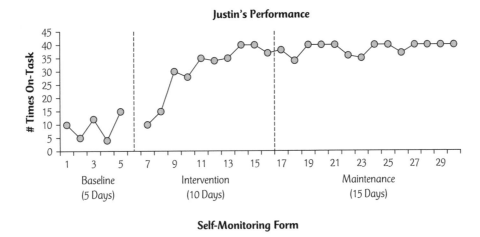

Self-Monitoring Form

Name _____   Class _____

Put a (+) when on-task and a (−) when off-task for each period assessed.

1. _____	11. _____
2. _____	12. _____
3. _____	13. _____
4. _____	14. _____
5. _____	15. _____
6. _____	16. _____
7. _____	17. _____
8. _____	18. _____
9. _____	19. _____
10. _____	20. _____

This self-monitoring procedure used with Justin could have been used with the whole class, and other target behaviors could be selected to monitor.

BY THE TIME I THINK ABOUT WHAT
I SHOULDN'T DO – I'VE ALREADY DONE IT!
(From Flick, 1998)

SUMMARY

Interventions for some of the core problems with students who have ADHD are explored. These include inattention and the often observed characteristic of off-task behavior. Impulsivity and hyperactivity are also discussed, as is following instructions, with interventions that target these problem behaviors. Noncompliance is reviewed along with an intervention that is designed to improve compliance. Social skills problems are further discussed. Aggression appears to be a major problem that is difficult to cope with; various types of aggression are discussed together with interventions to deal with them. The technique of self-monitoring is detailed, and a case study summarizes the use of some procedures.

While these applications of behavioral interventions for specific problem behaviors, often characteristic of ADHD, are basic and elementary, they do illustrate how to approach these problems in a systematic way. They are not the only behavioral interventions that might work, but they are some of the easiest ones to implement. The purpose of this clinical manual is to propose interventions that are easy to implement, that address the problem behavior, and that can be used *prior to* any formal interventions. These interventions can, therefore, be employed by all teachers—those in general education and those in special education. Of course, ancillary professionals (e.g., aides, school counselors) may also participate in these interventions.

8

Survival Techniques for Teachers

Key Points

- Changing teachers' coping strategies
- Relaxation/stress management
- Affirmations
- Assertion
- Broken record statement
- Mental health practices for teachers

Justin was an eight-year-old boy in the third grade. Justin took Ritalin-XR each day. While medication helped with Justin's impulsiveness, he was still disruptive by talking with other students, making faces at them, walking around the room, tapping his pencil, or using other objects to make noise. Teachers taught Justin to self-monitor and gave tokens for appropriate behavior as well as redirection for disruptive behavior; however, this program was generally ineffective.

What would you do to address these problems?

Teachers may experience a significant degree of stress in dealing with the child with ADHD. In the classroom, one of the greatest sources of stress for the teacher involves discipline of difficult-to-manage children. Children with ADHD can be included in the group. Teachers who leave the profession have often reported a lack of support regarding school discipline from the administration (Ingersoll, 2003; Johnson et al., 2006). It is a common observation that when children with ADHD are grouped together, in a family or in a classroom, a kind of synergistic effect occurs. The synergistic effect must be clearly differentiated from the contagion effect.

The term used to describe the spread of an emotional state from one individual to another is *emotional contagion*. . . . This mimicry appears to be the basic mechanism by which people "catch" emotions from others. (Brigham & Brigham, 2004, p. 8)

This effect has mostly applied to substance abuse (Rende, Slomkowski, Lloyd-Richardson, & Niaura, 2005) and suicide (Pearson-Gibson & Rang, 2006; Sudak & Sudak, 2005). The synergistic effect simply describes how two or more children with ADHD present more intense problems together than each one would separately. It is not a mimicry of behavior or emotional reactions; *synergistic* means that the sum is greater than the individual parts. In short, behavior problems may increase exponentially. Teachers might, therefore, experience burnout.

It's helpful to be aware that additional problems are created when the teacher of a child with ADHD also manifests residual symptoms and characteristics. In such cases, the child with ADHD is faced with a teacher who may be disorganized, inconsistent, impulsive, quick tempered, and poorly tuned in to the child's needs. Such teachers may have adopted a somewhat rigid routine and, therefore, lack flexibility in coping with difficult behavior. Interaction between these teachers with children who have more severe forms of ADHD and/or significant comorbid problems will thus be fraught with tension and might result in explosive consequences.

CHANGING THE TEACHER'S COPING STRATEGY

Teachers must not attempt to deal with too many problems at one time; they'll only feel overwhelmed and even give up as they frantically try to cope with all problems at once. These teachers should focus on one or perhaps two problems at a time, breaking larger tasks into smaller units, and they should prioritize problem behaviors. This does not mean dealing with the most severe behavior problem first; at times, teachers may discover that once a mild or moderate behavior problem is handled, other problem behaviors may not be so severe.

Just like the child with ADHD, teachers need breaks in their routine. Behavior problems will not be resolved overnight, and when some behavioral procedure seems not to be working, it may be helpful to stand back—retreat, if you will—and take a look at what's going on. On occasions, teachers become overfocused—concentrating on one aspect of a problem while failing to see the overall picture. It is important to use breaks in daily routine to incorporate pleasurable activities. Excessive pressure to perform may not only fail to achieve desired results but may also lead to the child's becoming depressed over failure to meet teacher expectations. Clearly, problems with depression appear most often in adolescents with ADHD.

What can teachers do to counteract and deal with the stress associated with managing the child with ADHD?

RELAXATION AND STRESS MANAGEMENT

Teachers can learn simple relaxation and stress management techniques. There are many relaxation tapes, and they are available in bookstores and CD and tape centers, as well as online. Some 5- to 10-minute tapes may be used on a daily basis. Even shorter relaxation exercises may be integrated within a hectic schedule. Some of these include (1) shrugging the shoulders and rotating them forward and backward in a circular motion three times each way; (2) rotating the head (for neck muscles) in a circular movement to the right (three times) and to the left (three times), being careful not to engage in this routine vigorously; (3) taking a slow, deep breath (from the abdomen) in through the nose and breathing out through the mouth; (4) repeating the previous procedure, this time saying "one" slowly with each exhalation; and (5) sitting very quiet and still while visualizing oneself in a calm, soothing, relaxing place (a kind of short mental vacation).

Another alternative is to use a kind of "stress inoculation" procedure that involves the self-talk method to aid in actively ignoring some behavior. This procedure may serve to reduce stress and at the same time maintain the proper course in working with the child. When a student's behavior is selected to be ignored, the child may become frustrated that he or she is not getting the usual attention. The student then escalates the intensity of affect associated with that behavior. If the behavior is whining, the whining becomes louder. If it is drumming a pencil on the desk, the drumming becomes louder. Teachers need to prepare in advance to "ride out" this more intense behavior by using a self-talk exercise that is designed to keep the focus on something other than the child. This may involve attempting to read a book or newspaper, work on a project, or grade papers. Teachers must, however, realize that no work will be accomplished during this time. This time is used to weaken the child's response eventually. Teachers must be prepared not to give in; giving in would certainly make the child even more persistent in the behavior, showing it at a more intense level. Teachers must keep the following internal dialogue in mind—and use it!

> Okay, I know this is going to get worse, but I can handle it. It's important for me to keep my attention on this newspaper (or grade book). I know I won't be able to concentrate very well, so I'm not concerned about getting anything accomplished—I just need to keep my attention on these materials.

> Typically, the intensity of the behavior will increase.

> Okay, I know his behavior is getting worse now. I expected that, so it's no surprise to me. What I need to do is continue my deep breathing and bring my attention back to my materials. I'm prepared for this to continue for a while and even get worse. I can handle this. I can continue to allow my muscles around my neck and shoulders to relax and let go. I can imagine the relaxation spreading to other muscles in my body. I'll just have to wait this out. I know that if I give in, he'll just be more persistent next time—and even more intense. I can handle this. I can remain calm and relaxed.

With a little practice, teachers can devise a self-talk procedure that best suits their style of conversation and their unique situation. Teachers should take a few moments to reflect on a situation where such a procedure would be helpful and write their own narrative script to use while ignoring some behavior. Remember that the child with ADHD exhibits many behaviors that may be physiologically determined, and such behaviors may never be totally removed or extinguished. It is, however, important to avoid adding a learned component to that behavioral pattern, which would make it even more difficult to handle. In short, many ADHD behaviors (e.g., wiggling, tapping, humming) might be diminished but never removed. The teacher should try out the self-talk exercise now.

DAILY AFFIRMATIONS

Using daily affirmations may also be useful for both parents and teachers. While some affirmations might have a religious content, others simply reaffirm the teacher's desire to change the way he or she responds to the child with ADHD. These statements may be repeated several times each day. It is, therefore, helpful to have them posted within view or easily accessible in a wallet, pocket, or purse. Some simple examples of these affirmations for parents and teachers are provided here.

Teachers' Affirmations

"I can now better understand the child with ADHD behavior, and I can be more flexible in dealing with it."

"I now know that I don't have to respond to every inappropriate behavior from the child with ADHD; I can ignore some of these behaviors, even though they may be annoying."

A book of affirmations by Tian Dayton (1991) is suggested as an additional reference. It is important that teachers develop their own affirmations that are specific to their situation and the problem behaviors they face. The teacher can use the previous affirmations as a guide and make sure to begin the statement with the pronoun *I*. Another book on affirmations for teachers has been developed by Withan (1995), and affirmations have been addressed further in Harvey and Chickie-Wolfe (2007).

BEING ASSERTIVE

Many children with ADHD firmly believe that they are in control—and in many cases they are. When misbehavior garners attention, such attention by teachers can be reinforcing. Even though much of this attention is negative or seemingly unpleasant, in fact, most attention directed at the child with ADHD is negative; thus, over time, even negative attention can be rewarding. It's simple—negative attention is better than no attention at all. Many children with ADHD learn which buttons to press to elicit attention from their teachers. After years of such experience, this pattern becomes almost like a game. Remember, the child with ADHD may be actively seeking to create some excitement or an uproar (i.e., self-stimulation). Sometimes the "punishment" may be well worth the laughs or upheaval created by the behavior. For many, "punishment" in school means being sent out of the classroom, which can actually be a reward for the child who thinks the class is boring. Escape further reinforces such behavior, as does the teacher's reaction.

Children with ADHD can almost predict when they will get in trouble, and some teachers have learned to recognize some of these signs as well. The main point here is that teachers must be able to resist attempts by the child to manipulate and control. Teachers who wish to survive teacherhood must be assertive with regard to behavioral procedures.

Using "Broken Record" Statements

Some behaviors of the child with ADHD can be quite resistant to change. Teachers must be just as resistant and persistent in not giving in to demands made by the child or to behaviors that are clearly manipulative in nature. A technique known as the "broken record" was first described by Cynthia Whitman (1991); it can be used when the child makes repetitive annoying requests or shows some other irritating behavior. The procedure is simple—just say NO! Repeating this statement and saying, "I'm sorry—you can't have what you want," may initially bring about an escalation of the intensity of the request (e.g., louder whining and perhaps temper tantrums, depending on the child's age) or repetition of some other annoying behavior designed to "punish the teacher" for not giving in to the demands (Flick, 1998).

It is important to state here that assertiveness is also needed in not allowing the child to name-call, curse, or threaten the teacher. Being assertive means requesting the respect that one deserves as a teacher. If disrespectful behaviors occur, it is important to state firmly, "I will not allow you to abuse me in that manner. It's OK to express your feelings; it's not OK to say what you said." Depending on the nature and severity of the abuse, the teacher may wish simply to turn away from the child and leave. Alternatively, a more formal punishment (i.e., behavior penalty or the overcorrection procedure) may be used. It is, however, important to consider the occasion for the child's verbal outburst. If the teacher used harsh words with the child, it is not unusual that the child will retaliate in a similar manner. It is again important for teachers to avoid harsh words or embarrassing language; in short, be positive and model appropriate behavior.

A good exercise would be for the teacher to write statements that can be used for certain behaviors—statements that would be appropriate for an "assertive stance." It is important to be prepared with these statements. They can be rehearsed so that when the behavior occurs, they will become almost automatic.

SUMMING UP TEACHER MENTAL HEALTH PRACTICES

To reduce and control the emotional stress associated with behavior management of the child with ADHD, teachers must address the following issues:

- *Accept the child.* ADHD is a neurobiological chronic problem, just like asthma or epilepsy. It can be controlled or managed but never (at this point in time) eliminated. Use of appropriate medications and/or behavioral strategies may result in improvement 80 percent of the time or better (Flick, 1998).
- *Know about ADHD and treatments that will make things better.* Knowing and understanding the nature of ADHD is an important first step. The teacher must also understand which behavioral techniques, used consistently, will make a difference in how the child responds. Medication often results in quick and sometimes dramatic behavior change, yet prior behaviors return when the medication wears off. It is equally important to teach the child with ADHD "skills that take the place of pills." These skills may be used as the child grows older and needs to cope with situations without medication. It is critical that the child learn to rely on his or her own resources and not turn to medication as a primary solution to problems. Keep

in mind that the best outcomes determined from long-term studies of children with ADHD as adults involve the use of behavioral techniques combined with medication. However, in many cases, behavioral intervention alone may suffice (especially when the problem behaviors are not severe).

- *Remain calm in crisis.* Utilize your relaxation and stress inoculation procedures. Calm creates the environment most conducive to maintaining close relationships and keeping children under control. Filters allow the teacher to focus on critical behaviors while ignoring the annoying ones.

- *Maintain a routine.* Teachers need to maintain structure in the classroom. Knowing what to expect—and when to expect it—is critical. So, too, is the development of habits. The trick is to have an established routine in which the components change to heighten and maintain the child's interest. Also include an allowance for transitions. Extensive planning and discussion of transition times will allow teachers to avoid considerable stress.

- *Keep communications clear.* This sounds simple, but poor communication may be the source of turmoil in classrooms. Remember that communications provide the basic structure in class. When these are unclear, the child may become confused. Teachers especially need to be clear and concise, giving instructions step-by-step, orally and—when possible—in writing. Mumbling, nagging, arguing, yelling, and trying to talk over "noise" will be ineffective.

- *Be aware of triggers to crisis events.* Most teachers are aware of those situations or occasions that are associated with, or directly bring about, an eruption of misbehavior. Restructuring such situations or occasions may be all that is needed to avoid escalation of misbehavior.

- *Stay positive.* More than any other recommendation, this one is crucial in maintaining relative calm at school. When negative attention is given, everyone becomes more tense. As behavior escalates, relationships are stressed, and the situation sometimes culminates in a violent interchange.

- *Use appropriate behavioral techniques.* Teachers are exposed to numerous variations of behavioral procedures. Sometimes inappropriate conclusions may be drawn when some techniques fail to work as they should. Many times, however, procedures are used inappropriately or perhaps not long enough to get results. Alternatively, the situation may simply be one in which nothing will work (i.e., the 20 percent of the time previously referred to). If teachers have a thorough knowledge of the behavioral techniques in this book, they will be better prepared to meet challenges in the classroom. However, any change in behavior occurs slowly; knowing what to do and actually doing it are two completely different things. It will require some practice and feedback to ensure that changes in the approach to behavior management have actually occurred.

- *Join a support group.* Many local and national organizations allow teachers to share information and to realize that they are not alone in dealing with the behavior of a child with ADHD. Teachers may benefit greatly by being able to exchange ideas and share feelings and common concerns. Typically, these support groups also have some of the latest information on new procedures, products, and services. The largest organization is CHADD (see the information listed in Resources at the back of this book).

- *General resources.* All teachers must stay abreast of new products, services, books, and so on. A list of centers that provide resources for parents and teachers, as well as children, is listed in Resources.

- *Consider adult ADHD:* Some teachers, as well as other professionals, may recognize characteristics of ADHD in themselves as they read and learn about problematic behavior in the children that they manage. For parents, this may not be at all unusual, since a strong genetic component is well documented for this disorder. While adult ADHD has not been a primary focus in this book, many other books, checklists, workbooks, and tests are oriented toward the adult with ADHD. Since this disorder may either be comorbid with or serve as a potential catalyst for several other significant clinical disorders, investigating ADHD may be an excellent way to begin looking at sources of problems encountered with children. It is reasonable to assume that when a parent is treated or becomes aware of such problems, that parent's orientation to and manner of coping with the child with ADHD often changes. As a result, the overall relationship changes, and the child's behavior may improve, even if nothing else does. A list of resources for children, adolescents, and adults with ADHD is provided in Resources.
- *Specific resources*: Refer to the information provided Resources at the back of this book to aid in the evaluation and treatment of ADHD.

THE FUTURE OUTLOOK

There have been several recent long-term or longitudinal studies of ADHD. Most studies indicate that ADHD is a chronic disorder that persists from childhood into adolescence and beyond (Barkley, 2005; Faraone, Biederman, & Mick, 2006). Short-term studies have also shown that children with ADHD continue to present variously with significant academic, cognitive, and behavioral problems through their teen years (Mannuzza & Klein, 1999). Studies have shown further that children with ADHD ultimately complete less of their education, get generally lower grades, fail more subjects, and are expelled more often than children without ADHD problems (Mannuzza & Klein, 1999). The children with ADHD were also found to show a greater risk for the development of a psychiatric disorder later in life; some develop conduct disorders. Children with ADHD are also more likely to abuse substances and are at a higher risk for antisocial behavior (Klein, 2001). Other studies indicated that children with ADHD are shorter and lighter than their peers after being on stimulant medication (DeNoon, 2006).

What does this mean? Specifically, teachers will be faced with the behavioral problems of children with ADHD for a considerable time. The data from long-term studies suggest that behavioral interventions are perhaps more heuristic and that stimulant medication incurs stunting of growth, as well as risk for significant psychiatric, substance abuse, and behavior disorders. Survey data indicate that teachers (and many parents) prefer the use of behavioral interventions first. Should behavior problems remain uncontrolled, medication can certainly be considered. It is far better to resolve significant behavior problems even temporarily than to allow them to continue. Thus, usually medication will require a choice between either stunting growth or enabling success in school, along with the prevention of other psychiatric problems and reduced rate of dropping out. The risks of not treating ADHD are thus significant in terms of long-term outcomes (Palumbo, as cited in DeNoon, 2006).

SUMMARY

This last chapter illustrates some of the techniques that can change the teacher's coping strategy. These include relaxation and stress management, affirmations, assertiveness, and using broken-record statements. There is also a summary of things that teachers can do to improve their chances of "survival" in managing the behaviors of a child with ADHD. Clearly, the behaviors of children with ADHD will remain intact for many years. Longitudinal studies reveal that ADHD does not "go away" or resolve itself by adolescence. It is, instead, a chronic disorder that persists even into adulthood. Studies also show that medication may be helpful in the short term, but there is little difference between children who have been on medication for many years and those who have not. There are advantages for having a child with ADHD on medication: research has shown that generally less medication than thought is needed, and children on medication may also be more amenable to behavioral interventions. Nevertheless, current research suggests that behavioral interventions might best be initiated first. Some children with ADHD may even be treated without medication. Medication may then be used if sufficient control is not obtained through the use of accommodations, general and specific suggestions, and informal behavioral interventions.

Appendix A

Answers to Problem Cases

Chapter 1

Jordan's target behaviors were working on-task and being nondisruptive. Consequences were class activities and special assignments (e.g., collecting papers, being line leader). Antecedent events were variable, but the main one was being assigned a task. Attention from the teacher and classmates seemed to maintain his behavior. Jordan learned more appropriate ways to obtain attention from the teacher and from the class. When he exhibited these behaviors, he was given a ticket (point), and the whole class received a mark on a card. When the whole class got 25 marks, the class would have a party. Jordan was also instructed in self-monitoring and marked a sheet for being on-task or off-task each time a tone sounded. If 90 percent of his marks agreed with the teacher's, he would get one ticket (point) for each completed task. Since he was able to complete three tasks per day, he was initially only required to complete four tasks for a ticket (point). This was gradually increased, as he gained competence, to five and then to six tasks per day. Jordan improved in his relations with others, as well as his work output.

Chapter 2

The target behavior for José was following directions without disruptive behavior. The usual consequences were class activities. No clear-cut setting events were identified. The antecedent event was stopping an activity he enjoyed to begin another task. José's problem behaviors were his noncompliance and his aggressive behavior (i.e., hitting and biting). José was provided with a model who showed what could be done in a calm manner. Regarding the antecedent strategies, José was allowed to continue his activity if he asked appropriately. Attention was withdrawn from any misbehavior. José was also rewarded with praise when he complied with simple requests (e.g., "Come over here so I can give you a treat"). Of course, he also got the treat for his appropriate behavior. Transitions were also modified so he was given advance warning (five minutes, three minutes, one minute). Much verbal praise was specific and delivered contingent on his completing tasks. In general, José improved, and no problem behaviors were noted after three months.

Chapter 3

Maureen's target behaviors were not to steal and to raise her hand to give answers. Consequences were small objects like pencils, paper, scissors, crayons, ruler, etc. Maureen received verbal praise and was given small rewards (e.g., pencils) when she did not steal from others. She was also reinforced for apologizing to her classmate. Since she did not know how to apologize, she was taught this skill in personal conferences with the teacher. When Maureen did steal an object, she was simply required to return it and apologize, and then she returned to the class activity. Little or no attention was given to her stealing behavior. She could also earn rewards for doing the appropriate thing in class (i.e., raising her hand to answer, instead of blurting out). Stealing decreased and raising a hand to answer increased in frequency.

Chapter 4

Marcus's desirable behavior consisted of attending and remaining in school and completing his work. Behavioral contracts were used. Consequences were things that were available in school but also things that he was interested in; some of his preferred activities were only available at home. Marcus was allowed extra time on the computer when he completed his work. Completing work in school also allowed him to have privileges at home (e.g., computer, phone, TV). Marcus was also allowed to read and work on topics where he showed greater interest (e.g., motorcycles, adventure, travel stories). This is a good example of a home-school program. Verbal praise was also given liberally for his appropriate behavior. Marcus showed a general increase in attendance and work completion as he was able to stay on-task for longer periods.

Chapter 5

Nothing further needs to be done in this case. If accommodations and basic behavioral techniques (e.g., praising) are sufficient, then no interventions need to be conducted. While the first step is to understand the function of the behavior, the second step is to employ the least invasive procedure to deal with the behavior. Teachers will only need to proceed further with interventions and/or an FBA and BIP should the prior step fail.

Chapter 6

Marvin's target behaviors were his working and completing tasks. Consequences would be ongoing class activities. Antecedent behaviors were simply assignments. Problem behaviors included being off-task and throwing occasional tantrums. His problem behaviors allowed him to escape difficult tasks, especially those that involved handwriting. Marvin was taught to self-monitor and to make a sheet indicating when he was on-task and when he was off-task each time a tone sounded (initially every minute, then every five minutes). In lieu of handwriting assignments, Marvin was allowed to complete written assignments on the computer. Productivity increased, and tantrums (related to off-task behavior) decreased.

Chapter 7

Milton's target behavior was primarily to complete his assignments. The antecedent was being given a worksheet in math. Milton's problem behaviors were crumpling up the worksheet, failing to complete his work, and making disrespectful comments to the teacher. Milton was first assigned a peer tutor who helped him with directions and with the actual work. He was also given study guides for math. Complex tasks were broken down, and he was given more time to complete tasks. For each completed task in math, he received one point. For every five points, Milton received a no-homework pass (good for no math homework for one night). Also, considerable verbal praise was given for his asking for help, completing tasks, and talking appropriately to the teacher. During the first week, he completed three tasks; during the second week he completed five tasks.

Chapter 8

Justin's target behaviors were to work on-task, follow directions, and show appropriate behavior in social interactions. He received tokens as a consequence for appropriate behavior. Much of his misbehavior occurred during independent seat work. His problem behavior was described as being "disruptive" to the class. The teacher decided to give attention only to those who did the right thing (i.e., clowing behavior received no adult attention). Since only those who showed appropriate behavior received attention, almost all students quickly followed this path. To replace the attention-getting behavior of clowning, Justin was to earn tokens for completed work. When he received 20 tokens, he was allowed five minutes to entertain the class. He could show and tell or simply tell jokes. Justin was also instructed on how to ask for a break. When this was done correctly, he got a five-minute break after completing 50 percent of his work. Completion of 100 percent earned a token. Justin's behavior and academic work improved.

Appendix B

Vanderbilt ADHD Diagnostic Teacher Rating Scale

Name: _____ Grade: _____

Date of Birth: _____ Teacher: _____ School: _____

Each rating should be considered in the context of what is appropriate for the age of the children you are rating.

Frequency Code: 0 = Never; 1 = Occasionally; 2 = Often; 3 = Very Often

1.	Fails to give attention to details or makes careless mistakes in schoolwork.	0	1	2	3
2.	Has difficulty sustaining attention to tasks or activities.	0	1	2	3
3.	Does not seem to listen when spoken to directly.	0	1	2	3
4.	Does not follow through on instruction and fails to finish schoolwork (not due to oppositional behavior or failure to understand).	0	1	2	3
5.	Has difficulty organizing tasks and activities.	0	1	2	3
6.	Avoids, dislikes, or is reluctant to engage in tasks that require sustained mental effort.	0	1	2	3
7.	Loses things necessary for tasks or activities (school assignments, pencils, or books).	0	1	2	3
8.	Is easily distracted by extraneous stimuli.	0	1	2	3
9.	Is forgetful in daily activities.	0	1	2	3
10.	Fidgets with hands or feet or squirms in seat.	0	1	2	3
11.	Leaves seat in classroom or in other situations in which remaining seated is expected.	0	1	2	3

(Continued)

(Continued)

12.	Runs about or climbs excessively in situations in which remaining seated is expected.	0	1	2	3
13.	Has difficulty playing or engaging in leisure activities quietly.	0	1	2	3
14.	Is "on the go" or often acts as if "driven by a motor."	0	1	2	3
15.	Talks excessively.	0	1	2	3
16.	Blurts out answers before questions have been completed.	0	1	2	3
17.	Has difficulty waiting in line.	0	1	2	3
18.	Interrupts or intrudes on others (e.g., butts into conversations or games).	0	1	2	3
19.	Loses temper.	0	1	2	3
20.	Actively defies or refuses to comply with adults' requests or rules.	0	1	2	3
21.	Is angry or resentful.	0	1	2	3
22.	Is spiteful and vindictive.	0	1	2	3
23.	Bullies, threatens, or intimidates others.	0	1	2	3
24.	Initiates physical fights.	0	1	2	3
25.	Lies to obtain goods for favors or to avoid obligations (i.e., "cons" others).	0	1	2	3
26.	Is physically cruel to people.	0	1	2	3
27.	Has stolen items of nontrivial value.	0	1	2	3
28.	Deliberately destroys others' property.	0	1	2	3
29.	Is fearful, anxious, or worried.	0	1	2	3
30.	Is self-conscious or easily embarrassed.	0	1	2	3
31.	Is afraid to try new things for fear of making mistakes.	0	1	2	3
32.	Feels worthless or inferior.	0	1	2	3
33.	Blames self for problems, feels guilty.	0	1	2	3
34.	Feels lonely, unwanted, or unloved; complains that "no one loves him/her."	0	1	2	3
35.	Is sad, unhappy, or depressed.	0	1	2	3

Performance						
		Problematic		*Average*		*Above Average*
Academic Performance						
1. Reading		1	2	3	4	5
2. Mathematics		1	2	3	4	5
3. Written expression		1	2	3	4	5

	Problematic		Average		Above Average
Classroom Behavioral Performance					
1. Relationships with peers	1	2	3	4	5
2. Following directions/rules	1	2	3	4	5
3. Disrupting class	1	2	3	4	5
4. Assignment completion	1	2	3	4	5
5. Organizational skills	1	2	3	4	5

This sample scale was reprinted with permission of the author, Mark Wolrich, MD. Available at http://www.vanderbiltchildrens.org/interior.php?mid=5734.

Appendix C

Medication Side Effects Rating Scale

Name: _____ **Date:** _____

Teacher: _____ **Grade:** _____ **Age:** _____

Medication/Dose: _____

Instructions: Please rate each behavior for this child. Use the following scale for each behavior/complaint: 0 = Absent, 1 = Mild, 2 = Moderate, 3 = Severe, 4 = Profound. Please rate each behavior in the morning and in the afternoon.

Morning		*Afternoon*	
Behavior	*Rating*	*Behavior*	*Rating*
Tremor	0 1 2 3 4	Tremor	0 1 2 3 4
Dry Mouth	0 1 2 3 4	Dry Mouth	0 1 2 3 4
Stomach	0 1 2 3 4	Stomach	0 1 2 3 4
Decreased Appetite	0 1 2 3 4	Decreased Appetite	0 1 2 3 4
Nausea	0 1 2 3 4	Nausea	0 1 2 3 4
Dizziness	0 1 2 3 4	Dizziness	0 1 2 3 4
Tics	0 1 2 3 4	Tics	0 1 2 3 4
Allergic Reaction	0 1 2 3 4	Allergic Reaction	0 1 2 3 4
Nervousness	0 1 2 3 4	Nervousness	0 1 2 3 4
Skin Rash	0 1 2 3 4	Skin Rash	0 1 2 3 4
Tiredness	0 1 2 3 4	Tiredness	0 1 2 3 4
Daydreams	0 1 2 3 4	Daydreams	0 1 2 3 4

(Continued)

(Continued)

Morning		Afternoon	
Behavior	*Rating*	*Behavior*	*Rating*
Less Talkative	0 1 2 3 4	Less Talkative	0 1 2 3 4
Irritable	0 1 2 3 4	Irritable	0 1 2 3 4
Sleepy	0 1 2 3 4	Sleepy	0 1 2 3 4
Crying	0 1 2 3 4	Crying	0 1 2 3 4
Sad Face	0 1 2 3 4	Sad Face	0 1 2 3 4
Euphoric	0 1 2 3 4	Euphoric	0 1 2 3 4
Hallucinations	0 1 2 3 4	Hallucinations	0 1 2 3 4
Anxious	0 1 2 3 4	Anxious	0 1 2 3 4

Most Serious: _____

Most Significant (Morning): _____

Most Significant (Afternoon): _____

Appendix D

Selecting Target Behaviors

Name: _____ **Grade:** _____ **Age:** _____

Birth Date: _____ **Diagnosis:** _____

Note: Select problem behaviors by priority.

Problem Behavior	Rate Frequency	Rate Severity
1.		
2.		
3.		

The frequency and severity of the behavior problems must be assessed during a baseline procedure. Thus, before any intervention, three problem behaviors must be selected to be addressed. Remember, you must be able to define the behavior accurately (e.g., Mark hit John three times today).

Problem Behavior	Definition
1.	
2.	
3.	

Appendix E

Behavioral Intervention Form

Name: _____ Grade: _____ Age: _____

Birth Date: _____ Diagnoses: _____

Problem Behavior Selected: _____

_____

Definition of Problem Behavior (How Measured): _____

_____

Choosing the Behavioral Intervention (Check all that apply):

Ignoring _____

Overcorrection _____

Withdrawal of Privilege _____

When-Then _____

Point System _____

Token System _____

Contracts _____

Modeling _____

Behavioral Intervention Program

Specify how the problem behavior will be addressed:

Appendix F

Social Rewards

Nonverbal Reinforcement

Pat child on shoulder.

Wink.

Give a thumbs-up.

Pat child on head.

Smile.

Give OK sign.

Hug.

Place arm around child.

Verbal Reinforcement

Good for you!

Great!

Terrific!

Nice going.

Exactly right.

You are learning fast.

I'm very proud of you.

Fantastic!

You are really learning a lot.

You really make my job fun.

Right on!

You haven't missed a thing.

I like that.

Good work!

You're really improving.

Congratulations!

Now you have the hang of it.

Super good!

Outstanding!

Keep working on it. You're improving.

Way to go!

You are doing that much better today.

You're doing fine.

That's the right way.

You remembered!

You're getting better every day.

Much better!

You've got it made.

That was beautiful.

You are a joy.

Tremendous!

That's better than ever.

It's such a pleasure to work with you.

You've got your brain in gear.

You've got that down pat.

Super!

Congratulations—you did it!

You're on the right track.

Good job.

That's it!

You must have been practicing.

That was first-class work.

Keep on trying.

That's right!

Superb!

Sensational!

I've never seen anyone do it better.

That's good.

You're really going to town.

You're really working hard today.

Well, look at you go!

Now you have it!

Keep it up!

Extraordinary!

You certainly did well today.

Now you've figured it out.

That's wonderful.

Wow!

That's really nice.

You've just about got it.

Fine!

That's coming along nicely.

Good going.

You did it that time.

I think you've got it now.

Nothing can stop you now.

Good remembering!

That's the best ever.

That's much better.

You did that very well.

I'm happy to see you working like that.

Marvelous!

Couldn't have done it better myself.

Wonderful!

You are very good at that.

Now that's what I call a fine job.

That's the right way to do it.

Perfect!

You did a lot of work today.

One more time and you have it.

That's how to handle it.

That's the best job you've ever done.

That's great.

I knew you could do it.

You're doing beautifully.

You outdid yourself today.

You've just about mastered that.

Good thinking.

Excellent!

You figured that out fast.

Keep up the good work.

That kind of work makes me happy.

That's better.

I'm proud of the way you worked today.

You're making real progress.

That's the way to do it.

You're doing a good job.

That's quite an improvement.

Appendix G

Common Classroom Rewards

Homework reduction

Physical contact (hugs, pats, closeness)

Playing game with a friend

Computer access

Additional recess

Free time in class

Run errand/collect or distribute papers/other class job

Field trip

Class games

Tickets/stickers/a certificate/play money

Small toys (marble, car, doll, clay) or other prize

Breakfast or lunch with teacher

Time to finish homework in class

Reading special magazine or book

Food (cookies, raisins, banana chips, candy, gum, popcorn)

Listening to music on tape recorder (headphones)

Working with clay or Play-Doh

Special pen or paper

Leading in a game

Being first in line

Skipping an assignment

Bringing something to class (show and tell)

Reduction of detention time

Appendix H

*Minneapolis Public Schools,
Special Education Department K–6*

*Children's Classroom
Reinforcement Survey for Teachers*

Student: _____ Age: _____

Date of Rating: _____ Rating: _____ Grade Level: _____

SURVEY GUIDELINES

The survey should be filled out in the presence of the student. Ask each question in the relevant sections, recording the student's response. If the student refuses to answer, rely on your own judgment or on that of the parent(s).

To determine the most desired reinforcer in each category, employ the data received from the student's responses. Use the "Teacher's Notations" section to record that information.

The suggested reinforcers listed are just that—suggestions. You and the student determine the best reinforcer in the particular situation. You will find that the lists will be especially helpful when the student has difficulty giving an answer (e.g., "I don't know").

You should feel comfortable with the student receiving the selected reinforcer, and you should feel the student is really motivated to work for it.

Try to determine social reinforcers or reinforcing school activities that will motivate the child before going on to material or home-administered reinforcers. This survey is designed to help you go only as far as necessary to find a functional reinforcer; use only as much of the survey as you need to find a reinforcer that your student will work for.

1. If you did a good job, who would you like to know about it?

2. The classmates you enjoy being with most are . . . ?

3. Your favorite adult at school is . . . ?

4. A person at school you would do almost anything for is . . . ?

5. If you did better at school, you wish your teacher would . . . ?

6. The friend or person you would most like to spend more time with at school is _____. What would you most like to do together?

TEACHER'S NOTATIONS

What social reinforcers do you and your child feel he or she will most want to earn?

People to send positive notes of progress to (in order of preference):

    1.

    2.

    3.

People to spend more time with and the activity:

    1.

    2.

    3.

SCHOOL ACTIVITY REINFORCERS

This part of the survey focuses on what the student does or would wish to do at school with additional free time (e.g., art projects, recess, monitor jobs).

1. If I had a chance at school, I sure would like to . . . ?

2. Something I really want to do at school is . . . ?

3. I feel terrific at school when I'm doing . . . ?

4. My favorite school subject is . . . ?

5. Use the following list only if the student is having difficulty thinking of activities he or she would like to work toward.

Which of the following would you most like to work toward?

_____Select topic for group to discuss.

_____Read to a friend.

_____Read with a friend.

_____Tutor a slower classmate.

_____Have free time in the library.

_____Be in a class play.

_____Discuss something with the teacher for five minutes.

_____Use radio with earphones.

_____Be first in line.

_____Assist teacher with teaching.

_____Help custodian.

_____Run errands.

_____Read a story.

_____Select game/object for recess.

_____Care for class pets/flowers, etc.

_____Earn time for the entire class to do a favorite activity.

_____Dust, erase, clean, arrange chairs, etc.

_____Work puzzle (free time).

_____Choose seat for specified time.

_____Choose group activity.

Which two would be your favorites?

1.

2.

TEACHER'S NOTATIONS

Which activities would the child most want to earn (in order of preference)?

1.

2.

3.

4.

Do *not* go beyond this if activity reinforcers prove adequate to motivate your child.

MATERIAL REINFORCERS

These are the things the child does not own or have ready access to that he or she would most likely work toward. Remember, be realistic and include the parent's financial support whenever possible.

1. What is your favorite food?

2. If I had my choice of any of the following foods, I would pick . . . ?

_____Ice Cream	_____Peanuts	_____Marshmallows
_____Soft Drinks	_____Animal Crackers	_____Apples
_____Cookies	_____Jawbreakers	_____Gum
_____Candy Bars	_____Lemon Drops	_____Crackers
_____Potato Chips	_____Raisins	_____Life Savers
_____M&M's	_____Cake	_____Candy Kisses
_____Candy Canes	_____Popsicles	_____Popcorn
_____Milk	_____Fruit	_____Candy Corn
_____Sugar-Coated Cereals	_____Cracker Jacks	

Check all of those named. (Use only if student has difficulty picking his or her favorite or the favorite initially chosen is not realistic.)

TEACHER'S NOTATIONS

Do I have the parents' financial support?   ____Yes   ____No

Limits?

With these limits in mind, the student's favorite foods would be (in order):

1.

2.

3.

4.

5.

Which three would be your favorites?

1.

2.

3.

TEACHER'S NOTATIONS

With the financial limits in mind, which material reinforcers would your child most want to work for (in order)?

1.

2.

3.

4.

If you feel this reinforcer would be sufficient to motivate this child, stop here and design a program around the chosen reinforcer. If not, go on to the next section.

HOME REINFORCERS

Home reinforcers should only be used with the complete cooperation of the parents. Use the relevant questions from the previous questions, if applicable.

My two favorite TV shows are . . . ?

1.

2.

The thing I like to do most with my mother is . . . ?

The thing I like to do most with my father is . . . ?

When I have money at home, I like to . . . ?

I spend most of my time at home . . . ?

Something I would like to do more of at home, but presently cannot, is . . . ?

When I have money, I like to . . . ?

If I had a dollar, I'd . . . ?

What is the best reward you could give me?

My favorite toy or game is . . . ?

If I could pick any of the following items to have, I'd pick (use only if having difficulty in isolating rewarding contingencies) . . . ?

____Balls	____Banks	____Boats
____Puzzles	____Rings	____Blocks
____Combs	____Flowers	____Comics
____Storybooks	____Miniature Cars	____Jump Rope
____Chalk	____Marbles	____Balloons
____Clay	____Toy Jewelry	____Medals
____Address Book	____Cups	____Fans
____Flashlight	____Silly Putty	____Stamps
____"Good Deed" Charts	____Whistles	____Bookmarkers
____Makeup Kits	____Bean Bags	____Toys
____Pencils With Names	____Jumping Beans	____Book Covers
____Cartoons	____Crayons	____Paints
____Stuffed Animals	____Coloring Books	____Straw Hats
____Pick-Up Sticks		

Which three of the above would you most want to earn?

    1.

    2.

    3.

Some place you would like to go, but have not been able to as much as you would like, is . . . ?

The person at home or in your neighborhood with whom you would most like to spend more time is . . . ?

What would you like to do with that person?

TEACHER'S NOTATIONS

Possible suggestions for home contingencies in order of practicality:

1.

2.

3.

4.

ADDITIONAL COMMENTS

Is there anything at all that was not already mentioned that you would be willing to work for or earn?

Is there anyone you would want to be like when you are x years old (five years older than student)?

TEACHER'S NOTATIONS

Additional comments:

This form is reprinted from http://pic.mpls.k12.mn.us/sites/97711090-59b5-4f98-964e-932ab29cf5be/uploads/BEH-RST.pdf; it was produced by the Minneapolis Public Schools.

Appendix I

Student Reinforcement Surveys

STUDENT REINFORCEMENT SURVEY #1

This survey can be used if you are attempting to discover activity reinforcers for students.

Activity Reinforcers

1. The activity I would like to do in school if I had a chance is . . . ?

2. Something that we should do at school is . . . ?

3. I feel great at school when I am doing . . . ?

4. My favorite class at school is . . . ?

5. My favorite activity that we do in class is . . . ?

6. After my work is done and when there is more time, I would like to . . . ?

7. When I have time to choose something to do quietly, I like to . . . ?

8. Circle three activities that you might like to do at school:

Reading with a friend	Being outside with friends	Working on a project
Having free time in the library	Listening to music with headphones	Drawing, painting, or using clay

Being in a class discussion	Being first to leave class	Talking with friends
Doing chores for a teacher friends	Running errands	Playing a game with
Talking with a teacher	Reading something I choose	Playing a class game
Eating lunch with an adult	Eating lunch in a classroom	Walking to a nearby restaurant

STUDENT REINFORCEMENT SURVEY #2

If you discover that a student prefers adult attention, this survey could help to identify the adults with whom a child wishes to spend more time or who would motivate a child.

Survey of Reinforcers

1. If I did well on an assignment, I would like for someone to tell this adult at my school:

2. My favorite adult in the school is _____
   because . . .

3. A person at school for whom I would do almost anything is . . .

4. If I did better at school, I wish teachers would . . .

5. The adult with whom I would like to spend more time at school is . . .

6. The member of my family I would most want to be proud of my progress at school is . . .

Appendix J

Basic Behavioral Questions

Name: _____ Grade: _____ Age: _____

Birth Date: _____ Diagnosis: _____

Problem Behaviors

What is the primary function of the problem behavior? _____

_____

Problem behavior gets (1) _____ (2) _____

Problem behavior allows child to avoid (1) _____ (2) _____

What are the setting events for the problem behavior (i.e., what seems to set it off or trigger it)? Antecedent:

_____

_____

What comes immediately after the problem behavior? Consequence:

_____

_____

Alternative Behavior

Define:

_____

_____

Reinforcement to be used:

_____

_____

_____

Appendix K

School Accommodations and Modifications

Some students with disabilities need accommodations or modifications to their educational program to participate in the general curriculum and be successful in school. While the Individuals with Disabilities Education Act (IDEA) and its regulations do not define *accommodations* or *modifications*, there is some agreement as to what these terms mean.

An *accommodation*, as used in this document, allows a student to complete the same assignment or test as other students but with a change in the timing, formatting, setting, scheduling, response, and/or presentation. This accommodation does not alter in any significant way what the test or assignment measures. Examples of accommodations include a student taking a Braille version of a test or a student taking a test alone in a quiet room.

A *modification*, as used in this document, is an adjustment to an assignment or a test that changes the standard or what the test or assignment is supposed to measure. Examples of possible modifications include a student completing work on part of a standard rather than the entire standard or a student completing an alternate assignment that is more easily achievable than the standard assignment.

Needed modifications and accommodations should be written into a student's Individualized Education Program (IEP) or Section 504 Plan. These changes should be chosen to fit the student's individual needs. It's important to include the student, if appropriate, when discussing needed accommodations and modifications. Asking the student what would be helpful is a good first step.

Here are some ideas for changes in textbooks and curriculum, the classroom environment, instruction and assignments, and possible behavior expectations that may be helpful when educating students with disabilities. When reviewing these ideas, keep in mind that any accommodations or modifications an IEP team chooses must be based on the individual needs of students, and the changes must be provided if included in the child's IEP.

TEXTBOOKS AND CURRICULUM

Books

- Provide alternative books with similar concepts but at an easier reading level.
- Provide audiotapes of textbooks and have the student follow the text while listening.
- Provide summaries of chapters.
- Provide interesting reading material at or slightly above the student's comfortable reading level.

- Use peer readers.
- Use a marker to highlight important textbook sections.
- Use word-for-word sentence fill-ins.
- Provide two sets of textbooks, one for home and one for school.
- Use index cards to record major themes.
- Provide the student with a list of discussion questions before reading the material.
- Give page numbers to help the student find answers.
- Provide books and other written materials in alternative formats, such as Braille or large print.

Curriculum

- Shorten assignments to focus on mastery of key concepts.
- Shorten spelling tests to focus on mastering the most functional words.
- Substitute alternatives for written assignments (clay models, posters, panoramas, collections, etc.).
- Specify and list exactly what the student will need to learn to pass. Review this list frequently.
- Modify expectations based on student needs (e.g., "When you have read this chapter, you should be able to list three reasons for the Civil War").
- Give alternatives to long written reports (e.g., write several short reports, preview new audiovisual materials and write a short review, give an oral report on an assigned topic).

CLASSROOM ENVIRONMENT

- Develop individualized rules for the student.
- Evaluate the classroom structure against the student's needs (flexible structure, firm limits, etc.).
- Keep workspaces clear of unrelated materials.
- Keep the classroom quiet during intense learning times.
- Reduce visual distractions in the classroom (mobiles, etc.).
- Provide a computer for written work.
- Seat the student close to the teacher or a positive role model.
- Use a study carrel. (Provide extras so that the student is not singled out.)
- Seat the student away from windows or doorways.
- Provide an unobstructed view of the chalkboard, teacher, movie screen, etc.
- Keep extra supplies of classroom materials (pencils, books) on hand.
- Use alternatives to crossword puzzles or word finds.
- Maintain adequate space between desks.

INSTRUCTION AND ASSIGNMENTS

Directions

- Use both oral and printed directions.
- Give directions in small steps and in as few words as possible.

- Number and sequence the steps in a task.
- Have student repeat the directions for a task.
- Provide visual aids.
- Show a model of the end product of directions (e.g., a completed math problem or finished quiz).
- Stand near the student when giving directions or presenting a lesson.

Time/Transitions

- Alert student several minutes before a transition from one activity to another is planned; give several reminders.
- Provide additional time to complete a task.
- Allow extra time to turn in homework without penalty.
- Provide assistance when moving about the building.

Handwriting

- Use worksheets that require minimal writing.
- Use fill-in questions with space for a brief response rather than a short essay.
- Provide a "designated note taker" or photocopy of another student's or teacher notes. (Do not require a poor note taker or a student with no friends to arrange with another student for notes.)
- Provide a print outline with videotapes and filmstrips.
- Provide a print copy of any assignments or directions written on the blackboard.
- Omit assignments that require copying, or let the student use a tape recorder to dictate answers.

Grading

- Provide a partial grade based on individual progress or effort.
- Use daily or frequent grading averaged into a grade for the quarter.
- Weight daily work higher than tests for a student who performs poorly on tests.
- Mark the correct answers rather than the incorrect ones.
- Permit a student to rework missed problems for a better grade.
- Average grades out when assignments are reworked or base grades on corrected work.
- Use a pass-fail or an alternative grading system when the student is assessed on his or her own growth.

Tests

- Go over directions orally.
- Teach the student how to take tests (e.g., how to review, how to plan time for each section).
- Provide a vocabulary list with definitions.
- Permit as much time as needed to finish tests.
- Allow tests to be taken in a room with few distractions (e.g., the library).
- Have test materials read to the student and allow oral responses.

- Divide tests into small sections of similar questions or problems.
- Use recognition tests (true-false, multiple-choice, or matching) instead of essays.
- Allow the student to complete an independent project as an alternative test.
- Give progress reports instead of grades.
- Grade spelling separately from content.
- Provide typed test materials, not tests written in cursive.
- Allow take-home or open-book tests.
- Provide possible answers for fill-in-the blank sections.
- Provide the first letter of the missing word.

Math

- Allow the student to use a calculator without penalty.
- Group similar problems together (e.g., all addition in one section).
- Provide fewer problems on a worksheet (e.g., 4 to 6 problems on a page rather than 20 or 30).
- Require fewer problems to attain passing grades.
- Use enlarged graph paper to write problems to help the student keep numbers in columns.
- Provide a table of math facts for reference.
- Tape a number line to the student's desk.
- Read and explain story problems or break problems into smaller steps.
- Use pictures or graphics.

Other

- Use sticky notes to mark assignments in textbooks.
- Check progress and provide feedback often in the first few minutes of each assignment.
- Place a ruler under sentences being read for better tracking.
- Introduce an overview of long-term assignments so the student knows what is expected and when it is due.
- Break long-term assignments into small, sequential steps, with daily monitoring and frequent grading.
- Have the student practice presenting in a small group before presenting to the class.
- Hand out worksheets one at a time.
- Sequence work, putting the easiest part first.
- Use photocopies, not dittos.
- Provide study guides and study questions that directly relate to tests.
- Reinforce student for recording assignments and due dates in a notebook.
- Draw arrows on worksheets, the chalkboard, or overheads to show how ideas are related or use other graphic organizers, such as flowcharts.

Behavior

- Arrange a "check-in" time to organize the day.
- Pair the student with a student who is a good behavior model for class projects.
- Modify school rules that may discriminate against the student.
- Use nonverbal cues to remind the student of rule violations.

- Amend consequences for rule violations (e.g., reward a forgetful student for remembering to bring pencils to class, rather than punishing the failure to remember).
- Minimize the use of punishment; provide positive as well as negative consequences.
- Develop an individualized behavior intervention plan that is positive and consistent with the student's ability and skills.
- Increase the frequency and immediacy of reinforcement.
- Arrange for the student to leave the classroom voluntarily and go to a designated "safe place" when under high stress.
- Develop a system or a code word to let the student know when behavior is not appropriate.
- Ignore behaviors that are not seriously disruptive.
- Develop interventions for behaviors that are annoying but not deliberate (e.g., provide a small piece of foam rubber for the desk of a student who continually taps a pencil on the desktop).
- Be aware of behavior changes that relate to medication or the length of the school day; modify expectations if appropriate.

This document was produced under U.S. Department of Education Grant No. H326A980004. No official endorsement by the U.S. Department of Education of any product, commodity, service, or enterprise mentioned in this report or on Web sites referred to in this report is intended or should be inferred.

This form is available from http://www.osepideasthatwork.org/parentkit/school_accom_mods_eng.asp.

Appendix L

504 Accommodation Checklist

If you have a child who does not qualify for special education under IDEA but has a mental or physical impairment that substantially limits one or more major life activity, including learning, that child may qualify for special help in a regular classroom setting under section 504 of the Rehabilitation Act of 1973.

The following is a list of accommodations that may help your child succeed in the classroom. This list can be used as a reference for parents and school personnel.

PHYSICAL ARRANGEMENT OF ROOM

- Seating student near the teacher
- Seating student near a positive role model
- Standing near the student when giving directions or presenting lessons
- Avoiding distracting stimuli (air conditioner, high-traffic area, etc.)
- Increasing distance between desks

LESSON PRESENTATION

- Pairing students to check work
- Writing key points on the board
- Providing peer tutoring
- Providing visual aids, large print, films
- Providing peer note taker
- Making sure directions are understood
- Including a variety of activities during each lesson
- Repeating directions to the student after they have been given to the class, then having the student repeat and explain the directions to the teacher
- Providing written outline
- Allowing student to tape record lessons
- Having child review key points orally
- Teaching through multisensory modes: visual, auditory, kinesthetic, olfactory
- Using computer-assisted instruction

- Accompanying oral directions with written directions on blackboard or paper for child to refer to
- Providing a model to help students and posting the model and referring to it often
- Providing cross-age peer tutoring
- Assisting the student in finding the main idea of a passage by underlining, highlighting, making cue cards, etc.
- Breaking longer presentations into shorter segments

ASSIGNMENTS/WORKSHEETS

- Giving extra time to complete tasks
- Simplifying complex directions
- Handing worksheets out one at a time
- Reducing the reading level of the assignments
- Requiring fewer correct responses to achieve grade (quality versus quantity)
- Allowing student to tape record assignments/homework
- Providing a structured routine in written form
- Providing study skills training/learning strategies
- Giving frequent short quizzes and avoiding long tests
- Shortening assignments; breaking work into smaller segments
- Allowing typewritten or computer-printed assignments prepared by the student or dictated by the student and recorded by someone else if needed.
- Using self-monitoring devices
- Reducing homework assignments
- Not grading handwriting
- Not allowing student to use cursive or manuscript writing
- Not marking reversals and transpositions of letters and numbers wrong, instead pointing them out for corrections
- Not requiring lengthy outside reading assignments
- Monitoring student's self-paced assignments (daily, weekly, biweekly)
- Arranging for homework assignments to reach home with clear, concise directions
- Recognizing and giving credit for student's oral participation in class

TEST TAKING

- Allowing open book exams
- Giving exams orally
- Giving take-home tests
- Using more objective items (fewer essay responses)
- Allowing student to give test answers on tape recorder
- Giving frequent short quizzes, not long exams
- Allowing extra time for exams
- Reading test items to student
- Avoiding placing student under pressure of time or competition

ORGANIZATION

- Providing peer assistance with organizational skills
- Assigning volunteer homework buddy
- Allowing student to have an extra set of books at home
- Sending daily/weekly progress reports home
- Developing a reward system for completion of in-school work and homework
- Providing student with a homework assignment notebook

BEHAVIORS

- Using timers to facilitate task completion
- Structuring transitional and unstructured times (recess, hallways, lunchroom, locker room, library, assembly, field trips, etc.)
- Praising specific behaviors
- Using self-monitoring strategies
- Giving extra privileges and rewards
- Keeping classroom rules simple and clear
- Making "prudent use" of negative consequences
- Allowing for short breaks between assignments
- Cuing student to stay on-task (nonverbal signal)
- Marking student's correct answers, not mistakes
- Implementing a classroom behavior management system
- Allowing student time out of seat to run errands, etc.
- Ignoring inappropriate behaviors not drastically outside classroom limits
- Allowing legitimate movement
- Contracting with the student
- Increasing the immediacy of rewards
- Implementing time-out procedures

This form may be found at http://www.come-over.to/FAS/IDEA504.htm.

Appendix M

Graphic Depiction of Rules

Name:	Response Cost Card					
Date:	M	T	W	Th	F	Total
Rule Above	Points Lost					

Name:	Response Cost Card					
Date:	M	T	W	Th	F	Total
quiets down						
Rule Above	Points Lost					

(Continued)

(Continued)

Name:	Response Cost Card					
Date:	M	T	W	Th	F	Total
raises hand						
Rule Above	Points Lost					
Name:	Response Cost Card					
Date:	M	T	W	Th	F	Total
pays attention						
Rule Above	Points Lost					
Name:	Response Cost Card					
Date:	M	T	W	Th	F	Total
waits turn						
Rule Above	Points Lost					

Name:	Response Cost Card					
Date:	M	T	W	Th	F	Total
works hard						
Rule Above	Points Lost					

Name:	Response Cost Card					
Date:	M	T	W	Th	F	Total
is positive						
Rule Above	Points Lost					

Name:	Response Cost Card					
Date:	M	T	W	Th	F	Total
uses manners						
Rule Above	Points Lost					

(Continued)

(Continued)

Name:	Response Cost Card					
Date:	M	T	W	Th	F	Total
 knows how to ignore						
Rule Above	Points Lost					

Appendix N

Example: Recording Sheet for Social Skills

Social Skill	M	T	W	Th	F	Totals
Listening						
Following Rules						
Sharing						
Working/Playing Cooperatively						
Problem Solving						
Controlling Anger						
Totals						

Behavior Check Card

Behavior	Mon	Tues	Wed	Thurs	Fri	Sat	Sun
Working Cooperatively							
Playing Cooperatively							
Cumulative Totals							
Date	**Point Total Goal This Week**						

Resources

BOOKS

Barkley, R. A. (1995). *Taking charge of ADHD: The complete authoritative guide for parents.* New York: Guilford Press.

DuPaul, G. J., & Stoner, G. (2004). *ADHD in the schools.* New York: Guilford Press.

Elliott, D. S., Hamburg, B. A., & Williams, K. R. (1998). *Violence in American schools: A new perspective.* Cambridge, England: Cambridge University Press.

Lougy, R. A., & Rosenthal, D. K. (2002). *ADHD: A survival guide for parents and teachers.* Duarte, CA: Hope Press.

Pierangelo, R., & Giuliana, J. D. (2007). *The educator's diagnostic manual of disabilities and disorders.* San Francisco: Jossey-Bass.

Rief, S. R. (2005). *How to reach and teach children with ADD/ADHD.* San Francisco: Jossey-Bass.

Rosenberg, M. S., Wilson, R., Maheady, C., & Sindelar, P. T. (2004). *Educating students with behavior disorders.* Boston: Allen & Bacon.

Sugai, G., & Horner, R. H. (2000). *Functional behavioral assessments.* Mahwah, NJ: Lawrence Erlbaum.

Watson, S. W., & Skinner, C. H. (Eds.). (2004). *Encyclopedia of school psychology.* New York: Springer.

Wright, P. W. D., & Wright, P. D. (2005). *Wrightslaw: IDEA 2004.* Hartfield, VA: Harbor House Low Press.

ARTICLES

Barkley, R. A. (1997). Behavioral inhibition, sustained attention, and executive functions: Constructing a unifying theory of ADHD. *Psychological Bulletin, 124,* 65–94

Barkley, R. A., Connor, D. F., & Kwasnik, D. (2000). Challenges to determining drug responding in an outpatient clinical setting: Comparing Adderall & methlphenidate in adolescents with ADHD. *Journal of Attention Disorders, 4,* 102–113.

Gottfredson, D. C. (1997). School-based crime prevention. In L. W. Sherman, D. C. Gottfredson, D. Mackenzie, J. Eck, P. Reuter, & S. Bushway (Eds.), *Preventing crime: What works, what doesn't, what's promising; A report to the United States Congress* (NCJ 171676; pp. 125–182). Washington, DC: U.S. Department of Justice, Office of Justice Programs.

Gunter, P. L., Denny. R. K., Jack, S. L., Sherer, R. E., & Nelson, C. M. (1993). Aversive stimuli in academic interactions between students with serious emotional disturbance and their teachers. *Behavior Disorders, 19,* 265–274.

Mayer, G. R. (1995). Preventing antisocial behavior in the schools. *Journal of Applied Behavior Analysis, 28*(4), 467–492.

Salend, S. J., Jantzen, N. R., & Giek, K. (1992). Using a peer confrontation system in a group setting. *Behavioral Disorders, 17,* 211–218.

Skiba, R. J., Peterson, R. L., & Williams, T. (1997). Office referrals and suspension: Disciplinary intervention in middle schools. *Education and Treatment of Children, 20,* 295–315.

Walker, H. M., Horner, R. A., Sugai, G., Bullis, M., Sprague, J. R., Brieker, D., et al. (1996). Integrated approaches to preventing antisocial behavior patterns among school-age children & youth. *Journal of Emotional & Behavioral Disorders, 4,* 193–256.

VIDEOS

Goldstein, S., & Goldstein, M. (1990). *Educating inattentive children.* Salt Lake City, UT: Neurology Learning & Behavior Center.

Rief, S. (1993). *Inclusive instruction and collaborative practices.* New York: National Professional Resources.

CATALOGS

ADD Warehouse
300 NW 70th Avenue,
Suite 102
Plantation, FL 33317
Phone: (954) 792-8944
Orders: (800) 233-9273

Childswork/Childsplay
135 Dupont Street
PO Box 760
Plainview, NY 11803-0760
Phone: (800) 962-1141
Web: http://www.childswork.com

INTERNET RESOURCES

Addressing Student Problem Behavior: Part 1 (1998): http://www.air.org/cecp/fba/problembehavior/main.htm

Addressing Student Problem Behavior: Part 2 (1998): http://www.air.org/cecp/fba/problembehavior2/main2.htm

Addressing Student Problem Behavior: Part 3 (1999): http://www.air.org/cecp/fba/problembehavior3/main3.htm

Lesson Plan for Teachers, Special Educators, etc.: http://www.youthchg.com

National Dissemination Center for Children With Disabilities (NICHCY) Publications: http://www.nichcy.org/pubs1.htm

One ADD Place: http://www.oneaddplace.com

Resources for Students in Transition: http://www.attainmentcompany.com

Resources for Students With Behavioral/Discipline Problems: http://www.taalliance.org/research

Special Education Resources and Information: http://www.educationworld.com

Teacher Education Videos and DVDs: http://www.business-marketing.com

Teacher Posters: Interventions for Students With Behavior Disorders: http://www.youthchg.com

Teacher's Guide to the U.S. Dept. of Education (2000): http://www.ed.gov/pubs/TeachersGuide/index.html

NEWSLETTERS

ITN (Innovative Teaching Newsletter): http://surfaquarium.com/NEWSLETTER
Mental Health Information (Disruptive Behavior Disorders): http://www.athealth.com/practitioner/
    newsletter/fpn_subscribe.html
My ADHD: ADD Warehouse: http://www.myadhd.com

ORGANIZATIONS/ASSOCIATIONS

America Counseling Association
Phone: (800) 347-6647
Web: http://www.counseling.org

American Academy of Child & Adolescent
    Psychiatry
Phone: (202) 966-7300
Web: http://www.aacap.org

American Academy of Special
    Education Professionals
Phone: (800) 424-0371
Web: http://aasep.org

American Federation of Teachers
Phone: (202) 879-4400
Web: http://www.aft.org
E-mail: online@aft.org

American Psychological Association (APA)
Phone (202) 336-5500, (800) 374-2721
Web: http://www.apa.org

Center for Effective Collaboration and
    Practice
Phone: (888) 457-1551
Web: http://cecp.air.org

Children and Adults With Attention
    Deficit/Hyperactivity Disorder (CHADD)
Phone: (800) 233-4050
Web: http://www.chadd.org

Council for Children With Behavioral
    Disorders (CCBD)
Phone: (913) 239-0550
Web: http://www.ccbd.net

Council for Exceptional Children
Phone: (800) 328-0272
Web: http://www.cec.sped.org

International Dyslexia Association
Phone: (800) 222-3123
Web: http://www.interdys.org

Learning Disabilities Association
    of America (LDA)
Phone: (412) 341-1515
Web: http://www.ldanatl.org

National Alliance on Mental Illness (NAMI)
Phone: (703) 524-7600
Web: http://www.nami.org

National Association of School
    Psychologists (NASP)
Phone: (301) 657-0270
Web: http://www.nasponline.org
E-mail: nasp@naspweb.org

National Association of Special Education
    Teachers (NASET)
Phone: (800) 754-4421
Web: http://www.naset.org

National Education Association
Phone: (202) 833-4000
Web: http://www.nea.org

National Information Center for Children
    With Disabilities (NICHCY)
Phone: (800) 695-0285
Web: http://www.nichcy.org

National Mental Health Information
    Center (SAMHSA)
Phone: (800) 789-2647
Web: http://mentalhealth.samhsa.gov

Positive Behavioral Interventions and Supports
    (OSEP Center on Effective Schoolwide
    Interventions)
Web: http://www.pbis.org

School Social Work Association of America
Phone: (847) 289-4642
Web: http://www.sswaa.org
E-mail: sswa@aol.com

Society for Developmental-Behavioral Health
Phone: (703) 556-4222
Web: http://www.sdbp.org

PUBLISHERS

Academic Therapy Publications
Phone (800) 422-7249
Web: http://www.academictherapy.com

Allyn & Bacon Longman
Phone (800) 947-7700, (866) 346-7314
Web: http://www.allynbaconmerrill.com

American Psychiatric Publishing
Phone (800) 368-5777
Web: http://www.appi.org

Barrons Educational Service Inc.
Phone (800) 645-3476
Web: http://barronseduc.com

Cambridge University Press
Web: http://www.uk.cambridge.org

Corwin
Phone (800) 818-7243
Web: http://www.corwin.com

Free Spirit Publishing
Phone (800) 735-7323
Web: http://www.freespirit.com

Guilford Press
Phone (800) 365-7006
Web: http://www.guilford.com

HarperCollins
Phone (800) 331-3761
Web: http://www.harpercollins.com

John Wiley & Sons
Phone (877) 762-2974
Web: http://www.wiley.com

Jossey-Bass
Phone (415) 433-1740
Web: http://www.josseybass.com

Magination Press
Phone (800) 374-2721
Web: http://www.maginationpress.com

New Harbinger Publications
Phone (800) 847-6273
Web: http://www.newharbinger.com

Paul H. Brooks
Phone (800) 638-3775
Web: http://www.brookespublishing.com

Pearson Higher Education
Phone (800) 526-0485
Web: http://www.pearsonhighered.com

Pro-Ed
Phone (800) 897-3200, (512) 451-3246
Web: http://www.proedinc.com

Research Press
Phone (217) 352-3273
Web: http://www.researchpress.com

SAGE
Phone (800) 818-7243
Web: http://www.sagepub.com

Scholastic Inc.
Phone (800) SCHOLASTIC or
   (800) 724-6527
Web: http://www.scholastic.com

Sopris West
Phone (800) 547-6747
Web: http://sopriswest.com

Specialty Press (ADD Warehouse)
Phone (800) 233-9273
eb: http://www.addwarehouse.com

Springer
Phone (781) 871-6600
Web: http://www.springer.com

Teachers College Press
Phone (800) 575-6566
Web: http://www.teacherscollegepress.com

Woodbine House
Phone (800) 843-7323
Web: http://www.woodbinehouse.com

BEHAVIORAL JOURNALS

Behavior Analysts Today
Web: http://www.behavior-analyst-online.org

Behavioral Interventions
Phone (800) 825-7550
Web: http://www3.interscience.wiley.com/journal/24375/home

Behavior Modification
Phone (800) 818-7243
Web: http://bmo.sagepub.com

Journal for the Education of Students Placed at Risk (JESPAR)
Phone (502) 852-0616
Web: https://louisville.edu/education/jespar

Journal of Applied Behavior Analysis
Phone (785) 841-4425
Web: http://seab.envmed.rochester.edu/jaba

Journal of Behavioral Education
Phone (212) 460-1500
Web: http://www.springerlink.com/content/105719

Journal of Positive Behavioral Interventions
Phone (212) 352-1404
Web: http://jpbi.sagepub.com

Journal of School Psychology
Phone (402) 472-5923
Web: http://www.elsevier.com/locate/jschpsyc

GLOSSARY

Behavioral Analysis Terms: http://www.coedu.usf.edu/abaglossary/main.asp

Behavioral Health Terms: http://www.uihealthcare.com/depts/uibehavioralhealth/patiented/glossary/html

Behavioral Intervention Terms: http://www.usu.edu/teachall/text/behavior/BEHAVglos.htm

Terms Used in Behavior Research: http://www.psychology.uiowa.edu/faculty/wasserman/glossary

Treatment Description: http://www.aacap.org/publications/factsfam/continum.htm

References

Acevedo-Polakovich, I. A., Lorch, E. P., Milich, R., & Ashby, R. D. (2006). Disentangling the relation between television viewing and cognitive processes in children with attention deficit hyperactivity disorder and comparison children. *Archives of Pediatric and Adolescent Medicine, 160*, 354–360.

Achenbach, T. M., & Rescorla, L. A. (2001). *Manual for the ASEBA School-Age Forms and Profiles.* Burlington: University of Vermont, Research Center for Children, Youth and Families.

Agran, M., Sinclair, T., Alper, M., Cavin, M., Wehmeyer, M., & Hughes, C. (2005). Using self-monitoring to increase following-direction skills of students with moderate to severe disabilities in general education. *Education & Training in Developmental Disabilities, 40*(1), 3–13.

Allen, K. E., & Cowdery, G. E. (2004). *The exceptional child: Inclusion in early childhood education* (5th ed.). Albany, NY: Thompson/Delmar.

American Academy of Pediatrics. (2000). Clinical guidelines: Diagnosis and evaluation of the child with attention deficit/hyperactivity disorder. *Pediatrics, 105*(5), 1158–1170.

American Psychiatric Association (APA). (2000). *Diagnostic and statistical manual of mental disorders* (4th ed., text rev.). Washington, DC: Author.

Anastopoulas, A. D., & Shelton, T. L. (2001). *Assessing attention deficit hyperactivity disorder.* New York: Kluwer Academic/Plenum Press.

Archer, A. & Gleason, M. (1989). *Skills for school success (Grades 3–6).* North Billerica, MA: Curriculum.

Azrin, H. H. & Holz, W. C. (1966). Punishment. In W. K. Homig, (Ed.), *Operant behavior: Areas of research & application.* New York: L Appleton Century Crafts.

Barkley, R. A. (1990). *Attention deficit/hyperactivity disorder: A handbook for diagnosis and treatment.* New York: Guilford Press.

Barkley, R. A. (2000). *Taking charge of ADHD: The complete, authoritative guide for parents* (Rev. ed.). New York: Guilford Press.

Barkley, R. A. (2002). Major life activity and health outcomes associated with attention-deficit-hyperactivity disorder. *Journal of Clinical Psychiatry, 63*, 10–15.

Barkley, R. A. (2005). *Attention-deficit hyperactivity disorder: A handbook for diagnosis & treatment* (3rd ed.). New York: Guilford Press.

Barkley, R. A., Fisher, M., Smallish, L., & Fletcher, K. (2002). The persistence of attentional-deficit hyperactivity disorder into young adulthood as a function of reporting source and definition of disorder. *Journal of Abnormal Psychology, 111*, 279–289.

Barkley, R. A., Fischer, M., Smallish, L., & Fletcher, K. (2006). Young adult outcome of hyperactive children: Adaptive functioning in major life areas. *Journal of the American Academy of Child & Adolescent Psychiatry, 45*, 192–202.

Barth, P. (2008, August 6). *Time out: Is recess in danger?* Retrieved August 12, 2009, from Center for Public Education Web site: http://www.centerforpubliceducation.org

Bender, W. N. (2007). *Relational discipline: Strategies for in-your-face kids* (2nd ed.). Charlotte, NC: Information Age.

Biederman, J., Faraone, S., Millberger, S., Guite, J., Mick, E., Chen, L., et al. (1996). A prospective 4-year follow-up study of attention-deficit hyperactivity and related disorders. *Archives of General Psychiatry, 53*(5), 437–446.

Biederman, J., Faraone, S., Monuteaux, M. C., Buber, M., & Cadogen, E. (2004). Gender effects on attention-deficit/hyperactivity disorder in adults, revisited. *Biological Psychiatry, 55*, 692–700.

Biederman, J., Mick, E., & Faraone, S. V. (2000). Age-dependent decline of symptoms of attention-deficit/hyperactivity disorder: Impact of remission definition and symptom type. *American Journal of Psychiatry, 157*, 816–818.

Bird, H. R., Canino, G. J., Davies, M. N., Ramirez, R., Shavez, L., Duarte, C., et al. (2005). The Brief Impairment Scale (BIS): A multidimensional scale of functional impairment for children & adolescents. *Journal of the American Academy of Child & Adolescent Psychiatry, 44*(7), 669–707.

Bohnert, A. M., Crnic, K. A., & Lim, K. G. (2003). Emotional competence and aggressive behavior in school-age children. *Journal of Abnormal Child Psychology, 37*, 79–91.

Borland, B. L., & Heckman, H. K. (1976). Hyperactive boys and their mothers: A 25-year follow-up study. *Archives of General Psychiatry, 33*, 669–675.

Boyajian, A. E., DuPaul, G. J., Handler, M. W., Eckert, T. L., & McGoey, K. E. (2001). The use of classroom-based brief functional analysis with preschoolers at-risk for attention deficit hyperactivity disorder. *The School Psychology Review, 30*(2), 278–293.

Boyd, R., & Richardson, P. J. (1985). *Culture and the evolutionary process.* Chicago: University of Chicago Press.

Brigham, F. J., & Brigham, M. M. (2004). *Processing emotions.* Charlottesville: University of Virginia, School of Continuing Education and Professional Studies. Retrieved August 12, 2009, from the University of Kansas Web site: http://www.specialconnections.ku.edu/~specconn/page/behavior/ub/pdf/casea/ProcessingEmotions-final.doc

Brown, R. T., Freeman, W. S., Pervin, T. M., Stein, M. T., Amler, R. W., Feldman, H. M., et al. (2001). Prevalence and assessment of attention-deficit/hyperactivity disorder in primary care settings. *Pediatrics, 107*(3), e43.

Brown, T. E. (2005). *Attention deficit disorder: The unfocused mind in children & adults.* New Haven, CT: Yale University Press.

Brown, T. E. (2009). *ADHD comorbidities: ADHD complications in children & adults.* Arlington, VA: American Psychiatric.

Bushman, B. T., & Anderson, C. A. (2001). Media violence and the American public: Scientific facts versus media misinformation. *American Psychologist, 56*(6/8), 477–489.

Campbell, S. B. (2006). Behavior problems in pre-school children: A review of recent research. *Journal of Child Psychology & Psychiatry, 36*(1), 113–149.

Carlson, G. L., & Mann, M. (2002). Sluggish cognitive tempo predicts a different pattern on impairment in the attention deficit hyperactivity disorder, predominantly inattentive type. *Journal of Clinical Child & Adolescent Psychology, 31*(1), 123–129.

Carr, E. G. (1977). The motivation of self-injurious behavior: A review of some hypothesis. *Psychological Bulletin, 84*, 800–815

Castellanos, F. X., Giedd, J. N., Marsh, W. L., Hamburger, S. D., Vaituzis, A. C., Dickstein, D. P., et al. (1996). Quantitative brain magnetic resonance imaging in attention-deficit-hyperactivity disorder. *Archives of General Psychiatry, 53*, 607–616.

Cavalier, A. R., & Bear, G. G. (2005). Behavior replacement techniques for correcting misbehavior. In G. G. Bear (Ed.), *Developing self-discipline and preventing and correcting misbehavior.* Boston: Allyn & Bacon.

Center for Education Policy (CEP). (2008). *Instructional time in elementary schools: A closer look at changes for specific subjects.* Washington, DC: Author.

Centers for Disease Control and Prevention (CDC). (2006). *School Health Policy and Programs Study (SHPPS) 2006: Overview.* Retrieved August 12, 2009, from http://www.cdc.gov/healthyyouth/shpps/2006/factsheets/pdf/FS_overview_SHPPS2006.pdf

Chamberlain, P., & Patterson, G. R. (1995). Discipline and child compliance. In M. H. Bornstrain (Ed.), *Handbook of parenting: Vol. 4. Applied and practical parenting* (pp. 205–223). Mahwah, NJ: Erlbaum.

Christophersen, E., & VanScoyoc, S. M. (2007). *What makes time-out work (and fail)?* Retreived August 12, 2009, from http://www.dbpeds.org/articles/detail.cfm?textID=739

Clark, L. S. (1985). *SOS! Help for parents.* Bowling Green, KY: Parents Press.

Cole, M., Cole, S. R., & Lightfoot, C. (2004). *The development of children.* New York: Worth.

Coleman, M. C., & Webber, J. (2002). *Emotional & behavioral disorders: Theory and practice* (4th ed.). Boston: Allyn & Bacon.

Cooper, C. S., Peterson, N. L., & Meier, J. A. (1987). Variables associated with disrupted placement in a select sample of abused & neglected children. *Child Abuse & Neglect, 11*(1), 75–86.

Cooper, L. J., Wacher, D. P., Brown, K., McComars, J. J., Peck, S. M., Drew, J., et al. (1999). Use of a concurrent operant paradigm to evaluate positive reinforcers during treatment of food refusal. *Behavior Modification, 23*(1), 3–40.

Cruz, N. V., & Bahna, S. L. (2006). Do food or additives cause behavior disorders? *Pediatric Annuals, 35,* 744–745, 748–754.

Dayton, T. (1991). *Daily affirmations for parents: How to nurture your children and renew yourself during the ups and downs of parenthood.* Deerfield Beach: Health Communications.

DeNoon, D. J. (2006). *Do ADHD drugs stunt kids' growth?* Retrieved August 12, 2009, from http://www.webmd.com/add-adhd/news/20060501/adhd-drugs-stunt-growth

DeShazo, B. T., Lyman, R. D., & Klinger, L. G. (2002). Academic underachievement and attention-deficit/hyperactive disorder: The negative impact of symptom severity on school performance. *Journal of School Psychology, 40,* 259–283.

Dixon, M. R., Horner, M. J., & Guercio, J. (2003). Self-control and the preference for delayed reinforcement: An example in brain injury. *Journal of Applied Behavior Analysis, 36,* 371–374.

Dunn, J., & Brunner, J. S. (2004). *Children's friendships: The beginning of intimacy.* Hoboken, NJ: Wiley-Blackwell.

DuPaul, G. J. (1991). Parent and teacher ratings of ADHD symptoms: Psychometric properties in a community-based sample. *Journal of Clinical Child Psychology, 20*(3), 245–253.

DuPaul, G. J., & Stoner, G. (2003). *ADHD in the schools: Assessment & intervention strategies* (2nd ed.). New York: Guilford.

DuPaul, G. J., Stoner, G., & O'Reilly, M. J. (2002). Best practice in classroom interventions for attention problems. In A Thomas & J. Grimes (Eds.), *Best practice in school psychology IV, Vol. 2* (pp. 1115–1127). Bethesda, MD: The National Association of School Psychologists.

DuPaul, G. J., & White, G. P. (2004). Counseling 101: An ADHD primer. *Principal Leadership, 5*(2), 11–15.

Eddy, J. M., Reid, J. B., & Curry, V. (2002). The etiology of youth antisocial behavior, delinquency and violence and a public health approach to prevention. In M. R. Shinn, H. M. Walker, & G. Stoner (Eds.), *Intervention for academic and behavior problems II: Preventive and remedial approaches* (pp. 27–51). Bethesda, MD: National Association of School Psychologists.

Ellison, A. T. (2002). An overview of childhood and adolescent ADHD: Understanding the complexities of development into the adult years. In S. Goldstein & A. T. Ellison (Eds.), *Clinician's guide to adult ADHD: Assessment and intervention* (pp. 1–23). San Diego, CA: Academic Press.

Emmons, P. G., & Anderson, L. M. (2005). *Understanding sensory dysfunction in learning, development and sensory dysfunction in autism spectrum disorders, ADHD, learning disabilities and bipolar disorder.* London: Jessica Kingsley.

Enger, T., Russell, N., Setzer, J., & Walkanoff, J. (1998). *Methods of improving active listening skills with relation to following directions.* Master's thesis, Saint Xavier University of IRI/Skylight, Chicago, 1998. (ERIC Document Reproduction Service No. ED420887)

Erchul, W. P., & Martens, B. K. (2002). *School consultation: Conceptual & empirical bases of practice* (2nd ed.). New York: Kluwer Academic/Plenum.

Fabiano, G. A., et al. (2007). The single and combined effects of multiple intensities of behavior modification and methylphenidate for children with attention deficit hyperactivity disorder in a classroom setting. *School Psychology Review, 25*(2), 195–216.

Faraone, S. W., Biederman, J., & Mick. E. (2006). The age-dependent decline of attention deficit hyperactivity disorder: A meta-analysis of follow-up studies. *Psychological Medicine, 36,* 159–165.

Finley, L. L. (2007). *Encyclopedia of juvenile violence.* Santa Barbara, CA: Greenwood Press.

Fischer, M., Barkley, R. A., Smallish, L., & Fletcher, K. (2002). Young adult follow-up of hyperactive children: Self-reported conduct problems and Teen CD. *Jounal of Abnormal Child Psychology, 30,* 463–475.

Flick, G. L. (1996). *Power parenting for children with ADD/ADHD: A practical parents' guide for managing difficult behaviors.* San Francisco: Jossey-Bass.

Flick, G. L. (1998). *ADD/ADHD behavior-change resource kit.* San Francisco: Jossey-Bass.

Flick, G. L. (2000). *How to reach & teach teenagers with ADHD: A step-by-step guide to overcoming difficult behaviors at school and at home.* San Francisco, CA: Jossey-Bass.

Flick, G. L. (2001). *Homework skills improvement kit: A training program to help children with ADD/ADHD.* Biloxi, MS: Seacoast.

Flick, G. L. (2002). Controversies in ADHD: Fundamental questions being answered slowly, but scientifically. *Advances for Nurse Practitioners, 10*(2), 34–36.

Forehand, R. L., & McMahon, R. J. (1981). *Helping the noncompliant child: A clinician's guide to parenting.* New York: Guilford.

Fox, C. L., & Boulton, M. T. (2005). The social skills problems of victims of bullying: Self, peer and teacher perceptions. *British Journal of Educational Psychology, 75,* 313–328.

Friedberg, R. D., & McClure, J. M. (2002). *Clinical practice of cognitive therapy with children and adolescents: The nuts and bolts.* New York: Guilford.

Goldman, L. S., Genel, M., Bezman, R. J., & Slanetz, P. J. (1998). Diagnosis and treatment of attention deficit/hyperactivity disorder in children & adolescents. *Journal of the American Medical Association, 279,* 1100–1107.

Goldstein, A. P., Harootunian, B., & Conoley, J. C. (1994). *Student aggression: Prevention, management, and replacement training.* New York: Guilford Press.

Goldstein, G., & Incagnoli, T. M. (Eds.). (1997). *Contemporary approaches to neuropsychological assessment.* New York: Plenum.

Goldstein, H. (2002). Communication intervention for children with autism: A review of treatment efficacy. *Journal of Autism & Developmental Disorders, 32*(5), 373–396.

Goldstein, S., & Goldstein, M. G. (1998). *Managing attention deficit hyperactivity disorder in children: A guide for practitioners.* New York: John Wiley & Sons.

Goldstein, S., & Teeter-Ellison, A. (2002). *Clinician's guide to adult ADHD.* New York: Academic Press.

Goodwin, D. W., Schulsinger, F., Hermansen, L., Guze, S. B., & Winokur, G. (1975). Alcoholism and the hyperactive child syndrome. *Journal of Nervous & Mental Disease, 160,* 349–353.

Graetz, B. W., Sawyer, M. G., Hazell, P. L., Arney, F. M., & Baghurst, P. A. (2001). Validity of DSM-IV ADHD subtypes in a nationally representative sample of Australian children & adolescents. *Journal of the American Academy of Child Adolescent Psychiatry, 40*(12), 1410–1417.

Gross-Tsur, V., Goldzweig, G., Landan, Y. E., Berger, R., Shmuelli, D., & Shalev, R. S. (2006). *Developmental Medicine & Child Neurology, 48*(11), 901–905.

Hamre, B. K. & Pianta, R. C. (2001). Early teacher-child relationships and the trajectory of children's school outcomes through eighth grade. *Child Development, 72*(2), 625–638.

Hartman, C. A., Willcutt, E. G., Rhee, S. A., & Pennington, B. F. (2004). The relation between sluggish cognitive tempo and DSM-IV ADHD. *Journal of Abnormal Child Psychology, 32,* 491–503.

Harvey, V. S., & Chickie-Wolfe, L. A. (2007). *Fostering independent learning: Practical strategies to promote student success.* New York: Guilford.

Hinshaw, S. P., & Park, T. (1999). Research issues and problems: Toward a more definitive science of disruptive behavior disorders. In H. C. Quay & A. E. Hogan (Eds.), *Handbook of disruptive behavior disorders* (pp. 593–620). New York: Plenum Press.

Hoch, H., McComas, J. J., Johnson, L., Faranda, N., & Guenther, S. L. (2002). The effects of magnitude and quality of reinforcement on choice responding during play activities. *Journal of Applied Behavior Analysis, 35*(2), 171–181.

Horner, R., Carr, E. G., Strain, P. S., Todd, A. W., & Reed, H. K. (2002). Problem behavior interventions for young children with autism: A research synthesis. *Journal of Autism & Developmental Disorders, 32,* 426–446.

Hubert, E. R., Weber, K. P., & McLaughlin, T. F. (2000). A comparison of copy, cover & compare and a traditional spelling intervention for an adolescent with conduct disorder. *Child & Family Behavior Therapy, 22*(3), 55–68.

Ingersoll, R. M. (2003). *Is there really a teacher shortage? A research report* (R-03-4). Seattle: Center for the Study of Teaching & Policy, University of Washington. Available August 12, 2009, at http://depts.washington.edu/ctpmail/PDFs/Shortage-RI-09-2003.pdf

Jackson, L. (2002). *Positive behavioral support in the classroom.* Baltimore, MD: P. H. Brooks.

Jarrett, O. S. (2002). *Recess in elementary school: What does the research say?* Retrieved August 12, 2009, from http://www.ericdigests.org/2003-2/recess.html

Jimerson, S. R., & Brock, S. E. (2004). Threat assessment, school crisis preparation, and school crisis response. In M. J. Furlong, M. P. Bates, D. C. Smith, & P. M. Kingery (Eds.), *Appraisal and prediction of school violence: Context, issues and methods* (pp. 63–82). Hauppauge, NY: Nova.

Johnson, D. E., & Conners, C. K. (2002). The assessment process: Conditions and comorbidities. In S. Goldstein & T. Ellison (Eds.), *Clinician's guide to adult ADHD: Assessment & intervention* (pp. 71–83). San Diego, CA: Academic Press.

Johnson, S. M., & The Project on the Next Generation of Teachers. (2006). Why new teachers stay. *American Educator, 30*(2), 8–21.

Kalb, L. M., & Loeber, R. (2003). Child disobedience and noncompliance: A review. *Pediatrics, 111*(3), 641–652.

King, R. A. et al. (1997). Practice parameters for the psychiatric assessment of children and adolescents. *Journal of the American Academy of Child & Adolescent Psychiatry, 36*(10 Suppl), 4S–20S. Available August 12, 2009, at http://www.aacap.org/galleries/PracticeParameters/Chiladol.pdf

Kolko, D. J., Bukstein, O. G., & Barron, J. (1999). Methylphenidate and behavior modification and children with ADHD and comorbid ODD or CD: Main & incremental effects across settings. *Journal of the American Academy of Child & Adolescent Psychiatry, 38*(5), 578–586.

Kendall, T. (1999). Sibling accounts of ADHD. *Family Process, 38*, 117–136.

Kern, L., & Dunlap, G. (1999). Assessment-based interventions for children with emotional and behavioral disorders. In A. C. Repp & R. A. Horner (Eds.), *Functional analysis of problem behavior: From effective assessment to effective support* (pp. 197–218). Belmont, CA: Wadsworth.

Kerr, M. (2002). *Strategies for addressing behavior problems in the classroom.* Upper Saddle River, NJ: Merrill.

Klein, R. G. (2001). MTA findings fail to consider methodological issues. *Archives of General Psychiatry, 58*, 1184–1185.

Koetz, L., & Pittel, A. (2009). *Contingency contracts to reduce disruptive classroom behavior: Recommendations for teachers.* Retrieved August 12, 2009, from the University of Delaware Web site: http://www.udel.edu/education/masters/psychology/handbook/recommendations/ContingencyContracts.doc

Krain, A. L., & Castellanos, F. X. (2006). Brain development & ADHD. *Clinical Psychology Review, 26*(4), 433–444.

Kutscher, M. L., & Puder, D. (2008). *ADHD—Living without brakes.* London: Jessica Kingsley.

Lahey, B. B., Pelham, W. E., Loney, J., Lee, S. S., & Willcutt, E. (2005). Instability of the *DSM-IV* subtypes of ADHD from preschool through elementary school. *Archives of General Psychiatry, 62*, 896–902.

Lahey, B. B., & Willcutt, E. (2002). Validity of the diagnosis and dimensions of attention deficit hyperactivity disorder. In P. S. Jenson & J. R. Cooper (Eds.), *Attention deficit hyperactivity disorder: State of true science* (pp. 1-1 to 1-23). New York: Civic Research Institute.

Lalli, J. S., & Casey, S. D. (1996). Treatment of multiply controlled problem behavior. *Journal of Applied Behavior Analysis, 29*, 391–395.

Landau, S., Lorch, E. P., & Milich, R. (1992). Visual attention to and comprehension of television in attention deficit hyperactivity disordered and normal boys. *Child Development, 63*, 928–937.

Lee, S. M., Burgeson, C., Fulton, J. E., & Spain, C. G. (2007). Physical education & physical activity: Results from the School Health Policies & Program Study. *Journal of School Health, 77*(8), 453.

LeFever, G. B., Kawson, K. V., Morrow, A. L. (1999). The extent of drug therapy for attention deficit hyperactivity disorder among children in public schools. *American Journal of Public Health, 89*, 1359–1364.

LeFever, G. B., Villers, M. S., Morrow, A. L., & Vaughn, E., III. (2002). Parental perceptions of adverse educational outcomes among children diagnosed and treated for ADHD: A call for improved school/provider collaboration. *Psychology in the Schools, 39*, 63–71.

Levine, M. D. (1993). *Misunderstood minds.* Retrieved August 12, 2009, from http://www.pbs.org/wgbh/misunderstoodminds/mathstrats.html

Levine, M. D. (1994). *Educational care.* Cambridge, MA: Educators.

Levine, M. D. (1997). *All kinds of minds.* Cambridge, MA: Educators.

Lindgren, S. D., & Koeppl, G. K. (1987). Assessing child behavior in a medical setting: Development of the Pediatric Behavior Scale. In R. J. Prinz (Ed.), *Advances in behavioral assessment of children and families: Vol. 3* (pp. 57–90). Greenwich, CT: JAI Press.

Lloyd, G., Stead, J., & Cohen, D. (2006). *Critical new perspectives on ADHD.* Abingdon, Oxon, England: Routledge.

Loe, I. M., & Feldman, H. M. (2007). Academic & educational outcomes of children with ADHD: A literature review and proposal for future research. *Ambulatory Pediatrics, 7,* 91–100.

Loeber, R., & Farrington, D. P. (2001). *Serious & violent juvenile offenders: Risk factors and successful interventions.* Thousand Oaks, CA: Sage.

Lovecky, D. V. (2004). *Different minds: Gifted children with ADHD, Asperger syndrome, and other learning deficits.* London: Jessica Kingsley.

Mannuzza, S., & Klein, R. G. (1999). Adolescent & adult outcomes in attention-deficit/hyperactivity disorder. In H. C. Quay & H. B. Hogan (Eds.), *Handbook of disruptive behavior disorders* (pp. 279–294). New York: Klumer Academics/Plenum.

Mannuzza, S., Klein, R. G., Klein, D. F., Bessler, A., & Shrout, P. (2002). Accuracy of adult recall of childhood attention deficit hyperactivity disorder. *American Journal of Psychiatry, 159,* 1882–1888.

Marcus, B. A., Vollmer, T. R., Swanson, V., Roane, H. R., & Ringdahl, J. E. (2001). An experimental analysis of aggression. *Behavior Modification, 25*(2), 189–213.

Marlow, A. G., Tingstrom, D. H., Olmi, D. J., & Edwards, R. P. (1997). The effects of classroom-based time-in/time-out on compliance rates in children with speech/language difficulties. *Child & Family Behavior Therapy, 19*(2), 1–15.

Martinez, C. R., Jr., & Forgatch, M. S. (2001). Preventing problems with boys' noncompliance: Effects of a parent training intervention for divorcing mothers. *Journal of Consulting & Clinical Psychology, 69*(3), 416–428.

Mash, E. J., & Barkley, R. A. (2005). *Treatment of childhood disorders* (3rd ed.). New York: Guilford.

McAfee, J. K., Schwilk, C., & Mitruski, M. (2006). Public policy on physical restraint of children with disabilities in public schools. *Education & Treatment of Children, 29,* 711–728.

McCartney, K., & Phillips, D. (2006). *The Blackwell handbook of early childhood development.* Hoboken, NJ: Wiley-Blackwell.

McNeill, S. L., Watson, T. S., Henington, C., & Meeks, C. (2002). The effects of training parents in functional behavior assessment on problem identification, problem analysis and intervention design. *Behavior Modification, 26*(4), 499–515.

Merrell, C., & Tymms, P. (2005, September). *A longitudinal study of the achievements, progress and attitudes of severely inattentive, hyperactive, and impulsive young children.* Paper presented at the Annual Conference of the British Educational Research Association, University of Glamorgan, Pontypridd, Wales, United Kingdom.

Meyer, A., Eilertsen, D. E., Sundet, J. M., Tshifularo, J. G., & Sagvolden, T. (2004). Cross-cultural similarities in ADHD-like behavior amongst South African primary school children. *South African Journal of Psychology, 34,* 123–139.

Milich, R. (1994). The response of children with ADHD to failure. *School Psychology Review, 23,* 11–18.

Miller, J. A., Tansey, M., & Hughes, T. L. (1998). Functional behavioral assessment: The link between problem behavior and effective intervention in schools. *Current Issues in Education, 1*(5). Retrieved August 12, 2009, from http://cie.asu.edu/volume1/number5/

Nadeau, K. (2002). Psychotherapy for women with ADHD. In K. Nadeau & P. Quinn (Eds.), *Understanding women with ADHD* (pp. 104–123). Silver Spring, MD: Advantage Books.

National Association of School Psychologists (NASP). (2003). *Position statement: Student grade retention & social promotion.* Silver Spring, MD: Author. Available August 12, 2009, at http://www.nasponline.org

Neef, N. A., Bicard, D. F., Endo, S., Coury, D. L., & Aman, M. G. (2005). Evaluation of pharmological treatment of impulsivity in children with attention deficit hyperactivity disorder. *Journal of Applied Behavior Analysis, 38*(2), 135–146.

Newcomer, L. L., & Lewis, T. J. (2004). Functional behavioral assessment: An investigation of assessment reliability and effectiveness of function-based intervention, *Journal of Emotional & Behavioral Disorders, 12*(3), 168–181.

Newstrom, J., McLaughlin, T. F., & Sweeney, W. J. (1999). The effects of contingency contracting to improve the mechanics of written language with a middle school student with behavior disorders. *Child & Family Behavior Therapy, 2*(1), 39–48.

Nigg, J. T. (2002). Neuropsychological executive functions & DSM-IV ADHD subtypes. *Journal of Child & Adolescent Psychiatry, 41*(1), 59–66.

Nigg, J. T. (2006). *What causes ADHD? Understanding what goes wrong and why.* New York: Guilford.

Nordquist, V. M., & McEvoy, M. A. (1983). Punishment as a factor in early childhood imitation. *Analysis and Intervention in Developmental Disabilities, 3*(4), 339–357.

Novak, G. P., Solanto, M., & Abikoff, H. (1995). Spatial orienting and focused attention in attention deficit hyperactivity disorder. *Psychophysiology, 32*, 546–559.

Olfson, M., Marcus, S. C., Weissman, M. M., & Jensen, P. S. (2002). National trade in the use of psychotropic medications by children. *Journal of American Academy of Child & Adolescent Psychiatry, 41*, 514–521.

Ollendick, T. H., & Schroeder, C. S. (2003). *Encyclopedia of clinical child and pediatric psychology.* New York: Kluwer Press.

Olmi, D. J., Sevier, R. C., & Nastasi, D. F. (1997). Time-in/time-out as a response to noncompliance and inappropriate behavior with children with developmental disabilities: Two case studies. *Psychology in the Schools, 34*, 31–39.

O'Riordan, M., & Passetti, F. (2006). Discrimination in autism within different sensory modalities. *Journal of Autism & Developmental Disorders, 36*(5), 665–675.

Owen Blakemore, J. E., Berenbaum, S. A., & Liben, L. S. (2009). *Gender Development.* New York: CRC Press.

Parker, H. C. (1992). *Listen, look and think: A self-regulation program for children.* Plantation, FL: Specialty Press.

Patterson, G. R. (1982). *Coercive family process.* Eugene, OR: Castalia.

Patterson, G. R., DeBaryshe, B. D., & Ramsey, E. (1989). A developmental perspective on antisocial behavior. *American Psychologist, 44*, 329–335.

Patterson, G. R., & Guillion, M. E. (1968). *Living with children: New methods for parents and teachers* (Rev. ed.). Champaign, IL: Research Press.

Pearson-Gibson, J. A., & Rang, L. M. (2006). Are written reports of suicide and seeking help contagious? High schoolers' perceptions. *Journal of Applied Social Psychology, 21*(18), 1517–1523.

Pelham, W. E. (2004, August). *Do stimulant drugs improve long-term outcomes in ADHD? Findings from the Pittsburg ADHD Longitudinal Study.* Paper presented at the annual meeting of the Children & Adults with Attention Deficit/Hyperactivity Disorder, Nashville, TN. Retrieved August 12, 2009, from http://www.allacademic.com/meta/p116696_index.html

Pelham, W. E. (2008). Against the grain: A proposal for a psychosocial-first approach to treating ADHD—the Buffalo treatment algorithm. In K. McBurnett & L. J. Pfiffner (Eds.), *Attentional deficit/hyperactivity disorder: Concepts, controversies, new directions* (pp. 301–316). New York: Informal Healthcare.

Pelham, W. E., Fabiano, G. A., & Massetti, G. M. (2005). Evidence-based assessment of attention deficit hyperactivity disorder in children & adolescents. *Journal of Clinical Child & Adolescent Psychology, 34*(3), 449–476.

Petermann, F., & Petermann, U. (1997). *Training with aggressive children.* Weinheim, Germany: Beltz.

Phillips, D. R., Schuen, V. L., & Saklofske, D. H. (1997). Treatment effects of a school-based cognitive-behavioral program for aggressive children. *Canadian Journal of School Psychology, 13*, 60–67.

Pisecco, S., Huzinec, C., & Curtis, D. (2001). The effects of child characteristics on teachers' acceptability of classroom-based behavioral strategies and psychostimulant medication for the treatment of ADHD. *Journal of Clinical Child & Adolescent Psychology, 30*(3), 413–421.

Power, T. J., Karustis, J. L., & Habboushe, D. F. (2001). *Homework success for children with ADHD: A family-school intervention program.* New York: Guilford Press.

Prout, H. T., & Brown, D. T. (2007). *Counseling and psychotherapy with children & adolescents: Theory and practice in school settings* (3rd ed.). New York: Wiley.

Quinn & Nadeau. (2002). *Gender issues and ADHD: Research, diagnosis and treatment.* Silver Spring, MD: Advantage Books.

Rapport, M. D., Scanlan, S. W., & Denney, C. B. (1999). Attention-deficit/hyperactivity disorder and scholastic achievement: A model of dual development pathways. *Journal of Child Psychology & Psychiatry, 40,* 1169–1185.

Reid, R. (1999). Attention deficit hyperactivity disorder: Effective methods for the classroom. *Focus on Exceptional Children, 32*(4), 1–19.

Reimers, C., & Brunger, B. A. (1999). *ADHD in the young child: Driven to redirection.* Plantation, FL: Specialty Press.

Rende, R., Slomkowski, C., Lloyd-Richardson, E., & Niaura, R. (2005). Sibling effects on substance use in adolescence: Social contagion and genetic relatedness. *Journal of Family Psychology, 19*(4), 611–618.

Reynolds, C. R., & Kamphaus, R. W. (2002). *The clinician's guide to the Behavior Assessment System for Children (BASC).* New York: Guilford Press.

Reynolds, C. R., & Kamphaus, R. W. (2004). *The Behavior Assessment System for Children* (2nd ed.). Circle Pines, MN: AGS.

Rief, S. F. (1993). *How to reach and teach ADD/ADHD children: Practical techniques, strategies, and interventions for helping children with attention problems and hyperactivity.* San Francisco: Jossey-Bass.

Robin, A. L. (1998). *ADHD in adolescents: Diagnosis and treatment.* New York: Guilford Press.

Robin, A., Schneider, M., & Dolnick, M. (1976). The turtle technique: An extended case study of self-control in the classroom. *Psychology in the Schools, 13,* 449–453.

Rosen, L. (2005). *School discipline: Best practices for administrators.* Thousand Oaks, CA: Corwin.

Rowland, A. S., Skipper, B., Rabiner, D. L., Umbach, D. M., Stallone, L., Campbell, R. A., et al. (2008). The shifting subtypes of ADHD: Classification depends on how symptom reports are combined. *Journal of Abnormal Child Psychology, 36*(5), 731–743.

Rubia, K. (2007). Neuro-anatomic evidence for the maturational delay hypothesis of ADHD. *Proceedings of the National Academy of Sciences of the United States of America (PNAS), 104*(50). Retrieved May 20, 2009, from http://www.pnas.org/content/104/50/19663.full

Samuels, C. A. (2009, April 17). Restraint, seclusion of students attracting new scrutiny: Watchdog agency preparing report on practices. *Education Week.* Retrieved August 12, 2009, from http://www.edweek.org/ew/articles/2009/04/17/29

Satterfield, J. H., & Dawson, M. E. (1971). Electrodermal correlates of hyperactivity in children. *Psychophysiology, 8,* 191–197.

Scahill, L., & Schwab-Stone, M. (2000). Epidemiology of ADHD in school-age children. *Child & Adolescent Psychiatry Clinics of North America, 9*(3), 541–555.

Scherer, M. (2006). Celebrate strengths, nurture affinities: A conversation with Mel Levine. *Educational Leadership, 64*(1), 8–15.

Schutte, R. C., & Hopkins, B. L. (1970). The effects of teacher attention on following instructions in a kindergarten class. *Journal of Applied Behavior Analysis, 3,* 117–122.

Scott, T. M., Nelson, C. M., Liapsin, C. J., Jolivette, K., Cristie, C. H., & Riney, M. (2002). Addressing the needs of at-risk and adjudicated youth through positive behavior support: Effective prevention practices. *Education & Treatment of Children, 25*(4), 532–551.

Shapiro, E. S., & Cole, L. L. (1994). *Behavior change in the classroom: Self-management interventions.* New York: Guilford Press.

Shapiro, E. S., & Kratochwill, T. R. (Eds.). (2002). *Conducting school-based assessments of child and adolescent behavior.* New York: Guilford Press.

Shaw, D. S., Winslow, E. B., Owens, E. B., Vendra, J. I., Cohn, J. F., & Bell, R. Q. (1998). The development of early externalizing problems among children from low-income families: A transformational perspective. *Journal of Abnormal Child Psychology, 26*(2), 95–107.

Shonkoff, J., & Phillips, D. A. (2000). *From neurons to neighborhoods: The science of early child development.* Washington, DC: National Academy Press.

Simonsen, B., Britton, L., & Young, D. (2009, January 20). School-wide positive behavior support in an alternative school setting: A case study. *Journal of Positive Behavior Interventions OnlineFirst.* Retrieved August 12, 2009, from http://jpbi.sagepub.com

Slough, N. M., & McMahon, R. J. (2007). Preventing serious conduct problems in school-age youth: The fast track program. *Cognitive & Behavioral Practice, 15*(1), 3–17.

Smalley, S. (2008). Reframing ADHD in the genomic era. *Psychiatric Times, 25*(7), 74–78.

Smallwood, D. L. (1997). Introduction. In S. L. Smallwood (Ed.), *Attention disorders in children: Resources for school psychologists.* Bethesda, MD: The National Association of School Psychologists.

Smith, M. R., & Lerman, D. C. (1999). A preliminary comparison of guided compliance & high-probability instructional sequences as treatment for noncompliance in children with developmental disabilities. *Research in Developmental Disabilities, 20*(3), 183–195

Sohlberg, M. M., & Mateer, C. A. (1989). *Introduction to cognitive rehabilitation: Theory & practice.* New York: Guilford Press.

Solanto, M. V. (2004, August). *Neuropsychological functioning in children with the predominantly inattentive subtype of ADHD.* Paper presented at the annual meeting of Children and Adults With Attention-Deficit/Hyperactivity Disorder (CHAD), Nashville, Tennessee. Retrieved May 20, 2009, from http://www.allacademic.com/meta/p116649_index.html

Solnick, J. V., Rincover, A., & Peterson, C. R. (1977). Some determinants of the reinforcing and punishing effects of time-out. *Journal of Applied Behavior Analysis, 10*(3), 415–424.

Spadafore, G. J., & Spadafore, S. J. (1997, April). *Spadafore Attention Deficit Hyperactivity Disorder Rating Scale: A new instrument.* Paper presented at the annual meeting of the National Association of School Psychologists (NASP), Anaheim, CA.

Spoth, R. L., Redmond, C., & Shin, C. (2000). Reducing adolescents' aggressive and hostile behaviors. *Archives of Pediatric & Adolescent Medicine, 154,* 1248–1257.

Steele, R. G., Elkin, T. D., & Roberts, M. C. (2007). Evidence-based therapies for children and adolescents: Problems & prospects. In R. G. Steele, T. D. Elkin, & M. C. Roberts (Eds.), *Handbook of evidence-based therapies for children and adolescents: Bridging science and practice* (pp. 3–8). New York: Springer.

Stokes, T. (2002). Terror and violence perpetrated by children. In C. E. Stout (Ed.), *The psychology of terrorism: Vol. IV. Programs and practices in response and prevention* (pp. 77–90). Westport, CT: Praeger.

Stoner, G., & Green, S. K. (1992). Reconsidering the scientist-practitioner model for school psychology practice. *School Psychology Review, 21*(1), 155–166.

Sudak, H. S., & Sudak, D. M. (2005). The media and suicide. *Academic Psychiatry, 29,* 495–499.

Swenson, N., Lolich, E., Williams, R. L., & McLaughlin, T. F. (2000). The effects of structured free time on request compliance and on-task behavior of a preadolescent with ADHD. *Child & Family Behavior Therapy, 22*(1), 51–59.

Swingle, P. G. (2008). *Biofeedback for the brain: How neurotherapy effectively treats depression, ADHD.* New York: Rutgers University Press.

Tallmadge, J., & Barkley, R. A. (1983). The interactions of hyperactive and normal boys with their father & mother. *Journal of Abnormal Child Psychology, 11,* 565–580.

Tannock, R. (2000). Attention-deficit/hyperactivity disorder with anxiety disorders. In T. E. Brown (Ed.), *Attention-deficit disorders and comorbidities in children, adolescents and adults* (pp. 125–170). Washington, DC: American Psychiatric Press.

Timimi, S. (2002). *Pathological child psychiatry and the medicalization of childhood.* Hove, East Sussex, England: Brunner-Routledge.

Todd, R. D., Huang, H., Smalley, S. L., Nelson, S. F., Willcutt, E. G., Pennington, B. F., et al. (2005). *Journal of Child Psychology & Psychiatry, 46*(10), 1030–1038.

Tsai, S. J., Wang, Y. C., & Hong, C. J. (2001). Allelic variants of the alpha 1a adrenoceptor and the promoter region of the alpha 2a adrenoceptor and temperament factors. *American Journal of Medical Genetics, 105,* 96–98.

Tsal, Y., Shalev, L., & Mevorach, C. (2005). The diversity of attention deficits in ADHD: The prevalence of four cognitive factors in ADHD versus controls. *Journal of Learning Disabilities, 38*(2), 142–157.

Tymms, P., & Merrell, C. (2004, April). *Screening & classroom interventions for inattentive, hyperactive and impulsive young children: A longitudinal study.* Paper presented at the annual meeting of the American Educational Research Association, San Diego, CA.

University of California—Los Angeles (UCLA). (1999). *Center for Mental Health in Schools.* Retrieved August 12, 2009, from http://smhp.psych.ucla.edu

U.S. Department of Education. (2006). *Teaching children with attention deficit hyperactivity disorder: Instructional strategies & practices.* Retrieved August 12, 2009, from www.ed.gov/rschstat/ research/pubs/adhd/adhd-teaching-2006.pdf

Vedantam, S. (2009, March 27). Debate over drugs for ADHD reignites: Long-term benefit for children at issue. *The Washington Post.* Retrieved August 12, 2009, from http://www .washingtonpost.com/wp-dyn/content/article/2009/03/26/AR2009032604018.html

Walker, H. M., Colvin, G., & Ramsey, E. (1995). *Antisocial behavior in school strategies and best practices.* Pacific Grove, CA: Brooks/Cole.

Walker, H. M., Ramsey, E., & Gresham, F. M. (2003/2004, Winter). Heading off disruptive behavior: How early intervention can reduce defiant behavior—and win back teaching time. *American Educator.* Retrieved August 12, 2009, from http://www.aft.org/pubs-reports/american_ educator/winter03–04/early_intervention.html

Watson, T. S., & Gresham, F. M. (1998). *Handbook of child behavior therapy.* New York: Plenum Press.

Webster-Stratton, C. (1998). Preventing conduct problems in Head Start children: Strengthening parenting competencies. *Journal of Consulting & Clinical Psychology, 66*(5), 715–730.

Weiss, G., & Hechtman, L. T. (1993). *Hyperactive children grown up: ADHD in children, adolescents, and adults* (2nd ed.). New York: Guilford Press.

Weiss, H., Caspe, M., & Lopez, M. E. (2006). *Family involvement in early childhood education.* Cambridge, MA: Harvard Family Research Project.

Welch, E., Fees, B., & Murray, A. D. (2001). *Parent-toddler play interaction and its relation to the home environment.* Retrieved August 12, 2009, from the Kansas State University Web site: http://www .kon.org/urc/welch.html

Whitman, C. (1991). *Win the whining war and other skirmishes: A family peace plan.* Pasadena, CA: Perspective.

Wilens, T. E., Beiderman, J., & Spencer, T. J. (2002). Attention-deficit/hyperactivity disorder across the lifespan. *Annual Review of Medicine, 53*, 113–131.

Willcutt, E. G., Chhabildas, N., & Pennington, B. F. (2001). Validity of the DSM-IV subtypes of ADHD. *The ADHD Report, 9*(1), 2–5.

Withan, A. P. (1995). *Dear teacher: Daily affirmations for teachers who inspire.* Fort Worth, TX: Brownlow.

Wolery, M., Bailey, D. D., & Sugai, G. M. (1988). *Effective teaching: Principles and procedures of applied behavior analysis with exceptional students.* Boston: Allyn & Bacon.

Wolfgang, C. H., & Glickman, C. D. (1986). *Solving discipline problems: Strategies for classroom teachers.* Boston: Allyn & Bacon.

Wolraich, M. L., Lambert, W., Duffing, M. A., Bickman, L., Simmons, T., & Worley, K. (2003). Psychometric properties of the Vanderbilt ADHD diagnostic parent rating scale in a referred population. *Journal of Pediatric Psychology, 28*(8), 559–568.

Wright, P. W. D., & Wright P. D. (2009). *Abuse & restraints in school.* Retrieved August 12, 2009, from http://www.wrightslaw.com/info/abuse.index.htm

Zeigler Dendy, C. A. (Ed.). (2006). *CHADD educator's manual on attention-deficit/hyperactivity disorder (AD/HD): An in-depth look from an educational perspective* (2nd ed.). Landover, MD: CHADD.

Zirpoli, T. J., & Mellow, K. J. (2001). *Behavior management: Application for teachers.* New York: MacMillan.

Zito, J. M., Safer, D. J., dosReis, S., Gardner, J. F., Boles, M., & Lynch, F. (2000). Trends in the prescribing of psychotropic medications to preschoolers. *Journal of the American Medical Association, 283*(8), 1025–1030.

Index

CORWIN

A SAGE Company

The Corwin logo—a raven striding across an open book—represents the union of courage and learning. Corwin is committed to improving education for all learners by publishing books and other professional development resources for those serving the field of PreK–12 education. By providing practical, hands-on materials, Corwin continues to carry out the promise of its motto: **"Helping Educators Do Their Work Better."**